"Anyone working in education or with children will be
book, with examples and insights from families and pro
I was especially interested in how early childhood anxieties and experiences
can impact on the way a child manages school—manifest in behaviour that's
immediately noticeable even if the reasons for it are not, or in behaviour that's
not initially concerning and "goes under the radar". The book made me consider
the work schools and psychotherapists need to do to ensure that our different
approaches complement each other in supporting the children and families we
work so hard with."

Don McGibbon, *Head Teacher, Fleet Primary School*

"An excellent resource for professionals in education, social care and child
mental health, and for parents who are unsure about their children receiving
therapeutic help at school. The editor and contributors remain true to the tradition
of psychoanalytic thinking about learning and teaching which has characterised
the Tavistock Clinic's approach for more than ninety years. At the same time, the
book is absolutely up-to-date with the current socio-political context in which
therapeutic services are based in schools, ensuring greater equity of access and
closer links between teachers, parents and clinicians. Chapters include interviews
with parents and teachers and vivid observations from classrooms and therapy
sessions, providing convincing accounts of the psychoanalytic perspective."

Biddy Youell, *Consultant Child and Adolescent Psychotherapist*

"This book provides detailed insight into children's emotional health and the
social/emotional factors that influence their well-being and ability to cope with
home and school life. It provides a real-life account of the challenges faced by
teachers and other professionals working with children with emotional difficulties
on a day to day basis. The need for specialist child psychotherapy is greater than
ever. The case studies and interviews demonstrate how child psychoanalytic
psychotherapists, families and schools working together can provide effective
intervention and support, allowing children's emotional obstacles to be explored
and overcome."

Karen Filiz, *Acting Deputy Head, Early Years Foundation Stage
and Inclusion Lead, Beckford Primary School*

CHILD PSYCHOANALYTIC PSYCHOTHERAPY IN PRIMARY SCHOOLS

This book investigates the experiences of severely troubled children and their families, teachers, and child psychoanalytic psychotherapists working together in primary schools.

The book begins by looking at children's emotional life during the primary school years and what can disrupt ordinary, helpful social development and learning. It examines what child psychoanalytic psychotherapy is, how it works, and why it is offered in primary schools. The following chapters intersperse accounts of creative child psychoanalytic approaches with interviews with parents, carers, teachers, and clinicians. A section focusing on mainstream primary schools presents parent–child interventions for a nursery class; child group psychotherapy with children from traumatized families; and consultation to school staff, with personal accounts from parents, a kinship carer, a family support worker, a deputy head, and a child psychotherapist. Chapters then focus on alternative educational settings, featuring a school for children with severe physical and cognitive disabilities; a primary pupil referral unit; and a therapeutic school. These chapters show psychotherapy with a non-verbal boy with autism; therapy groups with children who have missed out on the building blocks of development alongside reflective groups for school staff; and child psychotherapy approaches at lunchtime and in breaks, with insights from a parent, a clinical lead nurse, a head teacher, and a child psychotherapist. Finally, there is an evaluation of evidence about the impact of child psychotherapy within primary schools.

Recognizing the increasing importance of attending to the emotional difficulties of children whose relationships and learning are in jeopardy, this book will be invaluable to all those working in primary schools, to commissioners of child mental health services, to parents and carers, and to experienced and training clinicians.

Katie Argent is Head of Child and Adolescent Psychotherapy at the Tavistock and Portman NHS Foundation Trust. She has a special interest in the usefulness of psychoanalytic thinking outside the clinic.

Tavistock Clinic Series

Margot Waddell, Jocelyn Catty, & Kate Stratton (Series Editors)

Recent titles in the Tavistock Clinic Series

CHILD PSYCHOANALYTIC PSYCHOTHERAPY IN PRIMARY SCHOOLS

Tavistock Approaches

Edited by
Katie Argent

with interviews by
Milly Jenkins

LONDON AND NEW YORK

First published 2022
by Routledge
2 Park Square, Milton Park, Abingdon, Oxon OX14 4RN

and by Routledge
605 Third Avenue, New York, NY 10158

Routledge is an imprint of the Taylor & Francis Group, an informa business

British Library Cataloguing-in-Publication Data
A catalogue record for this book is available from the British Library

Library of Congress Cataloging-in-Publication Data
Names: Argent, Katie, 1958– editor.
Title: Child psychoanalytic psychotherapy in primary schools : Tavistock approaches / [edited by] Katie Argent, with interviews by Milly Jenkins.
Description: Milton Park, Abingdon, Oxon : New York, NY : Routledge, 2021. | Series: Tavistock series clinic | Includes bibliographical references and index.
Identifiers: LCCN 2021000862 (print) | LCCN 2021000863 (ebook) | ISBN 9781032029429 (hardback) | ISBN 9781032023182 (paperback) | ISBN 9781003185925 (ebook)
Subjects: LCSH: Child psychotherapy. | Child psychotherapy—Study and teaching. | Psychotherapist and patient.
Classification: LCC RJ504 .C475 2021 (print) | LCC RJ504 (ebook) | DDC 618.92/8914—dc23
LC record available at https://lccn.loc.gov/2021000862
LC ebook record available at https://lccn.loc.gov/2021000863

ISBN: 978-1-032-02942-9 (hbk)
ISBN: 978-1-032-02318-2 (pbk)
ISBN: 978-1-003-18592-5 (ebk)

DOI: 10.4324/9781003185925

Typeset in Palatino
by Apex CoVantage, LLC

*To our teachers
and to the school communities we have learned from*

CONTENTS

IV
Evidence from experience and audit

SERIES EDITORS' PREFACE

Since it was founded in 1920, the Tavistock Clinic—now the Tavistock and Portman NHS Foundation Trust—has developed a wide range of developmental approaches to mental health which have been strongly influenced by the ideas of psychoanalysis. It has also adopted systemic family therapy as a theoretical model and a clinical approach to family problems. The Tavistock is now one of the largest mental health training institutions in Britain. It teaches up to 600 students a year on postgraduate, doctoral, and qualifying courses in social work, systemic psychotherapy, psychology, psychiatry, nursing, as well as child, adolescent, and adult psychotherapy, along with 2,000 multidisciplinary clinicians, social workers, and teachers attending Continuing Professional Development courses and conferences on psychoanalytic observation, psychoanalytic thinking, and management and leadership in a range of clinical and community settings.

The Tavistock's philosophy aims at promoting therapeutic methods in mental health. Its work is based on the clinical expertise that is also the basis of its consultancy and research activities. The aim of this Series is to make available to the reading public the clinical, theoretical, and research work that is most influential at the Tavistock. The Series sets out new approaches in the understanding and treatment of psychological disturbance in children, adolescents, and adults, both as individuals and in families.

Child Psychoanalytic Psychotherapy in Primary Schools: Tavistock Approaches, edited by Katie Argent, brings together a range of perspectives on an endeavour that is becomingly increasingly important: that of attending to the emotional distress and disturbance of primary-school-aged children and their families, and doing so in the school setting itself. Written in a style refreshingly free of professional jargon, the book covers both mainstream and specialist schools and brings together the perspectives of child psychotherapists, school staff, and parents and carers. Interviews conducted and written up by Milly Jenkins and material from a research study conducted by Mel Serlin provide the means to bring in, respectively, the voices of parents and school staff and a grandparent "kinship" carer. These chapters beautifully offset those written by child psychotherapists, which bring the clinical work, and the presence of the children themselves, vividly to life.

The book is divided into four sections. In the first, the rationale for providing child psychoanalytic psychotherapy in primary schools is emphasized. Complementary chapters on children's emotional development and the nature and function of child psychotherapy articulate the importance of provision in the school setting, while Jenkins contributes a "brief history of a long relationship": namely, an account of the relationship between Tavistock child psychotherapy and schools. The latter includes the history of Tavistock teaching and training in this area, including most notably the Emotional Factors in Learning and Teaching course. Originally set up by Martha and Roland Harris in 1968, this course ran for many years and gave rise to the influential book *The Emotional Experience of Learning and Teaching* (edited by Isca Salzberger-Wittenberg, Gianna Williams, and Elsie Osborne), which was reissued in our Series in 1999. Jenkins then describes the history of two provisions: TOPS (Tavistock Outreach in Primary Schools), providing psychotherapy directly in mainstream primary schools; and Gloucester House, the specialist setting attached to the Tavistock, formerly referred to as the Mulberry Bush Day Unit (or just "Day Unit"). Both these innovative projects, in their current forms, are the focus of dedicated chapters later in the book.

Parts II and III focus on therapeutic work in mainstream and alternative provisions, respectively. The former attests to the range of styles of psychoanalytic work it is possible to offer in this setting, including a chapter on working in a school nursery by Kathryn Fenton and Anya Suschitzky, as well as a chapter on group psychotherapy by Marta Cioeta. The impact of child psychotherapy on parents and carers comes through powerfully here. The parents interviewed by Jenkins describe their child's psychotherapy with Cioeta and how they were able to work together to understand his difficulties in the context of the two cultures of their country of origin, and the UK, and of their own experiences as children. Their son's own voice comes in very powerfully in his parents' account: he "still talks about his therapists, asks if they are still here, talks about what they did together and the toys that were in the room". In Mel Serlin's chapter, a carer whose grandchild had therapy in TOPS describes her initial embarrassment—as though "I'm doing something wrong if she needs therapy"—and how her feelings were carefully attended to by school and therapist. The final chapter in Part II, an interview with a deputy head, a family support worker, and a child psychotherapist (Cioeta), illustrates the ways in which these professions can work together and the "constant communication" needed. As Cioeta notes: "the staff are excellent observers. And then, when we feed back . . . that can then help the school put a particular incident or behaviour into a frame of reference and understanding."

Turning to specialist provisions in Part III, we find chapters on psychotherapy within Gloucester House and within primary pupil referral units (PRUs) such as Robson House. Again the diversity of approaches is impressive. Carlos Vasquez writes of his work with a boy with autistic spectrum disorder in a special school; Fiona Henderson describes staff and children's groups in Robson House; and Ruth Glover explores the way a child psychotherapist's work in a therapeutic school extends outside the therapy room and into the corridors and even the school lunch-room. Glover, working at Gloucester House, is also interviewed in the final chapter in this section, along with its head teacher, and lead nurse/clinical lead. What comes across so clearly here, as throughout the book, is the power of conversation, within what Argent describes as a "framework of emotional relationships". The interview chapters weaving through the book's structure thus demonstrate the importance of the therapeutic dialogues that bring children, families, staff, and therapists together in diverse ways in these different primary school settings.

The final section of the book demonstrates a different sort of dialogue: between those who run therapeutic provisions and those who commission and fund them—a dialogue requiring "evidence" to justify continued financial support. Here, Cioeta (formerly the project lead for TOPS), together with one of us (JC), draws on her experience of evidencing the project over many years to think about the various creative ways in which this can be done. Using a report on one year of work in TOPS as its "case example", the chapter explores how such a project can be evidenced by collecting both quantitative data (such as "routine outcome monitoring" data collected through questionnaires to parents and teachers) and qualitative data (such as can be collected through formal questionnaires and clinical review meetings). This is a different sort of dialogue, but here, too, it is essential that the power of the therapeutic work shines through, to support the continuation of such endeavours.

This final chapter makes clear that projects such as TOPS cater for children with highly complex emotional and psychological needs, who are also usually from socioeconomically deprived groups. Since the book was written, the COVID-19 pandemic has arrived on our shores, which led to the closure of most schools in the UK to all but tiny numbers of children for many months; at the time of writing, schools have only recently re-opened. While the impact of this "lockdown" on children's mental health is yet to be clearly documented, evidence of its disproportionate impact on those already at a socioeconomic disadvantage is already emerging. *Child Psychoanalytic Psychotherapy in Primary Schools* articulates the significance of small specialist provisions like Gloucester House, which was allowed to remain open during the pandemic. At the same time, it highlights the careful yet profound therapeutic thinking of which, during these last months, significant numbers of children and their families will have been deprived. We can only hope that the "framework of emotional relationships" provided by such work is soon to be robustly reinstated.

ACKNOWLEDGEMENTS

First and foremost, the authors would like to thank the children, parents, and carers and all the staff in the schools we have worked in. Some families and school staff have given generous permission to use their own words, for which we are very grateful.

We would also like to thank:

» our child psychotherapy colleagues and trainees, for the shared thinking that has contributed to these chapters;

» Margaret Rustin and Biddy Youell, for their significant help with gathering our history and getting it in order for chapter 3;

» Graham Music, Victoria Blincow, and Myra Berg for their accounts of the primary-school-based child psychotherapy projects that feature in chapter 3;

» Dorette Engi and Myra Berg, for their invaluable support in running the children's group with Marta Cioeta;

» Andrea Tran, for kindly letting us reproduce his evocative picture in chapter 5;

» Kate Ronay, for her thoughtful observations and therapeutic work;

» Halima Mumin, for her skilful, sensitive, and vital work as interpreter and translator;

» Imke Ahlers, for her crucial role in analysing the TOPS data drawn on in chapter 14;

» Don McGibbon and the Arsenal in the Community project for letting us use the photograph on the cover;

» the Tavistock and Portman NHS Foundation Trust, for supporting our writing and editing with study and sabbatical leave;

» the Tavistock Clinic Foundation, for providing financial help with interview transcription, and Alma Dragush, who undertook this work meticulously;

» the Tavistock Clinic Series editors and Routledge for their encouragement and judgement.

Confidentiality

All chapters are written with identifying details changed or using composite cases to protect confidentiality. Generous permission was given by families and schools for the interviews and detailed clinical material.

ABOUT THE EDITOR AND CONTRIBUTORS

Katie Argent is Head of Child and Adolescent Psychotherapy at the Tavistock and Portman NHS Foundation Trust. She is a child and adolescent psychoanalytic psychotherapist in the Fostering, Adoption and Kinship Care Team and manages the Psychoanalytic Applied Portfolio in the Department of Education and Training. She has a background in public sector work in housing and homelessness and has a special interest in the usefulness of psychoanalytic thinking outside the clinic and in school-based child psychotherapy approaches.

Dexter Benjamin trained as a child and adolescent psychoanalytic psychotherapist, with a specialism in schools and Tier 3 adolescent outpatients services. He currently works for the Tavistock and Portman NHS Foundation Trust, as team manager and child and adolescent psychotherapist for the Fostering Adoption and Kinship Care team, and Course Lead for the Tavistock Centre/University of Essex MA in Psychoanalytic Studies. He is a clinical supervisor, group facilitator, and seminar leader on other courses in the trust and works in private practice with organizations and professionals working with children.

Francesca Benjamin worked for many years in music before moving into the field of social care and then training as a child and adolescent psychoanalytic psychotherapist at the Tavistock Clinic. She currently works as a child psychotherapist within the Tavistock, as part of teams offering treatment and consultation within primary school and specialist educational provision settings. She has previously taught on several courses in the Tavistock, as clinical supervisor and seminar leader, and is Course Lead for one of the Tavistock certificate courses, Reflective Mental Health Practice Today. She has a particular interest in the application of psychotherapeutic work in schools and other educational provisions.

Jocelyn Catty is a child and adolescent psychoanalytic psychotherapist and adult psychotherapist and research lead for the Child and Adolescent Psychoanalytic Psychotherapy doctoral training at the Tavistock Centre. She is also Principal Child Psychotherapist in a Child and Adolescent Mental Health Service (CAMHS) in South East London. She was formerly Senior Research Fellow in Mental Health at St George's, University of London.

Marta Cioeta is a child and adolescent psychoanalytic psychotherapist and deputy Course Lead for the Child and Adolescent Psychoanalytic Psychotherapy doctoral training at the Tavistock Centre. She currently works in the Autism and Learning Disabilities team at the Tavistock and previously worked as the project leader and lead therapist for the Tavistock Outreach in Primary Schools Project (TOPS).

Kathryn Fenton is a child and adolescent psychoanalytic psychotherapist working in North Camden Community CAMHS at the Tavistock and Portman NHS Foundation Trust. She is a tutor and clinical supervisor for the Child and Adolescent Psychoanalytic Psychotherapy doctoral training at the Tavistock Centre and Course Lead for the Tavistock Centre/ University of Essex MA in Perinatal and Early Years Work: A Psychoanalytic Observational Approach. Trained as a social worker, she has a strong interest in applied psychoanalytic work within a variety of settings.

Ruth Glover works as a child and adolescent psychoanalytic psychotherapist at Gloucester House, Tavistock Children's Day Unit. She is also co-principal child and adolescent psychotherapist at Open Door, an NHS Commissioned Charity for adolescents in Haringey. She teaches and supervises on the Child and Adolescent Psychoanalytic Psychotherapy doctoral training at the Tavistock Centre.

Fiona Henderson was trained at the Independent Psychoanalytic Child and Adolescent Psychotherapy Association (IPCAPA) at the British Psychotherapy Foundation (BPF) and worked in the Looked After and Adopted Team at Bromley CAMHS, Oxleas NHS Trust, until 2019. She is a member of the Whole Family Team, Tavistock and Portman NHS

Foundation Trust, and has worked for the Tavistock as a child psycho-analytic psychotherapist in a primary pupil referral unit for the last fifteen years.

Milly Jenkins is a child and adolescent psychoanalytic psychotherapist and deputy lead for the Tavistock Outreach in Primary Schools (TOPS) project. She also teaches on Tavistock courses. Before training as a child psychotherapist at the Tavistock, she worked as a teaching assistant, and, for three years, as an assistant therapist for TOPS in a Camden primary school. She trained and then worked in a Camden CAMHS team for eight years, including as CAMHS worker for five primary and secondary schools.

Mel Serlin is a child and adolescent psychoanalytic psychotherapist and member of the course organizing team for the Tavistock Centre/University of Essex MA in Working with Children, Young People and Families: A Psychoanalytic Observational Approach. Serlin leads the Tavistock Outreach in Primary Schools (TOPS) project and has an interest in the impact of intergenerational trauma, having worked for many years with looked-after children within residential, social care, and CAMHS settings. Serlin has completed a doctoral research study investigating the experiences of children living in kinship care.

Anya Suschitzky is a child and adolescent psychoanalytic psychotherapist at North Middlesex University Hospital and the Tavistock Outreach in Primary Schools project. She is a member of the course management team for the training in child psychoanalytic psychotherapy for the Child and Adolescent Psychoanalytic Psychotherapy doctoral training at the Tavistock Centre.

Carlos Vasquez is a clinical psychologist and child and adolescent psychoanalytic psychotherapist. He studied psychology in Peru, at the Pontificia Universidad Católica del Perú, and child and adolescent psychotherapy at the Tavistock Clinic in the UK. He has worked in clinical institutions in Peru and in the UK, including the Children, Young Adults and Families Department at the Tavistock Clinic and the Brent Centre for Young People in London. He has taught in Peru and at the Tavistock Clinic. Currently he works in private practice in Lima, Perú, with children, adolescents, and adults. He is a visiting lecturer on a Psychoanalytic Masters programme at the Pontificia Universidad Católica del Perú and teaches in various psychotherapy training institutes in Lima, including Intercambio and Centro de Psicoterapia Psicoanalítica de Lima.

Introduction

Katie Argent

This book offers teachers and school staff, clinicians, and primary education and child mental health providers and commissioners an understanding of the scope and limitations of locating highly specialist clinicians in primary educational settings. We hope it will also be useful to parents and carers wanting to know more about how a child psychoanalytic psychotherapy approach can help. It considers ways of bringing child psychotherapy into primary schools that can be timely, responsive, and effective for children and families with complex, chronic, and severe emotional difficulties. Our focus is the experience of children and their families, education professionals, and child psychotherapists engaged with Tavistock Clinic child psychotherapy approaches in a range of educational provision.

School learning happens in a framework of emotional relationships. School staff know that the quality of a child's adult–child and peer relationships will be a key indicator of the child's enjoyment of and success in school. This means that what happens in primary schools, alongside what happens at home, plays a critical part in children's emotional development as well as in their capacity to learn.

The immediate context is escalating worry about high levels of mental health difficulty for school-age children and young people. There is national concern about emotional help for children being available early enough and accessibly enough. The 2017–18 government Green Paper on transforming mental health care for children (Department of Health/

DOI: 10.4324/9781003185925-1

Department of Education, 2017) and the *NHS Long Term Plan* (NHS, 2019b) promote school-based child emotional health work. Schools are under pressure to demonstrate good practice in supporting whole-school emotional health as well as in responding to acute emotional problems. Meanwhile, Child and Adolescent Mental Health Services (CAMHS) are under pressure to reduce waiting times and speed up through-put with pared-back budgets. There is a political and financial push to provide services quickly at the lowest possible cost, so there is a need to be clear about why highly trained and skilled clinicians are critical to effective child mental health work.

Children go to school throughout their childhoods, and all have emotional difficulties at some points in their progress through the primary school years. Ordinary healthy development is about exploring and exercising emotional capacity when things are difficult as well as when they are easy. Most children need thoughtful, sensitive help with this from their families and schools. Usually everyday school interventions, such as extra classroom support, time with a learning mentor, or a period of art or drama therapy, in parallel with family care, is enough to help children manage the inevitable ups and downs of childhood.

In this book we concentrate on work with those children and their families about whom parents and carers, schools, GPs, and social workers are most worried. This is the small but significant number of children whose difficulties are severe and long-standing enough to meet the high threshold for referral to CAMHS but who, in a school's view, would not get to a CAMHS clinic. These are children who are likely to have had several supportive interventions already but have not been helped by this, or not helped enough. For these children and their families, a therapeutic approach that specifically works with precarious engagement and specializes in complex, challenging behavioural and non-verbal communication, including the extremes of withdrawal and aggression, is likely to be needed.

Schools—teachers, teaching assistants, school nurses, SENCos, office staff, playground and lunchtime staff—are in an unusually good position to observe children's interactions and to pick up when there are difficulties with relationships and with learning. Primary schools also see some of what happens between parents and children and make a relationship with parents as well as with children. Even for parents with an ambivalent relationship to their child's school—perhaps those whose own experience of school as children has been difficult—there is a relationship that can be built on, which can open the door to a child getting psychotherapeutic help.

Noticing that something is the matter is an essential first step in finding ways of helping, but it is not always straightforward. Children with chronic and severe difficulties may not show their worry, distress, confusion, anger, or fear in straightforward ways. Adults may find themselves provoked, enraged, or uninterested rather than curious and concerned. When communication is repeatedly fraught or stuck and emotional relationships become paralysed or volatile, this can suggest that the child's learning and emotional life at home and at school is in jeopardy.

Children and families who are referred to school-based child psychotherapy services often have a history of non-engagement with services. There can be considerable worry for parents or carers about being criticized or blamed for complex, chronic difficulties that may have affected a family across generations. The primary relationship for the family is with their child's school, and the school's hosting of other agencies, including psychotherapy, can help to ameliorate wariness and doubt about showing how hard things can be.

The chapters in this book show how child psychoanalytic psychotherapists work with fundamental anxieties and emotional conflicts that children and their families and schools may not be aware of, as well as with more identifiable problems, family and social/economic circumstances, developmental difficulties, and life events. It is often the less known-about fears—perhaps long-standing and deep-rooted, troubling, shameful, and distressing to put into words—that generate the hardest to resolve emotional obstacles to relationships and learning. Psychoanalytic psychotherapy attends to what is not or cannot be talked about or shown in straightforward ways. It draws on the feelings at play between the child, family, school, and therapist, gradually to build up a shared picture of the dynamics of a child's emotional experience in order to make emotional life more understandable and manageable for them in their family and school.

The following example provided by a child psychoanalytic psychotherapist gives a flavour of how school-based work can facilitate an immediate and tangible linking up that is helpful to families who tend to slip through the net.

Marie

Marie, who was 7 years old, had been in once-weekly psychotherapy in a mainstream primary school for some months. She was referred to the primary-school-based child psychotherapy service because of concern about her disruptive and aggressive behaviour, difficulties with concentration in class, and growing social isolation—friendships with peers were increasingly hard for her to sustain. Marie was a lively, wiry white girl who came across as bright, articulate, and sparky, with sudden mood changes. She could plunge into intense frustration and fury in a moment, overwhelmed by feeling unfairly treated. Other children found her controlling and often backed off. Teachers felt wary of her volatility and increasingly concerned that they could not support the considerable potential they saw in her.

This was a child who had caused a lot of worry in the school for a long time. Marie had been allocated additional support from a classroom assistant and a period of art therapy, but the difficulties continued. She was often to be found with the head teacher or deputy head, trying to work out what had caused the latest incident.

Marie lived with her mother, Bridget, and three older siblings. The family had lived in the area for several generations. There was a history of disruption, with dad coming and going unpredictably and the older children in and out of trouble at school and with the police. They were hard up financially, as were nearly all the families in school, and mum juggled different part-time jobs and seemed under significant strain. There had been a referral to Social Care, but the family did not meet the threshold for child protection, and it had been hard to arrange network meetings with Bridget and the professionals involved. There had also been a referral to CAMHS for Marie, but appointments were not attended.

The therapist's account

"As I ran down the school corridors after Marie, who had burst out of the therapy room when the session drew near the end, I had a familiar sense of disappointment. The play and talking for the previous 35 minutes seemed to count for nothing. I felt helpless and useless about not being able to keep Marie in the room. I anticipated my limitations being humiliatingly exposed as I tried to return her to the classroom without her injuring herself or someone else as she hurtled along.

I thought, by running off as the end of the session approached, Marie was giving me a taste of what it was like for her to come up against ordinary boundaries like a 'no' or a 'stop', making her feel small, powerless, and not in control. It was intolerable to her to have a sense of her own wants or needs and to feel that she might want or need something from someone else. She would rather be the one cutting short her own session time than the one left wanting. Adrenaline-charged excitement anaesthetized her from feelings of loss or from worry that there wasn't enough of what she needed available. She fought to stay feeling in charge by making others be the ones to get in a panic. Running around school was an effective way of heightening anxiety in the education staff and me. It generated confusion and an idea of emergency.

One day, after several weeks of running out, Marie started the session by winding Sellotape around the furniture in the therapy room, creating a woven, hanging, invisible hammock. She told me she wanted something that was just there, so she could lie there too, in the gap between the solid things: it wouldn't be like lying on something, nor like lying in something. I talked to her about her longing for there to be something around her, holding her in a hammock kind of way, suspended, letting her sink in as though she was weightless. She asked me to help her find the end of the tape and hold it, so she could cut it into strips, and I said she wanted me to help her—she gave me a suspicious look—but in an invisible kind of way.

Marie continued to weave the tape into a hanging, transparent mesh and then delicately positioned herself over the hammock. She lowered herself. The tape snapped under her weight. She leapt up yelling, 'Ow!', distressed and furious, shouting at me that I hadn't done it right. I said she felt that I had broken the hammock feeling. She shouted that I shouldn't have cut it like that. I said she felt I was someone who made her crash down with my bad cutting, she got a shock and shocks hurt. Marie was deflated and tearful, she said she wouldn't be able to make it again and now it was all in a mess. I said perhaps she wasn't sure that she and I could do something about the mess together. Marie watched sullenly as I started to pick up sticky tape from the floor and I said it looked like it was only me who thought we could do some sorting out after a mess. She got up and told me I had missed bits and began to unwind tape from the chairs and table, saying miserably that it always goes wrong and she can't make it strong enough. I said she had wanted something strong that would bear her weight and she wanted me to know about disappointed and panicky feelings when there was a crash. She gathered all the bits of sticky tape into a ball.

When the ball was round and firm, Marie said it could be a cricket ball, and now we had to make some strong bats to hit the ball and play. I said she wanted things between her and me to be ok after the crash and after she was angry with me—she wanted to check that I was sticking with her. I added that she wanted us to play something where we could hit the ball strongly with our weight, but we'd have to wait until the next session, because it was almost time to stop. Marie shouted that it wasn't time to stop, and it wasn't fair. She held the ball as though she was going to throw it at the window. I said she felt like throwing me, her stopping-things-therapist, and the ball out of the window. She hesitated, put the ball into her personal toy box, and carefully put the lid on."

* * *

Following this session, the therapist arranged to meet with the head teacher and SENCo. They discussed Marie's communication of urgency gathered over the last weeks. The therapist explained what she had understood both about Marie's need to protect herself from painful shocks by being the one to give them, and about her powerful longing for a supportive structure that could be reliable and robust while not intrusive or demanding. There were questions about what kind of communication structure could be put in place that would be helpful and respectful to the family and to Marie.

The head teacher met with Bridget to ask whether she would consider meeting with her regularly to keep the school and family linked up. She also suggested having frequent joint meetings together with the therapist to sustain a shared picture of Marie's development in her family and school contexts. Bridget began to meet weekly with the head teacher, and the complexity of what she was trying to manage became clearer, even though there were no immediate solutions. Marie started to stay in her session for the whole time and became less overwhelmed by her strong feelings of panic, fury, and distress. She was a little calmer in class, with less need to take up a controlling position. In review meetings Bridget let the head teacher and therapist know that she thought Marie did worry about things a lot. When the therapist suggested that Marie might be worried about how Bridget herself was feeling, she was able to acknowledge this.

Broadly speaking, schools and child psychotherapy share the aim of trying to maximize children's potential for learning. Both are interested in supporting children to use their minds in the service of helpful development. Both consider children's development as individuals and as members of family and peer groups. But education and psychotherapy approaches do not necessarily share working structures and boundaries or theoretical frameworks for understanding and managing behaviour and emotional states. Trying to address the emotional/behavioural needs of a class of 30 is a very different task from trying to understand the ways in which a specific child or group of children show their feelings. The differences in working culture can afford a rich range of perspectives on children's emotional lives; not surprisingly, this can also generate tension and friction between professionals. And there is a history of conflict between Education and Health at local-authority and central-government levels in terms of who is responsible for what and where the funding comes from.

This book presents an exploration of the dynamics at play when child psychoanalytic psychotherapy is offered within primary school settings. We look at mainstream and alternative educational settings

and at individual, family, group, and staff consultation child psychotherapy approaches. We look at the challenges for education and child
psychotherapy workers: the potential for disagreement and discomfort,
as well as for creativity and collegiality. Questions are raised for child
psychotherapy culture and therapeutic technique, and issues emerge for
schools as hosts to specialized child psychotherapy projects.

Psychoanalysis—including child psychoanalytic psychotherapy—
has sometimes been thought of as privileging individual internal or
emotional life and not paying enough attention to the realities of experience in a world of structural inequalities, including structures of class,
race, gender, sexuality, and disability. Working in schools, particularly
the inner-city primary schools that feature in this book, requires us to
be in contact with the emotional reality of all aspects of children's—and
our own—identities and the way in which who, what, and where we are
is fundamental to emotional, relational development. Working as child
psychoanalytic psychotherapists in primary schools makes us investigate our own clinical theory and practice, and so this book also presents
a process of question and doubt and change in our work.

The idea of a book presenting different Tavistock child psychotherapy approaches in primary schools arose from supervision discussions
with colleagues working in mainstream and alternative education settings. We were keen to hear from each other about what worked, how,
and why. What we had learned from conversations with families and
teachers about their experience of in-school psychotherapy was central
to our project, and we wanted the book to put this across. Milly Jenkins
undertook a series of individual and group interviews with parents and
school staff, and these conversations are interspersed with chapters on
child psychotherapy approaches throughout the book.

Psychoanalytic thinking frames the child psychotherapy perspectives and practice represented here, though we use few psychoanalytic
technical terms. We decided to try to write in a descriptive way, much
as we would talk when at work in schools.

Part I presents the context in terms of children's emotional development during the primary school period, the place of child psychoanalytic psychotherapy in meeting complex emotional needs, and the
background of Tavistock child psychotherapy approaches in schools.

The first chapter in part I looks at children's ordinary emotional
development during primary school. Dexter Benjamin and Francesca
Benjamin consider the emotional factors at play when a child starts
school, including the impact of children's early experience on how they
manage the transition into school culture. They explore children's different ways of coping with anxiety associated with ordinary development,

the painfulness of change and loss, as well as the pleasure in growth and learning, and how, without being aware of it, this informs the kinds of emotional connections children create—or cut—within their own minds. These connections are integral to children's capacity to make relationships and learn. Benjamin and Benjamin explore the ways in which school offers children contact with peer and social/cultural groupings, contributing to the ongoing development of a sense of self linked to emotional experiences in groups, as well as with parents or carers and family. In a good-enough school environment, children can explore aspects of their own emerging personalities through their involvement in social dynamics, while at the same time social dynamics have a bearing on individual identity formation.

In chapter 2, I set out my view of what child psychoanalytic psychotherapy is, and how it works. I consider why this highly specialized approach can be particularly helpful to children with complex and chronic difficulties that are affecting their developmental and learning potential and impacting on their families and schools; and I discuss the usefulness of offering child psychotherapy approaches within primary schools.

Milly Jenkins ends part I with a brief history of the long relationship between Tavistock child psychotherapy and schools. The chapter captures some of the key initiatives and developments in the twentieth and twenty-first centuries.

Part II presents accounts of child psychoanalytic direct work with children and families and interviews with parents and teachers in mainstream primary school settings.

In chapter 4, Kathryn Fenton and Anya Suschitzky write about working in a school nursery with young children and their parents or carers in the context of the UK government's early intervention agenda. They discuss the helpfulness of careful, detailed nursery observation in working with families and the school to understand difficulties with separation and other issues. A shared picture of the underlying anxieties for the child and the family is developed through a focus on the emotional meaning of a child's behaviour. This shared picture is fundamental to establishing therapeutic relationships with parents who are wary of engaging with professionals or agencies.

Chapter 5 investigates the usefulness of a children's psychotherapy group in primary school. Marta Cioeta considers what is offered by child group psychotherapy and the benefits and demands of delivering this within schools. Faced with paralysing dynamics in a group of children whose families had histories of traumatic loss and dislocation, Cioeta and her colleague consulted with parents and teachers and adapted their technique.

The perspective of parents is foregrounded in Milly Jenkins' interview with Isha and Sheikh in chapter 6. Isha and Sheikh are the parents of Mohamed, who was 9 years old when the school referred him to the Tavistock Outreach in Primary Schools in-school team and whose anger and aggression had become increasingly difficult for his parents and the school to understand or manage. They talk frankly of their doubts and concerns as parents about the possibility of psychotherapy for Mohamed. Jenkins interviews them together with Marta Cioeta, the lead child psychotherapist in school, about their experience of Mohamed being in individual therapy for two years.

A grandmother's experience of her granddaughter, Kayla, for whom she is the kinship carer, having child psychoanalytic psychotherapy is explored in chapter 7. Mel Serlin introduces the complex situation of kinship care arrangements and draws on interviews with Kayla's grandmother, Eileen, her teacher, and the psychotherapist in discussing the developing relationship between family, school, and child psychotherapy service.

Part II ends with a conversation, chapter 8, between a deputy head, a family support worker, and a child psychoanalytic psychotherapist working together in a primary school. Milly Jenkins invites discussion about what working together has been like for each of them. They consider the benefits for children, families, and school staff, as well as the discomfort and conflict encountered in work across education and mental health cultures.

Part III is about work in alternative educational settings: a school for children with severe physical and cognitive disabilities; a primary pupil referral unit (PPRU); and a therapeutic school.

Chapter 9 starts part III with Carlos Vasquez's account of individual psychoanalytic psychotherapy with a 6-year-old boy with autism in a special school. Kevin was non-verbal and extremely withdrawn. Building an understanding of him relied on the psychotherapist noticing and examining his own changing states of mind, particularly states of hopelessness, in response to small changes in Kevin's behaviour and attitude. Vasquez notes how school culture lent itself to extending his usual approach, including using non-verbal forms of communication himself.

In chapter 10, Fiona Henderson describes a developmental child psychotherapy approach with excluded children in a PPRU. Opportunities for ordinary, small steps in helpful emotional development emerge through running therapeutic groups for children. This is supported by a thoughtful school culture that is enhanced by a reflective group for education staff. Henderson gives an account of therapeutic groups for younger and older children and of the group for school staff.

Following this, in chapter 11, Lena, the mother of Alek, a 7-year-old boy in the PPRU, talks to Milly Jenkins about what the move from mainstream primary school to the PPRU was like for her and her son. Lena is joined by Fiona Henderson in a frank discussion about the experience of individual and group psychotherapy for Alek.

Working in a therapeutic school involves having an active role in all aspects of the school community and structure, inside and outside the therapy room, at playtimes and lunchtimes as well as in therapy sessions. This is the setting for chapter 12. Ruth Glover writes about the contribution of child psychoanalytic psychotherapy to the thinking and dynamics of a therapeutic school day unit for children with complex and pronounced emotional, behavioural, and educational difficulties.

The last chapter in part III, chapter 13, presents interviews conducted by Milly Jenkins with the therapeutic school's head teacher, lead nurse/clinical lead, and child psychotherapist. Each interviewee talks to Jenkins about what they see working and what the obstacles are in bringing together educational and psychotherapy approaches in a setting where the needs of the children and the demands on staff are extreme.

The final part of the book, "Evidence from Experience and Audit", considers the difference that having child psychotherapy within primary schools makes to children, families, and teachers and to what schools can offer in relation to helpful emotional development.

Chapter 14 provides an analysis and discussion of quantitative and qualitative audit data from a Tavistock child psychotherapy outreach in primary schools project. The project stands as a case study of child psychoanalytic work in primary schools, and the data is investigated in terms of measurable outcomes that are meaningful for families, schools, and commissioners. The reality of data collection for busy clinicians, teachers, and families is also considered.

PART I

WHY HAVE
CHILD PSYCHOANALYTIC PSYCHOTHERAPY
IN PRIMARY SCHOOLS?

CHAPTER ONE

Ordinary emotional development in the primary school years

Dexter Benjamin & Francesca Benjamin

The idea of developmental milestones can evoke a picture of slow, steady progress made from year to year, and yet when one thinks about the experience of approaching the school gates for the very first time as a child or parent, a rather more complex and dynamic picture of emotional tumult comes to mind. For children, there can be excitement, anticipation, and a sense of pride at being more grown up and ready for big school. However, alongside the promise of new relationships and discoveries, there are often feelings of bewilderment, dread, and loss. Similarly, parents and carers commonly experience pride and pleasure in their child's readiness for the challenges ahead, alongside sadness at the loss of their baby.

This chapter draws on psychoanalytic concepts in presenting our understanding of emotional development in the primary school years. We begin with some thoughts about the impact of early experience and relationships on starting school. Then we explore factors at play in school transitions and new relationships and in forming individual and group identities. We consider the importance of individual and group identity formation as key aspects of developing the capacity to contain oneself, which is intrinsic to learning and emotional life.

DOI: 10.4324/9781003185925-3

Early experience and new beginnings at school

As school life begins, parents and child have to adapt to a new routine and culture, one that is quite different from their familiar home environment. In particular, the movement from being within a close-knit family, a small child-minding group, or even in a lively nursery setting to being part of a large classroom environment asks of children that they gradually acclimatize to a greater level of structure. They will have to make do with fewer opportunities for free play and self-expression, or one-to-one time with adults. Navigating this challenge can afford children an experience of growing braver and more independent; and becoming embedded in the world of school, with its hints of the grown-up world of work, can still be anchored in imaginative play.

Games of Hide and Seek and Mummies and Daddies are classic examples of play as the vehicle through which children begin to negotiate key developmental experiences of separation and loss. In ordinary circumstances, children come to realize that they can be held in mind by someone who is elsewhere, and that their memory of that person can keep the relationship alive when separated.

Taiwo

> Taiwo, a 4-year-old reception-class girl, is playing in the home corner of the classroom with another child, Ennio, as the teaching assistant looks on. She rather earnestly gathers a toy phone, keys, and a thick book into an old lunchbox and explains that she is putting her laptop and lunch into her briefcase and that she is running late and must hurry to work. She turns to a slightly bemused Ennio and blows him a kiss, before waving and rushing to an empty desk a few metres away. Seconds later, she hurries back into the home corner, exclaiming, "I am back from work!" and asking the teaching assistant how her day has been. She repeats this sequence a few times before asking Ennio now to go to his work, and asks him to pick her up from school later. As these scenarios play out, the atmosphere becomes lighter, and Taiwo's brow less furrowed. Ennio begins to complain about the traffic and, smiling at Taiwo, comments on the need to pick up some yoghurt and grapes on the way home.

This vignette illustrates Taiwo's increasingly creative way of managing significant goodbyes and absences that form an integral part of starting primary school. Through repetition and elaboration, she starts to experience what is initially serious play as a more playful business, where Ennio and the teaching assistant's identities and agency are more recognized in their own right and where there is greater scope for improvisation and reciprocity.

This example highlights the way in which the benefits of play are enhanced by opportunities to join in, from small group to entire class levels, offering a collective ability to think and imagine from multiple perspectives. Through this process, the group's knowledge and understanding of the world is deepened and its capacity for creativity made greater than the sum of its parts.

Creative play, such as seen above, is more likely to be in evidence where there have been, over time, repeated good-enough early experiences of care, which helps children with current experiences in terms of getting it right and recovering from getting it wrong. In families, the interplay of positive early experiences with a child's own capacity to build on these helps to establish a secure parent–child connection. Children and parents are then better able to tolerate the ordinary pain and anxiety stemming from ordinary separations that predate the beginning of school, such as weaning, bedtimes, and the return to work after maternity or paternity leave. This process forms the bedrock of negotiating the significant emotional changes and accompanying loss of earlier aspects of the parent–child relationship that are linked with starting school. As we see with Taiwo, this is also the platform for forming positive relationships with adults and children.

Graham Music (2016) grounds these emotional dynamics in an understanding of early brain development. He describes the importance of *biological or physiological templates*, which can shape the types of relationships that a child is likely to have, as well as their physical and cognitive skills and functioning.

Alongside the negotiation of anxiety and loss is the potential expansion of curiosity and a love for knowledge offered by school life. The reception-aged child often shows a strong desire both to know more about the familiar and to discover uncharted worlds beyond the home, forming new relationships with school staff and other children and accumulating countless interesting facts about tadpoles and planets. During this developmental phase, there is a gradual gathering of understanding about the world, both from emotional experience and from classroom learning. Through primary school, there is essential learning about one's feelings and one's identity, about what it means to have different kinds of relationships within one's own mind and with others, and about feelings of belonging to or being excluded from social/cultural groups, in preparation for adolescence.

With so many individual, interpersonal, biological, and group-dynamic factors, it is inevitable that the process of learning about self, identity, and relationships will not be steady or linear. If one's early experiences of being cared for are distorted or disrupted, then future attachments, relationships, and capacity to engage with the emotional fabric of the school in general may be influenced or compromised.

Ordinary anxieties about separation or new relationships sometimes feel overwhelming and can lead to unhelpful coping strategies. We may see this in children who, on starting school, become exceptionally clingy or rejecting, over-familiar or distant, overly compliant or resistant to boundaries, and unpredictable or intolerant of change. If anxiety is intense, play and learning may become characterized by excessive rigidity, a tendency to chaos or artificiality: adopting a superhero or know-all stance or repeatedly finding ways of escaping notice, for example. There may be times when a child seems prone to getting lost in the school building, withdraws from peer and adult relationships, is unable to stay in class, or does not want to go to school at all.

The following vignette describes the struggle of Matthew, a 7-year-old boy, to stay in school. Matthew was an only child whose family had had ongoing Social Care involvement for a number of years. There was chronic domestic violence, leading to the recent separation of Matthew's parents, which had increased their acrimony. In addition, both Matthew's maternal grandmother and his aunt, to whom he was close, had passed away during the previous six months. Matthew had become increasingly anxious and reluctant to leave his mother in the mornings, and teachers were concerned about his aggressive behaviour in school.

Matthew

> Matthew is deeply engrossed in a task involving the creation of a three-dimensional cardboard house, when another child speaks to him, saying, "You've done it wrong—that's not what you were supposed to do." Matthew immediately lashes out at the child, before moving around the room, frenziedly knocking other children's work onto the floor, upturning tables and chairs, and physically turning on the teaching assistant who attempts to intervene. Upon being told that he would have to go home, he immediately calms down, waiting in the corner of the classroom to be collected by his mum.

Matthew's behaviour seems to show the importance of a secure emotional base in order to engage with the school environment and learning tasks and to manage provocation from peers. Perhaps, working hard at the learning task, Matthew is trying to create the feeling of a solid, stable home, something that is particularly difficult for a child whose home life has been so upsetting. At the same time, he may feel worried about—and, at some level, even responsible for—his parents' separation, his mother's wellbeing, and the involvement of Social Care, with its implications of further separations and losses. This may be why he finds his classmate's interruption and criticism unbearable, connecting to a terrible worry that his own getting things wrong has made everything go wrong at home. One could view Matthew's violent outburst both as an expression of the chaos and conflict he feels in his life at the moment and as a means to get back home, where he can check on his mum, making sure he doesn't lose her too.

Progress and pitfalls in transitions

It is not only the big transition from home to school that carries such weight in the world of the young child. Children need to negotiate many daily transitions at school, such as the change from one class to another, the beginnings and endings of playtimes and lunchtimes, and changes in subject or activity. Children also need to cope with the relational shifts that accompany changes in class teachers, playground supervisors, classroom assistants, and peers, which can feel enormously unsettling. The strength of the child's emotional resources and the extent to which these times can be prepared for and facilitated by others are significant factors in how the child will tolerate both progression and loss, not just in the early years, but throughout life.

Priya

Priya is a quiet girl in Year 1, who seems untroubled by separations and leaves her mother readily at the gates, settling into classes quickly after arriving. On closer observation, however, it is noticed that she never actually says goodbye to her mother or hello to her class teacher. In the classroom, she goes fairly unnoticed for long periods of time, although, when asked, both teachers and children report liking her. Priya is a bright girl, but teachers can feel frustrated that she becomes distracted and therefore does not always reach her potential. In addition, Priya frequently gets lost between the classroom, dinner hall, and playground, even when walking with her friends or with a member of staff. She daydreams, dawdles behind others, stares at the artwork on the walls, and as a result she often gets left behind. When spotted by a member of staff or a friend, Priya can sometimes seem unsure of where she has been and where she is going. But she recovers her bearings quickly, checking where it is she should be.

Priya could be understood to be managing moments of transition and separation throughout the day by ignoring them. But without these important punctuations there is no distinction between one activity or experience and another, so the emotional meaning of the movement and changes in her day becomes increasingly confused. In these moments, she seems to feel less held together and literally loses her direction. In the face of moving into a physical space or situation with different rules, Priya enters into a dreamy state, where she is harder to notice, and where her sense of time and space is blurred. It is the focused quality of her friends' and teachers' attention that allows her to notice she has become lost or preoccupied, find her sense of agency again, and reengage with the environment and where she needs to go.

As well as ordinary moments of transition throughout the school day and week, there are, of course, more substantial transitions, such as the ending of term, changes of class at the end of the school year, and ultimately the transition from primary to secondary school, which is often in the minds of children and their parents well before starting Year 6. A child's inclination to tolerate these shifts without becoming excessively anxious or derailed is dependent on their capacity to work through and recover from the ordinary losses accompanying development. Losing one teacher at the end of the school year and gaining a new teacher at the beginning of the next is a usual experience for most primary school children. Any type of weaning—that is, in this context, the need to relinquish the old class teacher as a source of emotional comfort and intellectual nourishment—can stir up much earlier experiences of loss: a process that Freud (1917e) called mourning.

A child who is able to experience some degree of sadness, disappointment, anxiety, or anger at the end of the year about having to lose a teacher they feel particularly close to is likely also to hold onto positive aspects of their relationship with their teacher during and after the transition. They are then less likely to become unhelpfully preoccupied with, for example, a belief that no other teacher could match up to their predecessor. Instead, they will have a greater proclivity to get to know a new teacher, a desire to find out about them and to share things about themselves. In other words, a process of mourning can enable a child to encounter new experiences and people optimistically, relatively unencumbered by the past.

One of the ways that children manage experiences of loss, change, and separation during the early years is through the use of what Winnicott (1953) referred to as the transitional object. This often manifests in younger children as an attachment to a physical object such as a blanket or a teddy but can also be a rhyme or song, experienced by the child as belonging to them while being separate from them—partly "not me" and partly "me". Transitional objects represent important aspects of the parent–child bond and of the experience of being cared for, so children often respond very powerfully to their presence or absence. In primary-school-aged children, transitional objects might appear in other ways, such as a well-chewed sleeve or endless updates of interactions with the family dog. Such phenomena help children to tolerate anxieties about being separate from parents or carers and also connect them to the supportive structures in their older-child world, such as effective communication between parents and school and within the school system. This allows children to begin to let go of earlier ways of relating and communicating with others in a familiar environment and sets up the conditions for them to continue this process successfully once the transition has been made.

It will come as no surprise to teachers and parents that the outward signs of potential pitfalls inherent in emotional transitions can take very ordinary forms, such as unfinished cornflakes at breakfast, dragging feet on the way to school, or rambunctiousness in the corridors between lessons and break times. Schools can be painfully aware of the impact on children of losing a class teacher or teaching assistant, as mentioned above, especially when it has taken time and hard work to build those relationships with children who find separations hard. It can be particularly difficult to contain despair and frustration when witnessing a child responding to loss with the kind of regression that leaves staff and parents feeling as if they, too, are back to square one. One way of understanding this behaviour is as a communication by the child that they do feel as if they have lost everything. Faced with the experience of transition as a disaster, children may express anger and reproach, feeling that the adults are ruining everything by ending a fun lesson, or break time, or academic year. It is important to consider, in terms of what can go wrong, that children's accusations of ill-treatment can provoke irritation or defensiveness from adults rather than straightforwardly communicating feelings of loss and sadness that might elicit a sympathetic response.

School relationships and school learning

A central determinant in a child's ability to thrive in school is being in a psychological state of containment (Bion, 1962): that is, having the experience of feeling safe, held in mind, and belonging to a place where a holistic picture of them, warts and all, is known about, well enough understood, and reasonably accepted. A child's earliest relationships form the environment within which they start to explore their feelings and begin to develop the capacity to think and make sense of their experience. If parents or primary carers can help a baby show their needs and wants relatively freely, absorb the emotional intensity the baby communicates, and respond in a way that leaves the baby feeling carefully attended to and enabled to carry on communicating, this is a helpful, containing basis from which a child can take steps in learning about their world and themselves. In the previous section we linked early relationship-based experience to the way in which a child manages to begin school; here we connect school learning both to the child's emotional base in family relationships and to new, school relationships (Youell, 2006).

A containing school environment may manifest in many ways: from friendly dinner ladies and caretakers to differentiated learning and learning support, personalized education plans, and parent evenings. At a different level, consistency of classroom and wider school routines and expectations, as well as the familiarity of the building and the space to be creative and discover, all contribute to a child's experience of containment.

At the heart of all of this is the child's relationship with educational staff: primarily, but not always, the class teacher. School staff can serve as sources of knowledge, safety, and authority, and as parental figures during the school day. In relationships with their students, school staff help children learn to manage the most powerful of emotions, ranging from love to hatred, which might otherwise overwhelm them.

One of the ways in which children communicate and so develop these key relationships is through processes of identification: that is, putting themselves in the shoes of others and finding ways of putting others in their own shoes (Klein, 1946). They communicate in a myriad ways, including through physical and verbal expression and the ways in which they work and learn in class. Every communication is suffused with a range of emotions. The child's manner or style of metaphorically wearing their own shoes and giving them to others to wear, adds nuance.

For example, some children may play at being the teacher: here the child may be working through daily interactions to explore both positive and negative aspects of their particular pupil–teacher relationships, such as expectation and disappointment, accomplishment and hubris, curiosity and assumption. Play or playful communication may also invite a complementary means of being discovered. We see this in children who bring passion and interest to their relationships, sparking curiosity and reflection about them (and the relationship with them) in the teacher's mind.

Other children, however, may play as if they really are the teacher. In this version of play, they may be mimicking very accurately what a teacher does rather than allowing themselves to explore their ideas and feelings about the teacher. These children may have a knack of getting under the skin of those around them, often in a way that evokes rejection. In this kind of play the primary preoccupation may be more to do with needing to get rid of a feeling than trying to making sense of it. Appropriating the role of teacher might also be a child's way of feeling in charge and in control so as to avoid feeling small and powerless, or simply uncomfortable in their own skin.

Daily, ordinary experiences of relating between pupil and school staff are often linked to the historical relationships of both child and adult. Perhaps unsurprisingly, the picture of teacher–child interaction can be incredibly vivid, involving strong emotions such as hate, fear, and love.

Similar dynamics, which contribute to the development of a child's social skills, can be seen in peer relationships and friendships, as described below.

Charlotte and Layla

Charlotte and Layla have been friends since they were sat next to each other in Mrs Barlow's class at the start of Key Stage I. Charlotte is a confident, bright, and articulate girl, who is very good at leading imaginative games, often involving mummies and babies, or doctors and nurses. These characterize her genuinely caring and thoughtful side, despite her appearing at times as totally carefree, and being affectionately known in the staff room as a chatterbox. Layla, on the other hand, is a shy but thoughtful girl, often reluctant to put her hand up in class. She is much more likely to follow games led by others but seems to possess a quiet strength, which has the effect of calming those around her. In the playground, the two friends are near the climbing frame when Charlotte jumps up excitedly and says, "I know, let's climb to the top of the mountain!" A little unsure, Layla responds, "It is awfully high!" but follows anyway. As they begin their ascent, Charlotte skilfully climbs to the highest rung, while Layla cautiously negotiates the lower part of the frame. "Come on Layla, come on! We are mountain lions!" Layla giggles, roaring timidly, as she climbs a little higher. The two are surveying the playground below, when the lunch bell rings. When climbing down, Charlotte briefly loses her footing. Her demeanour suddenly changes, and worriedly she tells Layla that she is stuck. Layla climbs carefully down and moves around to Charlotte, earnestly telling her, "I'll rescue you." She holds her hand up towards Charlotte and guides her down.

As older siblings, both girls are not strangers to looking after others, and this is part of what has brought them together. Charlotte has a younger brother, who is reserved and, like Layla, tends to follow others. Layla's younger sister is known as the family entertainer, often daring Layla into mischief. Charlotte and Layla find in each other not only someone to look after, but someone with whom they can explore other aspects of sibling dynamics, including feelings of vulnerability and dependency. Since the birth of her brother, Charlotte has compensated for the loss of exclusivity with her parents by focusing on mastery—of her feelings, of her environment, and of her needs. Layla, on the other hand, has developed a degree of withdrawal from feelings and the world around her. Through their friendship, both can flexibly and safely take turns to experience what it is like to have something to offer and to need something from the other.

Inevitably, limitations in the containing nature of school routines and relationships arise, even if these are often temporary. This can happen if emotional pain and pressure is too great for a relationship to bear: for example, when a child tries to rid themselves of angry feelings by goading their teacher, leading to an uncharacteristically angry and punitive reaction from the teacher in question. The containing relationship can also be compromised by pressures in the wider system: in relation to governmental targets, austerity measures, and Ofsted inspections, for example, or familial experiences of poverty, bereavement, and societal discrimination, which feed into the dynamics of school life. At the level of the playground, a tendency to communicate through ridding oneself of painful feelings can lead to excessive conflict, bullying, or being bullied, as well as social isolation and scapegoating: dynamics that can, in turn, lead to low self-esteem and further negative reinforcement of challenging behaviours.

Identity development and links with learning

The capacity to contain oneself becomes increasingly important for older children attempting gradually to establish relationships away from the family and to approach school learning with greater independence. In this section we suggest that individual and group identity formation are a central aspect of the capacity to contain oneself.

It is easy to underestimate the multitude of environmental and biological differences, and their interplay, which influence the formation of identity. From our earliest moments, social expectation and conditioning meet genetic predisposition, linked to such absolute or contested aspects of life as gender and temperament. Furthermore, each individual will incorporate and use in their own way the many psychological traits passed on through early bonding experiences within the family milieu. Boys and girls can be seen as living and developing within socially defined boundaries about what is acceptable or unacceptable for them, including what colour clothes they should wear, what toys should interest them, how much they should cry, their language development, and to what extent they can express their physicality and aggression. This is further complicated by social constructions of sameness and difference pertaining to race, class, and family composition that are intrinsic to emotional life and personal identity. A child's educational journey is informed even before they are born by intergenerational narratives of success and failure, linked to structural inequalities.

These factors play a part in shaping the identity and role, on the spectrum between fitting in and non-conformity, that children adopt within their social networks at home and in school. Different ways of responding to outside cues, influenced by genetic predisposition and environmental opportunity, can become habitual, a default mode of functioning, whether helpful or unhelpful in nature.

A reasonably consistent facilitating school environment plays a crucial role, not only as a point of reference in others' understanding of the child's ever-shifting emotional world, but also in a child's own establishment of a consistent sense of self and their ability to be separate and comfortable in their own skin. To have an experience relatively unimpeded by worries or distractions allows for curiosity and creativity to come to the fore in the classroom setting—something essential in independent and group learning. In a psychological state of receptiveness and readiness, an activity or task can be appreciated and engaged with in its own right, not unduly limited by a child's needing to deal with being alone and how he or she manages that, for example. Confidence gained from combining creativity, knowledge, and skill establishes a virtuous cycle, whereby the child's positive sense of identity is further strengthened, especially in relation to the capacity for self-containment and independence.

Joshua

Joshua is a Year 5 student of slightly above-average intelligence and exceptional enthusiasm, who has recently transferred from another school. One morning, the class is learning about Henry VIII. As has been typical in History, Joshua's favourite subject since starting at the school, he frequently puts up his hand to answer questions, even when he doesn't fully know the answer. His teacher is keen to nurture his ability and preserve his enthusiasm but also feels frustrated and undermined by the ongoing impingement on Joshua's and his classmates' learning. Aware of his relative newness and accompanying worries, she decides to focus on supporting the understanding in his incomplete answers, simultaneously drawing in other members of the class. After this particular lesson, she also makes an extra effort to make contact with and find out about him in other ways during the school day. Over time, Joshua begins to make friendships in the class and also becomes appropriately hesitant and uncertain in relation to knowing the answers, waiting before raising his hand to ask questions. Slowly, his academic levels improve, a little beyond what has been predicted for him.

Here, we see Joshua as a boy without a settled place and sense of belonging, using his cognitive capacities as a way of trying to establish himself with the teacher and classmates. One could understand his fascination with Henry VIII as a wish to be powerful and admired, ensuring place and status, to defend himself—without being aware of this—from the discomfort of uncertainty, of not knowing where he stands socially and academically, and the threat of going unnoticed. While his interruptions push him into the minds of others for a time, it is at the expense of discovering something not already known and of his potential pleasure in learning new things. Without support, a child in this position might continue to behave as if they knew everything already, apparently performing well while not open to learning anything new, not able to show vulnerability and so not easily letting a teacher help. In Joshua's case, his teacher's capacity to hold in mind his vulnerability as a new student meets an awareness that his pushiness and wish to be cleverest serves as protection from feeling small and lost. She is able to adopt an inclusive, whole-class approach and, crucially, avoid using her own intellect or cleverness to manage her frustration and unhelpfully silence his worries. This allows him to feel that he does have a place, in the minds of both teacher and classmates. Such a sense of belonging leaves him better equipped to tolerate the frustration of not-knowing and so gradually become open to curiosity and freer learning.

As children move through primary school, one-to-one relationships develop and best friends are made within a world of ever more sophisticated social interaction. We see with increasing clarity the way in which children start to adopt roles that may both suit their personality and express something on behalf of the school class or social group (Bion, 1961, pp. 117–119). We might see a class clown ramping up their acting out during the introduction of a topic that is particularly difficult to understand, and a group of children only too welcoming of the distraction. Children may find themselves assigned a litany of roles: black sheep, scapegoat, class-clown, little-miss-perfect, swot, wimp, the bullied, or the bully. Some children may play these parts all too readily, and struggle to give them up. At the same time, each child develops their capacity to choose different sorts of intimate friendships and extend their reach into the social world. These more varied peer relationships offer greater opportunities for learning about oneself and others, consolidating a sense of identity. However, increased confidence and freedom of thinking can, paradoxically, be experienced as overwhelming or frightening. Greater independence inevitably brings a starker experience of being separate and exposes the developing child to loneliness or feelings of abandonment: "Will the teachers still think about me if I can manage by myself?"

Loneliness and the sense of abandonment can, however, be mitigated by the child having a real experience of belonging to a group beyond the family. Developing a sense of an independent self is inextricably linked to, and in constant interplay with, having an actual place in relation to a wider socio-cultural history and context.

At worst—for example in scapegoating, bullying, and the out-of-control classroom—this process can happen in a primarily defensive way, which seeks to idealize characteristics like strength, power, and ruthlessness, while disavowing what are felt to be weak aspects of the self, such as vulnerability, dependency, and shame. Such disavowal can then compromise the capacity for compassion and empathy. This process contains many features of what Bion (1961) called basic assumption functioning, where a group, and the individuals in it, are concerned mostly with defending against anxiety, often linked to trying to achieve a task (in the classroom this might be the task of trying to learn as a group). As a counterbalance to the depressingly familiar resistance to learning captured in this dynamic, Armstrong (2010) helpfully reminds us that Bion (1961) also describes, alongside the pull towards basic assumption functioning, a group and its individuals as being "hopelessly committed to a developmental procedure" (p. 89).

It is our belief that the development of a true sense of self emerges in learning from the emotional experience of group dynamics; that the development of individual and group identity are intimately connected. This learning brings the possibility of simultaneously feeling oneself to be alive as an individual with a sense of agency and belonging to, but also being represented by, something greater than oneself. The extent to which a child can be aware of and tolerate feelings about what they are leaving behind is therefore crucial not only to that child's relationships, but also to the continuing development of his or her group and individual identity. This is dependent on whether the child's own capacity to feel held in mind is supported by ongoing important relationships in their life and the way in which their progress and achievements can be facilitated by those around them.

Towards the end of primary school, many children have to contend with the onset of puberty. This brings an awareness of both emotional and physical change, at once exciting and bewildering. Anxieties associated with bodily changes and sexual development manifest in a range of preoccupations with body type and attractiveness. The recent explosion of awareness about gender identity questions highlights another dimension of complexity in negotiating the transition from childhood into adolescence. This can be understood not only in relation to environmental and societal pressures, but also in terms of changes in how it actually feels for young people to inhabit their bodies.

At around this time, technology starts to establish itself as a pivotal part of everyday social life and social interaction with family and peers. Comparisons with others, in terms of physical appearance, dress sense and popularity, are intensified through social media apps and accounts, online group activity, and even whether or not one owns a phone or tablet.

We have explored the importance of learning about oneself through others during the primary school years. The interplay of individual and group identity development helps children to start to find a sense of themselves as relational beings outside as well as inside the family and to manage emotional and classroom learning while gradually developing the capacity to contain themselves.

Given the ordinary considerable challenges of identity development and the importance of the group to the individual, real experiences of prejudice and discrimination severely heighten anxiety, attacking a child's emerging sense of individual and group identity and so threatening their growing self-containment. In the classroom, as in society, discrimination seems commonly to relate to physical differences such as gender, size, skin colour, attractiveness, and those differences created by physical disability or less visible differences such as social status, intelligence, and emotional security or vulnerability. Such factors interact in a complex way, both protecting and threatening a child's identity in the group. We might see this in the intelligent child who is both disparaged and admired by his or her peer group. Equally, the reality of developing with a physical or cognitive disability can influence adult expectations of a child's potential progress and, in turn, affect the way in which children present and relate to their own needs, both ordinary and special.

Prejudice and discrimination pressurize identity development, impacting on a child's capacity to face emotional life without excessively constraining their relationships or curiosity. The attack on identity includes provoking a wish to protect the self through inhibition, acting out, and, crucially, restricted friendship formation, which can, in turn, constrain individual and group learning.

Simon

Simon, a 9-year-old boy who emigrated from Kenya with his family aged 5, has joined a large group of children who are milling around on the grass after lunch, arguing about what to play next. He confidently and clearly suggests first Pokemon, then Star Wars, and finally British Bulldog, but his suggestions are ignored or rejected, with some of the children caricaturing his faint accent. Becoming more agitated, louder, and less coherent, he becomes part of the clamour, desperately trying to find a route into the centre of the throng. Without an obvious resolution or consensus, the group divides into teams to play World Championship Wrestling, and Simon drifts uncertainly to the fringes of the group nearest to him. As the others engage in reciprocal body slams, suplexes, and a variety of creative throws and submissions, Simon's engagement becomes more erratic and rough. He is noticeably sweating, and his eyes flit around wildly. However, whenever he attempts to negotiate a wrestling sequence, or "tag in" with one of his team, he is again ignored. Gradually, the other children, including those on his team, become either exasperated or fearful as Simon becomes increasingly disinhibited and eventually loses control, hurting another child, at which point the playground supervisor intervenes, sending Simon inside.

It would seem that Simon is a reasonably confident and able child, who joins a group in some turmoil at the start of lunch play, struggling to find leadership and direction in their play. Viewing this as an example of Bion's concept of basic assumption mentality, one might understand that while all attempts at control of the group are being quashed or sabotaged, Simon's unremarkable bid for leadership, or for otherwise belonging, is set aside for different treatment. Noticeably different from the others in terms of skin colour and, to a degree, his accent, Simon appears to be collectively sequestered by the group—not quite allowed to join in on the same basis as the other children. In particular, it is his efforts to fit in that seem most unwanted, leaving him increasingly ostracized, feeling helpless, angry, and desperate. This seems to offer the group respite from its own struggles and anxieties around leadership, and it is then that the group is able to settle on a game to play. Any attempt by Simon to escape the role of pariah in which he finds himself is thwarted or even provokes further marginalization, until he seems to lose hold of all aspects of himself other than those acknowledged by the group: his different ethnicity, need for others, helplessness, anger, and, finally, loss of control.

Some children may have individual and environmental emotional resources to overcome such discriminatory pressures, for example by becoming more appreciative of community or being driven towards greater achievement. Schools can play a vital role in supporting young people and families in this regard, creating a protective space within which children can freely draw on the lived experience of being and relating from their particular cultures. This allows for an authentic discovery about self, others, and the world at large and, at its best, enriches the learning milieu of the school.

If children are not able to express themselves reasonably freely, they may fail to establish a clear-enough sense of their identity, becoming, for example, highly impressionable, clingy, easily forgotten or otherwise superficial, and false. Those finding progress and achievement too unsettling or suffused with loss may gain a reputation for self-sabotage. It is important for individuals, families, and schools to be able to challenge these identities when they become rigid and unchanging, as difficult as this may sometimes be.

Conclusion

We have attempted to draw together an overview of the emotional development context for primary school children's thinking and learning, including the supportive function of the imagination and reflectiveness of teachers in relation to children's social development and academic achievement.

The title of this chapter belies the extraordinary sprawl and intricacy of processes that contribute to the progression of the kind of emotional life in the primary school years that could be thought of as normal or unremarkable. For children, the start of school life brings the tremendous challenge of successfully joining and embedding into a new environment, managing fear and excitement about the unknown, while simultaneously finding a way to cope for extended periods without (usually) their greatest sources of safety and comfort. The negotiation of transitions is seen as an uncompromising game of snakes and ladders, where the child's own steps towards progress, development, and achievement are tempered by how well they cope with the unpredictability and severity of setbacks and failures. At once far from ordinary in terms of complexity and yet commonplace are the wide-ranging modes of verbal and non-verbal communication, epitomized in play, that allow children and teachers to recognize and empathize with emotional states in themselves and others. It is in this context that children and teachers have to learn and educate.

The chapter touches on the way in which past relationships and emotional experiences are brought to bear on the current situation. We highlight the importance to us all, as social creatures, of the classroom and the wider school system, which can organize itself around the task of work and learning, but can also mobilize individuals in the service of avoiding shared anxieties provoked by being in larger groups. At the same time, we have tried to illustrate the way in which the group environment in a school helps individual children not only to think, learn and manage emotion, but also to socialize, adopting ways of being that collectively constitute their sense of identity and gradually help to give meaning to who they are. The mastery of conflicting senses of self as an individual and as a group member is a fine balancing act, and the chapter presents the maze of issues for children in negotiating this challenge, in earnest perhaps for the first time, in preparation for secondary school. Although the complexity of the emotional task of development in the primary school years can look less tumultuous than that in the child's early years and adolescence, it is of paramount importance in terms of social identity and relationships and in establishing a safe and stable staging post before the upheavals of puberty kick in.

CHAPTER TWO

Using child psychoanalytic psychotherapy in primary schools

Katie Argent

Complex needs

Children's emotional health is informed by their social, cultural, and economic circumstances and family context, as well as by who they are and how they function individually, as discussed in chapter one. There are all sorts of emotional and practical obstacles in childhood that must be grappled with; families are children's most important resource for helping with this, and schools are also central.

In every school there are some children whose difficulties arise from a combination of environmental factors, family circumstances, and individual propensities or vulnerabilities, including ways of responding to experiences and physical or biological aspects of genetic inheritance. Trauma in the child's own life or in the lives of previous generations often plays a part in what is called adverse childhood experiences. Trauma can include experiences of neglect and abuse, dislocation, persecution, prejudice, intergenerational disadvantage, and/or physical or cognitive disability.

This mixture of individual, family, and environmental factors and the impact of repeated shocking experiences can lead to a child finding ways of managing emotional life that severely limit their capacity for curiosity and exploration in order to protect themselves from unmanageable distress and anxiety. This is not a cognitive, rational process. The child is not aware of protecting themselves from emotional contact through aggression or withdrawal. What the school or the family or others encounter

    DOI: 10.4324/9781003185925-4

in the child might be rejecting, contemptuous, or hostile behaviour and language at one end of the scale, or retreat, passivity, and silence at the other. We, the adults, may find ourselves responding in ways we don't understand—such as suddenly becoming uncharacteristically angry or wanting to get away from the child or feeling stupid and useless. Children with conditions described in mental health guidelines as co-morbid, where there is more than one major problem, often generate sharp feelings of anxiety or disturbance in others.

Becoming aware of such uncomfortable feelings can be helpful in identifying that something is seriously the matter. It is also valuable because it means that the child is continuing to communicate, even if this is at a level they do not notice. If parents, professionals, and support systems stop feeling and registering the disturbance, then there is a risk that we shut down communication and lose touch with the emotional needs of the child. This may make it easier for a child mental health or education system to operate in the short term, but, as schools and families know, complex emotional needs get knottier if they are not attended to.

It is not unusual for initial or new difficulties with eating, sleeping, toileting, concentrating in class, or peer friendships to appear solvable with additional support, only to reappear in a chronic form or to be replaced by a different problem. If difficulties become long-standing and if they interfere with a child's good-enough capacity to make and sustain relationships with others and to make and build on the connections within their own mind that are necessary for learning, then there may be a more complex emotional situation that needs further help.

In 2019 the Department for Education estimated that, in the average state primary school, there were 14 children whose complex, co-morbid condition was likely to require highly specialist intervention (DfE, 2019).

Highly specialist assessment

Where there are complex needs, there is usually an account of additional family and school support not having helped or not having helped enough, and the combination of individual and environmental factors having been compounded by the situation going on for a long time. A referral for highly specialist assessment and treatment may have been precipitated by an escalation of difficulty or by a recognition that the difficulties have become entrenched and are impacting on the child's emotional and learning development. Referrals are often made to specialist services when children are approaching a transition, such as from home or nursery school into reception class, from infant school into junior school, or from primary to secondary school, and there are worries about whether this will be manageable. The family, the school, and the child themselves cannot make sense of what is happening, of why the child is doing or saying things (or not doing and not saying things); what the child is showing seems to be outside their own understanding and control.

A careful, coherent, responsive, effective intervention requires different perspectives and skills and takes time. The development of a shared understanding with the child and family or carers about the current situation and the possible factors contributing to this is essential. A highly specialist assessment does not seek to give a definitive narrative of what has happened and why. It seeks to untangle and explore the factors at play in a way that makes sense to the child, family, and school.

An initial assessment needs to gauge the range and level of current emotional difficulty and need. This entails mapping the child's developmental history and the child–family relationship history; taking into account significant life events and circumstances; paying attention to the specific family culture and wider cultural context; gathering feedback from relevant professionals and agencies; and getting a flavour of the way in which the individual child and their parents or carers manage their emotional lives through first-hand clinician interaction. This is necessarily a relationship-based assessment approach, with the experience of the child and their family or carers at the centre. In an initial assessment, where there are complex needs, what takes time is building relationships, including ensuring that there is opportunity to admit uncertainty and doubt in the family, network, and clinicians and to address the feelings from hope to despair ordinarily stirred up by the offer of help.

Hassan

Hassan was a 7-year-old boy who was referred to the in-school psychotherapy service because of long-standing concern on the part of his teachers about his difficulties concentrating in class, angry outbursts, and fighting with other children. He was considered to be bright but was significantly under-achieving in reading, writing, and maths. He was described as confused and confusing.

There was a history of domestic violence, and Hassan and his younger brother now lived with their mother, Khadija. The school did not know whether there was contact with father. Khadija had told the school that there were no problems at home. Initiatives undertaken by the school to make a stronger home–school connection had not been sustainable.

Hassan had had a series of supportive interventions in and out of the classroom.

Although Khadija had agreed to the referral, she did not attend several appointments to meet with the child psychotherapist, Miri, and did not respond to phone messages or letters. The therapist talked to the referrer, the SENCo, who thought it might help if he offered to come to the first appointment together with Khadija, because they had known each other for several years, and although their relationship had not always been easy, he thought the relative familiarity might provide a bridge.

Khadija was initially reticent and then a bit indignant at the first appointment. She did not seem worried about her son and said he did not get angry or confused at home. The therapist found herself making a huge effort to engage mum and realized that she felt disbelieved, as though she was making up the concerns. The SENCo encouraged mum to bring Hassan to introduce him to the therapist the next time.

Hassan came to the second appointment with mum and sat next to her quietly. He was a slight, serious-looking boy, who glanced up quickly if invited to say something and then looked down or looked at his mum. Miri, the therapist, was aware of being particularly careful with what she said to him, and that she modulated the tone and volume of her voice. Hassan did start to look at the toy animals and figures that were on the table, eventually picking them up and gathering them into family groups. Meanwhile mum talked about both children being fine, her pregnancies had been normal, and there hadn't been any real concerns about either child's development; they managed well, she and the children. She told the therapist that the children's dad did not live with them. When the therapist asked about contact with dad, Khadija did not reply, and Hassan stopped investigating the toys. The therapist said she'd noticed that what she'd just said about contact with dad had had an impact, and mum smiled at Hassan and told the therapist that he was a sensitive boy. The therapist asked whether mum would like to talk with her on her own next time, and whether Hassan would like to be introduced to a colleague and see whether he'd want some space for himself as well.

Khadija came to meet the second therapist, Jo, with Hassan. Hassan looked anxiously at mum and said he wasn't sure about seeing this other therapist, but when mum said she thought it was a good idea, Hassan relaxed a little and agreed.

In the following weeks, bit by bit, Khadija let Miri know about a complicated family situation. She was close to her own mother and siblings but ostracized by her extended family, who disapproved of her relationship with the children's father. Her housing situation had been terrible while the children were small. She was living far from her close family, in flats that were damp, cramped, and infested, and she thought this had affected her children's health. Despite being a good eater, Hassan often had stomach upsets and intermittent asthma. Their current accommodation was slightly better but still too small, and mum had to sleep on the sofa. The rent was not entirely covered by state benefits, so they were in arrears, which meant that they were unlikely to be allocated a larger flat.

Khadija explained that her own parents had come to the UK as asylum-seekers from an East African country. They had left other family members, friends, and their home in order to seek safety. Links with their community in the UK were important to the family not only because of sharing a distressing history, but also because of the struggle to make a home in the UK in an environment that was not reliably welcoming and could be hostile.

Miri was aware of feeling kept at a distance by Khadija's matter-of-fact way of speaking, despite being told about painful family experiences. She remembered Khadija's reluctance to come to appointments and her reticence and annoyance to begin with. She said maybe Khadija was not sure about coming to talk to a white UK therapist like her in case she met racist criticism rather than a respectful welcome. Khadija said that she had not known what to expect.

Khadija said that the children had only once witnessed violence from their father towards her, and she had told the children that this was play-fighting, not real. She was sure that the children had no idea that this was anything other than playing and that they had not known about the violence on any other occasion.

After she left the children's father, a couple of years ago, Khadija worried that the father would turn up at school and try to take the children. This is why, for several months, the children did not go to school, which precipitated local authority concern about the children's well-being. Khadija said that now dad is meant to see the children on Sundays but is often late or does not arrive at the meeting place at all. She herself sometimes changed the arrangements at short notice. The social worker who'd got involved when the children were not going to school had talked to both parents about needing to make changes to arrangements in advance.

Khadija told Miri that for a long time she had hoped things would get better with her former partner. She had tried talking to her immediate family but felt so ashamed, particularly because the wider family had not approved of the relationship; she did not tell them quite how bad things were, and so they did not take it seriously. Even when the social workers got involved, she felt they did not believe her, and it was pointless trying to talk to them about how frightened she was. She felt she just had to cope on her own.

The therapist realized that her initial feeling of being disbelieved by Khadija might be useful information—a communication from Khadija about how she felt. Miri and Khadija talked about how confusing, distressing, and enraging the experience of not being believed could be. Khadija seemed relieved that this was understood.

She talked about Hassan being very much aware of his parents' separation and that he would often ask where his father was. She was proud of him being a sensitive boy; he helped her at home and was no trouble.

Miri talked with Khadija about Hassan's sensitivity. Gradually they started to explore the possibility that he was very tuned in to how she was and had perhaps been alert to the atmosphere at home during the time that dad lived with the family, even though Khadija had wanted to protect her children from knowing what was happening. The wish to protect them was strong partly because she had grown up knowing that her parents and grandparents had lived through terrible violence and had endured dislocation and loss of home in order that the next generations should not have to suffer in the same way. This played a part in making her own domestic situation feel shameful to her and unimportant, compared to the unhappiness that had gone before. It had often felt impossible for her to convey to others the seriousness of her situation, and now she found herself not knowing how seriously to take what the school was saying about her son.

Meanwhile, in his individual assessment sessions with Jo, Hassan quickly showed other sides of himself. Hassan's play was sometimes marked by its dreamy quality. With the toy figures and animals, he would present unstructured, shifting relationships between characters. His narratives had sudden gaps in meaning, and he would often forget a simple word or part of a word. Usually he would then continue as though there had not been a gap. When Jo asked about what had happened, or if occasionally he himself noticed the forgetting, he turned to Jo with a mixture of expectation and demand, as though she was meant to fill in the gaps of meaning for him.

In his play with toy figures and animals, Hassan seemed to identify himself with a strong male figure, a fantastical persona, who could be a helpful rescuer but could have more destructive qualities. By the second individual session, there were times when Hassan behaved towards Jo in a domineering, disdainful, angry fashion. Jo could see that this mood was triggered by Hassan becoming confused or uncertain in response to something she said, which he seemed to experience as being slighted or badly treated. His mood shifted quickly, and his level of aggression rose sharply at these moments. In the powerful male role, he treated Jo as a pathetically weak female worthy of contempt. He would make as though to hit or punch Jo, or poke her in the eye, but always stopped short of actually doing this. Jo noticed how an atmosphere of constant threat was generated, so that even when Hassan was playing in a more ordinary, companionable way, the tension did not ever go away.

Jo started to think about Hassan slipping into survival mode when he encountered what he experienced as a turning away from or against him. Hassan would attack first with his words or demeanour in order to pre-empt the attack he believed would come from Jo. Jo noticed that when he was feeling under attack, Hassan became worried about somebody coming into the therapy room and was vigilant about noises he could hear from outside. When in this anxious, volatile state, Hassan found it hard to tell the difference between what was real and what was in the realm of play—a game or the imagination. This seemed to tally with the school's concern that Hassan could easily end up involved in playground fights when play fighting spilled into real aggression.

The differences between Hassan and Jo in terms of race and religion, evident in terms of Jo being white and not showing religious observance in her dress and Hassan being black and from an observant Muslim family, as well as in relation to gender were integral to the developing therapy relationship in the early assessment sessions. Feelings of superiority and inferiority, power and powerlessness, potency and helplessness infused the interactions in the assessment sessions. Jo not being a Muslim heightened Hassan's expectation that she could not understand him and his funda-mental fear that he was not understandable. This fuelled his taking up an all-knowing, omnipotent position in order not to feel terribly alone and hopeless. It was important for Jo to talk openly about the differences between them, her not knowing all about him and needing to get to know him. It was also important to keep in mind the reality of prejudice and discrimination faced by the family—that the family's community was at the receiving end of racist threat locally and in the current political and social context. Hassan knew about being under attack, and not only because of what had happened between his parents in his home.

It was striking that Hassan did play and did talk to Jo from the beginning of the assessment. Although the way that he related to her was troubling, he was a powerful communicator, and she needed to be affected by him in order to start to understand his emotional experience. He seemed to feel relief when Jo talked to him about not being there to tell him off, but to try to understand him. With the emotional temperature a little lower, Hassan introduced the idea of having what he called "a meeting" within the session, for Jo to say what she had understood. There was an opening, a wanting to be understood, albeit at his command. These meetings within sessions also came with the risk that Hassan would feel not sufficiently understood and would need to protect himself immediately.

After a few appointments for Hassan alongside meetings between Khadija and Miri, Miri convened a wider meeting, with Khadija, the school SENCo, Hassan's class teacher, and Jo. By this point, Khadija seemed to feel supported enough to give weight to the perspectives of the class teacher and SENCo and to hear what Jo had learned about Hassan's emotional state. This left Khadija feeling more worried about Hassan than she had been before. She wondered whether he was so good at home because he didn't want to upset her. In fact, he had become stroppier at home recently, she told the meeting, and she had had to be more authoritative. It was distressing for Khadija to realize that her children had been more exposed to the violence at home than she had thought, and that finding ordinary ways of showing ordinary feelings might have become very difficult for Hassan, particularly if he felt he must protect his mum and not upset her.

There was a shared understanding of the ongoing impact of Hassan's early confusing and frightening experiences in his immediate family (perhaps, as Khadija and Miri had started to talk about, combined with a wider family history of violent trauma that continued to reverberate) and his individual way of managing this by becoming big and strong and powerful in his imagination. It seemed especially difficult for Hassan to know about and express his own ordinary aggressive feelings in manageable ways, which all children need to be able to do in order to take the small risks that are part of learning and social relationships. This helped the meeting see why Hassan hardly ever put his hand up or put himself forward in class, and why an ordinary disagreement could escalate suddenly into violence. There was shared worry about the extent of his propensity to muddle up reality and fantasy and the potential risk of harming others or himself. It was agreed that the level of confusion and anxiety shown by Hassan needed monitoring, with the possibility of requesting a psychiatric consultation from CAMHS.

Khadija did not want Hassan to be referred to CAMHS at this point, feeling that the school setting was easier both for him and for her. During the early assessment period, the social worker had offered to help to establish more regular and reliable contact for the children with their father; he also took on board the family's cramped housing conditions, which did not allow Hassan or his brother room to play or give Khadija a room of her own, though he was not optimistic about the chances of getting anywhere with this. However, by the end of the assessment the social worker was no longer involved and, with Khadija's permission, the therapist and the SENCo made a referral to Early Help in the hope of getting family support. Options for further work with the child psychoanalytic psychotherapy service in the school were considered: family work that would include Hassan's younger brother, group or individual work for Hassan, and parallel parent work with Khadija were all possibilities.

Guidelines for evidence-based treatment provided by the National Institute for Clinical Excellence (NICE) are an important starting point in considering options for ongoing therapeutic work. However, when considering complex emotional difficulties, or co-morbidity, assessment clinicians and teams usually find that guidelines cannot encompass the full picture gathered by the assessment process. NICE acknowledges the need for clinical decisions to go beyond the guidelines where there is complexity. This puts weighty responsibility on the assessment process having established good-enough communication between families, clinicians, and the network to arrive at a full-enough shared picture of what the matter is, so that a sensible decision can be made about what might help.

Trying to make sense of how a child interacts in their family and at school, communicates verbally and through their behaviour with peers and adults, shows their thoughts and feelings, and manages school learning is key to the role of a highly specialist clinician. Working together with the family, school, and network, highly specialist clinicians bring to the team around the child their experience and expertise in the area of child emotional needs and mental health. Following assessment, a specialist clinical intervention may be offered directly to the family, and/or consultation, training, and advice could be provided to the network and school, who have direct contact with the family. This may take place in a Child and Adolescent Mental Health Service clinic, in a school or other community setting, or in a third-sector or private setting.

The contribution of child psychoanalytic psychotherapy

The particular contribution of child psychoanalytic psychotherapy to an understanding of a child's emotional life in their home, school, and wider cultural context is both knowledge of non-verbal communication and skill in recognizing the thoughts and feelings that lie behind what is said and done. Underlying this is a comprehensive grasp of ordinary and unusual emotional development from birth to young adulthood; expertise in linking the current emotional situation with the individual child and family's particular history; and experience of interacting and communicating with children in an age-appropriate way.

As illustrated in the case example of Hassan, a child psychoanalytic approach involves a focus on emotional states that are not immediately observable or rationally known about. The approach uses sustained attention to the fine detail of someone's interactions, style of speaking, and behaving, as well as to the emotional states that interaction with the child creates in other people, including within the clinician. This is a way of trying to understand what a child and the people in the child's life are communicating at a fundamental emotional level: the fears, confusion, and powerful feelings that are not easy to put into words or show in manageable ways because they do not lend themselves to reasoned narrative.

The approach uses the emotional experience of the therapist as a way of making sense of a child's feelings. There is an exploration of the impact on the therapist of the child's way of being, and on the child of the therapist's way of being. This includes exploration of the emotional meaning for child and therapist of their difference and sameness. As with all relationships, where, who, and what someone is, including their cultural and social identity and history, is intrinsic to how contact develops. This means that the therapist has to be open to noticing dimensions of difference in emotional life that are integral to individual and group identity. There is not, of course, an equation of the clinician's subjective experience with the child's. The therapist must be able to differentiate their own emotional preoccupations from the child's, parent's, or carer's. This requires the therapist to know about their own limitations in terms of experience and their own areas of prejudice and ignorance.

A focus on the feelings behind behaviour and language is particularly valuable when communication is not working and relationships have got stuck, which are indicators of complex emotional difficulties. Without being aware of it, children and their parents or carers may have developed ways of dealing with emotional life that manifest as behaviour that it is hard for others to relate to or even to tolerate.

Working with extremes of hostility and passivity and a spectrum of challenging, rebuffing, depleting, and defeating ways of relating requires considerable capacity to know about and manage high levels of anxiety in the clinician. It is essential not to emotionally push away, judge, or normalize the worrying, painful, bewildering states stirred up by close contact with a child with complex difficulties. The task is to find a way of having emotional contact at the child's level, bit by bit, that helps the child and their family and school to start communicating in a more manageable way.

Working at the child's level means being open to how they show feelings and thoughts through imaginative play, playing games with rules, playing sport (up to the limits set by the available room and the available physical capacity of the therapist), drawing and making things, being active, being still, talking and being quiet. Child psychoanalytic psychotherapists may literally put themselves at the child's level, sitting on the floor or using the whole room to engage in play, while maintaining safe, consistent boundaries. The approach is led by how the child interacts, plays, and talks. This can be used in individual child, parent–child, family, and group work and drawn on in work with parents and carers and in consultation and training with other professionals and professional networks.

Child psychoanalytic psychotherapy with children and families where there are pronounced and entangled emotional needs usually takes place within a team context. This may be a multidisciplinary CAMHS team or a community-based multi-agency, multi-professional team organized pragmatically according to the circumstances of a particular child or family, as seen in the case of Hassan.

Child psychoanalytic psychotherapists have established school-based assessment and treatment approaches throughout the UK. In subsequent chapters in this book we look specifically at a range of initiatives developed under the umbrella of the Tavistock Clinic; an evaluation of effectiveness is offered in chapter 14.

Getting to CAMHS

When environmental and emotional obstacles cannot be managed even with the help of family and school, to the extent that children's relationships, learning, and potential for development are in jeopardy, and when ordinary additional support has been tried and has not helped enough, then a referral to CAMHS is usually considered. The purpose of a multidisciplinary CAMHS team with expertise in a range of areas is to bring together different, highly skilled perspectives so that the knot of child and family experiences and histories can be untangled and gradually understood and worked with.

However, the current reality is that even for children and families where complex difficulties have been recognized, the threshold for referral to CAMHS is extremely high, the availability of highly skilled clinicians is increasingly limited, and waiting lists can be long. Some CAMHS clinicians report that new referrals are limited to high risks of suicide or serious self-harm (ACP, 2018).

There is also estimated to be a significant number—829,000 in 2019, estimated by the Children's Commissioner—of vulnerable children whose needs have not been noticed and are not known to services and so are nowhere near a CAMHS referral (Children's Commissioner, 2019). Some of these children may not be attending school.

And there have always been families who did not get to CAMHS either because they did not want to be referred in the first place or because they did not attend appointments. These families and children are likely to be among the more than 700,000 estimated by the Children's Commissioner to be known to services where the level of support is unclear (Children's Commissioner, 2019).

Worry about the stigma of mental ill health, or that having a look at what the matter is could make things worse, can be powerful. There can be wariness about getting caught up in a system where the family or the child will be treated as the problem. Anticipation of blame and criticism can be paralysing. We all work hard to manage ordinary feelings of guilt and shame throughout our lives, including as parents and carers. Having to recognize that a child has severe emotional difficulties that we, as parents or carers, have not been able to help with and fear we may have contributed to can generate overwhelming guilt. For families who have faced prejudice and discrimination, there may be additional concern about attitudes and assumptions they could meet in the clinic and about whether clinicians will know anything of the reality of this. It is a big step to agree to a CAMHS referral and then to trust clinicians with getting to know about what goes in a child's mind—perhaps things that cannot be seen or heard directly.

While providing child mental health services in schools may be a more realistic option for some families, it is, of course, essential to establish robust links with local CAMHS if the school service does not directly come under the CAMHS remit. Children and families with complex difficulties may need to access mental health assessment and ongoing therapeutic work in the school setting; they may also need a range of clinical perspectives and input from CAMHS, which could include a referral onwards or bringing additional expertise into the school. It is partnership between CAMHS, school-based child mental health resources, and education services that offers children and families the integrated resource that is needed.

The primary school setting

The 2017 Government Green Paper, "Transforming Children and Young People's Mental Health Provision" (Department of Health/Department for Education, 2017), and the 2019 "NHS Long Term Plan" (NHS, 2019b) propose that school-based services are key to addressing the mental health needs of children as part of integrated care systems in the next ten years. The plan gives emphasis to training school-based mental health staff quickly so that children's emotional difficulties can be spotted and responded to as early as possible. The experience of Tavistock child psychoanalytic psychotherapy approaches in schools suggests that an integrated care system with capacity to address the needs of children causing the most concern requires highly specialist clinical resources, linked in to local CAMHS in order to ensure multidisciplinary input and safe practice, alongside resources to identify and support children with less complex difficulties.

School-based psychotherapy does not work best for all children and families. Some families prefer to come to a clinic setting precisely because it is separate from home and school and feels more private. If input is needed immediately from a multidisciplinary clinical team rather than a multi-agency multi-professional team around the child, then a CAMHS setting will be more sensible.

There is already considerable experience of working across education and child mental health in the UK, of bringing highly specialist clinical resources—usually CAMHS clinicians—into primary schools. This book focuses on a child psychoanalytic psychotherapy approach in the primary school setting because of the importance of working with non-verbal and extreme forms of communication in meeting complex emotional needs.

While the objectives of child mental health services and schools overlap in relation to maximizing children's capacity to develop and learn, institutional culture and practice differs significantly, and there has not always been an easy relationship. At the same time, both state schools and child mental health clinics have had to manage reductions in public sector funding in meeting the undiminished needs of the communities they serve. Pressure on other public sector services, such as Social Care, also contributes to education and child mental health workers having to expand their responsibilities in order to provide a reasonable level of support, within which school learning and mental health work can take place. This leaves teachers and clinicians clinics wary of proposals that could increase government and public expectations of education and health and blur the distinction between specialist and generic roles.

Negotiating practicalities and governance issues, such as room availability, the boundaries of confidentiality, referral systems, and appointment schedules, are the bricks and mortar of building relationships between education and child mental health in primary schools. This entails handling associated anxieties about compromising both the educational and clinical settings.

For schools, hosting child psychoanalytic psychotherapists has involved being prepared to manage disruption and upset as well as reallocating physical space and staff time in prioritizing the needs of some children and families. The pragmatic, flexible use of limited space that schools rely on in order to organize necessary support outside the classroom is curtailed by protecting therapy space, for example. Even if therapy session times are adjusted to better fit the teaching timetable, the fluctuating support needs of hundreds of children still have to be met, with less space available.

Within school culture, confidentiality principles, including assessment of who needs to know what, are carefully held. Bringing psychotherapy approaches into schools introduces another layer of confidentiality that can feel excluding and obstructive to teachers and education staff, who have children's best interests at heart. Child psychotherapists share with parents or carers, and with education staff also working with a child, general feedback about how a therapeutic intervention is going, but unless there is concern about risk or the child has specifically given permission, they do not share detail from sessions. This can generate strain between teachers—who spend many hours every weekday with a child—and psychotherapists—who usually spend no more than an hour a week with that child. This can be intensified with a child psychotherapy approach, where the emphasis includes exploring thoughts and feelings that the children, families, and teachers are not aware of. Without respectful, frequent therapy/school communication, the difference in approach can become divisive.

Teachers know that being in therapy can at times stir up all sorts of difficult feelings for children. Not only does a child miss lesson or playtime for therapy sessions, they may also—usually temporarily—become more demanding and difficult to manage, which can have a detrimental impact on the other 29 or so children under a teacher's care in class. This is something that therapists working in schools need to be aware of and sensitive to.

For child psychoanalytic psychotherapists, working from a primary school base has meant adapting the therapy setting to make clinical approaches relevant and effective. The clinical setting, including boundaries of consistent time and place, is considered fundamental to the therapy relationship between child or family and therapist. In a clinic, psychoanalytic psychotherapy tries to provide a stable, neutral-enough setting with a constant neutral-enough therapist, so that a child or family can be as free as possible to find out about feelings and thoughts they are not easily aware of, which may be thoughts and feelings that critically inform their emotional life.

A crucial aspect of the therapy relationship is the opportunity to take into account how ordinary boundaries are treated. Ways in which the time boundary of sessions is complied with, investigated, or pushed against by the child; how the room and what is allowed there is enjoyed, tolerated, or disparaged; and whether simple toys and art materials are played with, ignored, or destroyed are all suggestive of the extent to which the therapist and the therapy are felt to be anchoring, facilitating, frustrating, restrictive, withholding, or punishing, for example. A child's or family's feelings about this change all the time, and investigating this is intrinsic to the therapy dynamic.

How the therapist sustains privacy for the sessions and consistency of room, furniture, and toys is bound to play a part in how the therapist is experienced by the family or child. A setting that in itself detracts from the emotional dynamic between the child or family and the therapist can hinder the possibility of feelings emerging that can be examined. Establishing a reasonable consistency of clinical setting in a contemporary CAMHS clinic is demanding enough. Working in a school, clinical sessions are permeated by sounds of lessons and playground, the smell of school dinners, other children and school staff coming into the room by mistake or expecting to use the room themselves due to timetabling mishap, and by evidence of what else the room is used for in changes to room layout and furniture. Clinical contact in a school is more liable to disruption and distraction than in a clinic. In these ways a school setting challenges child psychoanalytic perspectives and practice.

Child psychotherapists always work with the child's world of home, school, and other agencies. This is primarily because children are dependent on the families and organizations they live within, so any development in a child's emotional functioning has to be supported by development in the family or caring system in order to be sustainable. A question for psychoanalytic psychotherapy has sometimes been whether child psychotherapy has become overly oriented towards working with and understanding the impact of environment and context, at the expense of looking closely at how a child uses their own mind, making or cutting connections in the process of generating or restricting emotional meaning. There can be concern about detracting from a focus on what happens in the therapy relationship and the understanding this offers about emotional functioning that is not rational and not available to be rationally known about, which is the approach particular to psychoanalytic psychotherapy. If the job of psychotherapy is to help someone to realize and try to understand what they feel and how they manage their feelings, opening up the possibility of reality-based individual change to make the most of the capacities they do have, then there can be unease about psychotherapy getting involved with the child's social world. From this standpoint, school-based psychotherapy, with its fabric of interruption and inconsistency—the persistent presence of school life in the setting—could compromise the therapy relationship.

But for some child psychoanalytic psychotherapists, a key dimension of partnership with primary schools has been the opportunity to grasp the nettle of a perception of psychotherapy as cut off from the social reality of peoples' lives and only interested in individual emotional experience in an abstract way. Being based within a school brings us into direct contact with how the child lives and allows a different kind of relationship with the child's family. What goes on within a child's mind—the specific ways in which they experience actual or imagined relationships and events; how freely or restrictively they make, defend against, or attack anxiety-provoking associative links, and the extent to which this activity is within or outside awareness; and their individual means of communicating all of this—is a crucial part of the picture. What is different is the opportunity to learn about the child's context from being in it, to work closely with the child's teachers and other education staff who are in the same place at the same time, and to get to know the family in a setting that the family is familiar with.

Importantly, the social meaning of family and community circumstances for a child's emotional development, including their individual and group identity, necessarily has prominence for a psychotherapist working in school. What it means at a group as well as an individual level to be a member of the school and wider community, including the resonance of structural social and economic inequalities, is intrinsic to the dynamics of school life and to the relationship between school and psychotherapy cultures.

In chapter 1, the beginnings of group identity in the primary school years were described as a valuable aspect of extending the capacity to contain oneself in the process of managing separation from primary carers. For children, playing out wishes and fears about what and who they are in relation to others and starting to make accommodation to where they find themselves on the basis of experience is fundamental to development in primary school. It is not surprising that the nature of primary school institutional life and the preoccupations of primary school children can bring questions of difference and sameness into the school-based psychotherapy relationship more robustly than is possible in a clinic. While the social realities of class, race, and other areas of difference and sameness are arguably always embedded in the inter-personal and intra-personal dynamics at play in the therapy relationship, this dimension can be less available to be thought about in a mental health service that is set apart from home and school, the two centres of emotional life for a child. Working in primary schools has helped to widen the scope of what child psychotherapy seeks to explore and understand.

Some aspects of what it is like for schools and psychotherapists to work together closely is shown in the following chapters.

CHAPTER THREE

Tavistock child psychotherapy in schools: A brief history of a long relationship

Milly Jenkins

C hild psychotherapists and teaching staff have a long history of working together and learning from each other. Since child psychotherapy's emergence in the early twentieth century, and still today, many child psychotherapists began their working lives as teachers or support staff in schools, going on to retrain as therapists and then returning to schools to work in a different capacity. Over the years, many teaching staff have also come to the Tavistock, not to train as therapists, but to do observational, child-psychotherapy-informed courses, often run by former teachers, to think about the emotional experience of learning and to deepen their understanding of the children in their classrooms.

Perhaps child psychotherapists and teachers have needed each other's mutual support to survive in two of what Freud (1937c) gloomily called the three "impossible" professions—psychotherapy, education, and government, "in which one can be sure beforehand of achieving unsatisfying results" (p. 248). Or, perhaps, these are professions where the work is often too complex and multi-layered to be proven a clear success by testing, outcome measurements, and league tables.

Mental health and teaching staff together have also had to ride waves of reform and restructuring in education and health. At times these have seen child psychotherapists working in education, employed by local authorities and schools, and at other times employed in the NHS, largely working in clinics but always trying to find creative ways to go

DOI: 10.4324/9781003185925-5

on thinking with teaching staff in a linked-up way about vulnerable children's mental health and education.

This chapter is not intended to be an official or comprehensive history. It is based on conversations with Tavistock staff and their memories of how schoolwork developed: an uneven history of the uneven development of Tavistock child psychotherapy in schools—with apologies, in advance, for any omissions.

Psychoanalysis and education—the early days

Although Freud was thinking and writing about infants and children from the 1890s on, it was not until the 1920s and 1930s, with the pioneering work of child psychotherapists Melanie Klein and Anna Freud, that psychoanalytic therapeutic ways of working with children came into practice.

The first child therapists were, like Anna Freud, often teachers, and from the start they were thinking about how to apply psychoanalytic thinking to education. There were, initially, ambitious attempts to reform education and establish progressive schools. These were largely unsuccessful experiments, and Anna Freud, who set up the Hampstead Clinic—later the Anna Freud Centre—is described as having instead become increasingly interested in a more modest and practical approach aimed at supporting teachers in mainstream schools. "Psychoanalysis could not 'solve' the problems of education", wrote Nick Midgley of her work. "But it could help those working as teachers develop a deeper psychological understanding of children in a developmental context, and to appreciate the complex unconscious dynamics at play in the classroom setting" (2008, p. 40).

Another pioneer, Susan Isaacs, a teacher of young children, an adult and child psychoanalyst, and an associate of Melanie Klein, also experimented in progressive schools before shifting her focus back to mainstream education. In 1933 she became the first Director of the Department of Child Development at the Institute of Education in London, paving the way for child-centred educational approaches. She is described in the *Oxford Dictionary of National Biography* as "the greatest influence on British education in the twentieth century" (Pines, 2004). She also influenced ideas on parenting, for many years writing a weekly agony aunt column in *The Nursery World* under the pseudonym "Ursula Wise".

A new profession, reaching into schools

Child psychotherapy was not formalized as a training and profession until the late 1940s. Before and after the war, child psychotherapists often worked in local Child Guidance Clinics—the forerunners of today's Child and Adolescent Mental Health Services (CAMHS), funded by local authority education budgets rather than by the NHS— so through the 1940s and 1950s they continued to be linked to education and schools. Child psychotherapy has, it seems, always been "applied": taken out of clinics and adapted to community settings, not just in schools, but in GP surgeries and, later, Children's Centres, too. "Child psychotherapy in the UK has its roots both in the world of the psychoanalysis of children and in the public sector", says Isobel Pick, Chair of the Association of Child Psychotherapists (ACP), which was established in 1949, soon after the founding of the National Health Service (personal communication).

During those years the Tavistock Clinic moved under the umbrella of the new NHS, with John Bowlby, founder of attachment theory, leading its Department of Children and Parents with a new vision for child mental health work. "The pre-war child guidance model of parallel work with children and mothers was expanded", wrote Margaret Rustin (2007, p. 355). "The wider context of the children's lives was to be taken account of through attention to the child's school experience and the involvement of fathers in the clinical work." Bowlby also saw the need for a child psychotherapy profession and in 1948 invited Esther Bick, a child psychoanalyst with a background in child development, to set up a training. The cornerstone of this was infant observation, a method developed by Bick and based on the thinking of Melanie Klein.

When Martha Harris, another former teacher turned child psychotherapist, took over from Bick in 1960, she further extended the reach of child psychotherapy into education, developing the practice of consultation to schools, whereby therapists went into schools on a regular basis to listen to teaching staff's dilemmas about individual children and think together about what might help. Married to a teacher and educationalist, Roland Harris, then deputy head of Woodberry Down, a model London comprehensive, Martha Harris and child psychotherapist Edna O'Shaughnessy were employed as part-time staff at the school in a two-year pilot project. (O'Shaughnessy also taught the child development course at the Institute of Education.)

The main focus at Woodberry Down School was on supporting staff, but Harris and O'Shaughnessy also helped teachers to run small groups with children and linked the school up with the local Child Guidance Clinic, so they could liaise in relation to pupils seen there. A former Woodberry Down teacher, Jack Whitehead, has written about his experience of working with Harris: "She came into my Houseroom at lunch time every Thursday for about a year. I interviewed my problem cases and she observed and gently joined in. Her help was invaluable" (Whitehead, n.d.).

It was also Harris who developed the idea of a "work discussion group", now a key component in the training for child psychotherapists and other professionals, as well as a service offered by child psychotherapists working in schools. She and O'Shaughnessy ran one such group for teachers at Woodberry Down. Harris (1968) wrote:

> [We] met regularly for thirty minutes each week before lunch—too brief a time, which often extended into the lunch hour. . . . Discussions with this group ranged from queries posed by particular children to general problems of child development, the influence of social and environmental factors, the teacher's own part in relationships with groups and with individual children, and the influence of the school structure and hierarchy on the teacher's own capacity to function well. As the group grew more familiar with the consultant and with each other there was much discussion of the particular emotional stresses and strains in teaching, of ways in which teachers could be trained to cope with them, and to help with younger colleagues encountering difficult classes for the first time. [p. 321]

For child psychotherapists, wrote Harris, the project highlighted the large number of children and families with

> critical or more chronic problems who either would not or could not be dealt with in a clinic setting; also the difficulties in finding the time and appropriate setting within [schools] to deal with individual problems.
> On the other hand it brought home to [us] the exceptional possibilities of the school situation in detecting and modifying some of these problems (which usually have to be carried willy-nilly), and of the school as a potential therapeutic as well as an educational institution. [p. 341]

The support of the head teacher was key, concluded Harris, to making such projects work. He or she needed to have "sufficient confidence in both her own teachers and in the consultant to allow them to get together without forcing matters, and to take a positive attitude in helping to resolve any discords that might occur" (pp. 341–342). She thought that many schools would benefit from having permanent, even full-time, specialists working alongside staff, foreseeing the potential for the school counselling and therapy services that were to emerge decades later.

Ad hoc and formal: a new course for teaching staff, the Day Unit, and group work in schools

Another outcome of the Woodberry Down project was the Tavistock's Counselling Course, a ground-breaking course for school and higher education teachers set up by Martha and Roland Harris in 1968. It ran for many years and combined "clinical thinking and expertise in educational theory and practice . . . with child psychotherapists and educationalists working closely together" (Youell, 2006, p. 1). It was later called "Emotional Factors in Learning and Teaching: Counselling Aspects in Education" and run by Isca Salzberger-Wittenberg. The course approach and concepts were summarized in *The Emotional Experience of Learning and Teaching* by Salzberger-Wittenberg, Gianna Henry, and Elsie Osborne, first published in 1983 and still read by child psychotherapists and teaching staff today.

Margaret Rustin, later head of the Tavistock Child Psychotherapy Training, remembers this as a period "when Tavistock approaches to thinking about schools began to take shape more systematically". Alongside this formalization of ideas, teaching, and training, child psychotherapists and those training to become child psychotherapists also continued to work in education in improvised ways, finding opportunities to learn and share thinking in schools with head teachers open to new ideas and ways of working.

Rustin, recently graduated from university, found herself working in an "ad hoc" way in Essendine Primary School in Paddington in 1966 and 1967, running groups for children who struggled to manage as a group in the classroom. She had been encouraged to do this by Martha Harris and John Bowlby after joining a work discussion group facilitated by them and including, among others, several educational psychologists. Harris and Bowlby had suggested she get experience with children to help her to decide whether she wanted to train as a child psychotherapist, and the work discussion group gave her somewhere to think about the children as well as learn about working with teachers.

"The children were extremely demanding", she says, "but I did have a lot of freedom." The group cooked and sang together and played music as a band. Rustin brought in a tape recorder, and some of the children, especially a selectively mute girl, were fascinated to hear their own voices. She visited their homes and got to know their families; she even went to some first communions and, in the holidays, drove them in her car to the airport to see planes taking off and landing. "This was before seatbelts", she says. "Can you imagine? Definitely *not* the Tavistock approach."

Another development in the late 1960s was the opening of what is today called Gloucester House, the Tavistock's specialist day school for 5–14-year-olds. Back then it was called the Child Guidance Centre; later, in the 1980s, it became part of the Tavistock Children and Parents Department and was re-named the Mulberry Bush Day Unit (twinned with the specialist Mulberry Bush School in Oxfordshire, also still open today).

At the Day Unit, child psychotherapists were members of a team in which health and education staff worked together in a way not dissimilar from today (see chapters 12 and 13). "The Unit is a team comprising a psychiatrist, a psychiatric social worker, an educational psychologist and a child psychotherapist", wrote Dilys Daws, who worked there, in *The Child Psychotherapist and the Problems of Young People* (Daws & Boston, 1977).

> The staff also consists of three teachers, employed by the ILEA (Inner London Education Authority), together with three assistants who are employed by the Health Service. [p. 86]

She described the benefits and challenges of the work:

> One of the satisfying aspects of the Day Unit is working alongside teachers who are with children all day. It can be supportive for teachers and therapist alike to share the burden of working with disturbed children. . . . The teachers with whom I work of course don't need advice from me on handling a child as such, but I hope that their own intuition is enhanced by a shared insight into the unconscious processes at work within their pupils. [p. 99]

In the late 1960s and the 1970s, Tavistock child psychotherapists, again supported by Martha Harris, further developed and formalized group psychotherapy for children in primary schools. Susan Reid, Eva Fry, and Maria Rhode began running groups in London primaries, realizing they could reach children unlikely to attend individual therapy at clinics and whose parents might have been anxious about the stigma of this. School group work, they observed, took the pressure off teachers, "relieving him or her for a while of the most troublesome children". They could also help staff by being "a sympathetic listener and a source of new ideas" and found "the willing ear of the worker also relieved some of the pressure usually carried by the head" (Reid, Fry, & Rhode, 1977, pp. 57–58).

Reid (1999) later wrote about group psychotherapy having a natural home in schools, because it helps children struggling to make and keep friends, giving them a safe space to think about these difficulties. "Because the therapy takes place in the company of their peers, there is often a rapid carry over in terms of improvements into their school lives", she wrote. "For many children, group psychotherapy is sufficient to get them on the pathway of healthy and happy development" (p. 258). Group therapy also worked well in schools because groups could be co-facilitated with teaching staff in multidisciplinary work where "each discipline's training brings its own particular skills [that] often complement each other in a particularly helpful way" (p. 249).

The 1980s and 1990s: new ways into schools and education

Child psychotherapists continued to be dual citizens of health and education. In the mid-1970s they formally became NHS employees but continued to take their work into schools over the coming decades, with schools often contracting Tavistock services. In the 1980s Jane Maltby, head teacher of Sacred Heart Junior primary school for 18 years, studied at the Tavistock and asked one of her seminar leaders, Shirley Burch, another former teacher, to come into her school to help her think about particular children. Maltby then went on to train as a child psychotherapist, to work in Child Guidance Clinics, and to write about her own consultation work to schools (Maltby, 2008).

It seems this is when child psychotherapists began working more directly with individual children and families in schools, offering meetings and sessions in any available private spaces that could be found. While some schools were—and are—able to provide dedicated therapy rooms, in others child psychotherapists have had to make do with whatever is available. In a paper called "Standing Next to the Weighing Scales" Dilys Daws (1985) wrote about her work over several decades in the baby clinic of a Camden GP surgery. Child psychotherapists who work in schools might, similarly, describe their experience as "Perching in the First Aid Room". Working in schools required, and still does, fitting into tight spaces and timetables, snatched corridor conversations with teachers, long searches for children in the playground, and climbing many flights of stairs.

While some child psychotherapists continued to work in an ad hoc way in schools, others were beginning to set up more formal services. In the 1990s Maltby, together with the Tavistock's Judith Edwards, started the Bishop Harvey Family Service in Barnet—a voluntary sector project that worked closely with local schools and offered a five-session model of family work, taking referrals from teachers and seeing families in their project base as well as in schools (Edwards & Maltby, 1998). A series of Tavistock child psychotherapists also worked at William Tyndale Primary School in Islington. Others worked in ILEA special schools. Eileen Orford, a child psychotherapist described by Biddy Youell as "deeply rooted in education", worked in schools for children with emotional and behavioural difficulties, ran a service at North Westminster Community School, consulted to staff in pupil referral units, and offered work discussion groups at Robson House, Camden's pupil referral unit for primary-age children. (See chapters 10 and 11).

Youell describes the 1990s as "heady years" that saw a significant expansion in Tavistock school services and education courses. Together with Hamish Canham, she was the Course Lead for "Emotional Factors in Learning and Teaching", which continued to be an important hub for teachers and child psychotherapists. She later wrote *The Learning Relationship* (2006), based on the course, and with contributions from the work of Canham, another key text on psychoanalytic ideas in education. Teaching staff who enrolled not only took the thinking back to their schools but also helped to create new services. One of these was at New Rush Hall, a specialist school for 5–16-year-olds in Redbridge, where a teacher who had attended the course asked Tavistock child psychotherapists to run work discussion groups, later expanded into an in-school psychotherapy service, with a small team providing assessment and treatment for children and families.

By now there was a pre-clinical training course for child psychotherapists, set up by Martha Harris, that, as well as being a route into the child psychotherapy training for a wide range of professionals, including school staff, was also a valued source of continuing professional development. Today it is called "Working with Children, Young People and Families: A Psychoanalytic Observational Approach". The success of these courses, says Youell, was based on the stance that: "Child psychotherapy isn't a secret methodology that only child psychotherapists can use. It is a way of understanding children and influencing practice, something far bigger than just a treatment."

Meeting the demand for services in the community: TOPS and the Camden CAMHS school project

Tavistock child psychotherapists also began setting up services in schools across several London boroughs. Graham Music developed the Tavistock Outreach in Primary Schools (TOPS) project, which has now been running for nearly 20 years; its work is described in several chapters of this book.

According to Graham Music (personal communication, 2008), "supported by Lisa Miller, then Chair of the Child and Family Department, we cobbled the service together with no resources, slowly applying for funding. It was important to integrate this outreach work with core services by ensuring good links were made with local children's mental health teams. Also, to offer support and work discussion groups to staff, from Learning Support Assistants to senior management, as well as in-service training."

While making a strong case for child psychotherapy in schools and the idea that schools could support children with much more than education, Music also thought realistic expectations of what could be achieved were needed, warning against a simplistic approach that might expect teaching staff and child psychotherapists to fix complex, ingrained social problems:

> We should perhaps be wary of the idea that either schools or child psychotherapy can solve the kind of social issues of which an unhappy child might represent the symptom. Nonetheless the skills of a psychoanalytic child psychotherapist can certainly go some way to changing both how a child feels, how parents feel, and also how school staff and other professionals perceive the children in their care. [Music & Hall, 2008, pp. 59–60]

Funding, when it came, was initially from the Camden's Children's Fund, a government initiative launched in 2000 and aimed at early identification and support for children and young people at risk of social exclusion. TOPS was soon working in five schools across the borough, offering assessment, individual therapy, and parent work, as well as group work, under-fives work, and consultation and support for staff. It aimed to be holistic, not just providing one-to-one work with children but also working closely with parents and teachers, thinking about the child's whole context. Over the years, Katie Argent and Marta Cioeta successfully sought grant funding from charities and financial commitment from participating schools. TOPS has expanded to work in eight Camden schools, and its team now includes an adult therapist and advocacy worker.

The government was by then putting a greater focus on child and adolescent mental health, with the consolidation of services and the establishment of CAMHS teams across the country, beginning in the mid-1990s. In 2004 the Department of Health published the *National Service Framework for Children, Young People and Maternity Services*, a ten-year plan to which child psychotherapists—among other mental health professionals—contributed, which for the first time set national standards for children's health and social care. It called for the growth and expansion of CAMHS services, with a new emphasis on working in the community, including in schools. It sat alongside *Every Child Matters*, the government paper published after the death of Victoria Climbié, with its five key outcomes for children and young people and new frameworks for improving multi-agency work (Department of Education and Skills, 2003).

Between 2008 and 2011, the Tavistock ran a pilot project in eight local schools, led by Victoria Blincow, in partnership with the Anna

Freud Centre, and funded by the government's Targeted Mental Health in Schools (TAMHS) programme. By now the Tavistock had been contracted to run the CAMHS services for the London Borough of Camden, and, in 2011, following on from the success of the TOPS and TAMHS projects and thanks to a determined NHS commissioner, Sarah Brown, it was decided to place CAMHS clinicians, including child psychotherapists, in 55 schools across the borough; working in secondary schools for one day a week, in primaries half a day a fortnight, and in special schools for two or more days a week. The schools service continues today, managed by Victoria Blincow. It has short waiting times and can fast-track children and young people into CAMHS if needed.

There were other developments during these years. By the early 2000s, the "Emotional Factors" course was in demand outside London, with Biddy Youell and Lydia Hartland-Rowe running one-day workshops across the North of England. Teaching staff who attended often went on to train as clinicians, including at new child psychotherapy training schools by then established in Scotland (1993), Birmingham (1995), and, later, Leeds (2003). Some of their graduates later set up school services, such as Impact North, a social enterprise that provides therapy in primary and secondary schools in Leeds.

Emil Jackson wrote about developing work discussion groups with school staff (Jackson, 2002, 2008) and pointed to evidence of the positive impact of work discussion on staff morale and sickness levels. Jackson's work was highlighted as a model of good practice in a government report on the implementation of the NSF.

The borough-wide school services provided by Camden CAMHS are still unusual today. In recent years schools have mostly been left to fend for themselves in providing mental health and pastoral care support for their pupils, especially since the advent of academies, with schools managing their own budgets and buying in services rather than using those provided by local authorities. Now, however, following years of rising concern about child and adolescent mental health and about the impact of cuts to services, the government is proposing increased new mental health services in schools, as outlined in the 2017 Green Paper, "Transforming Children and Young People's Mental Health Provision" (Department of Health/Department for Education, 2017).

This reflects the growing recognition that many children and young people who are struggling with, or at risk of, mental health problems can most easily be identified and helped in schools. But there are concerns, too, that if not properly funded and specialized, the new mental health services in schools will not be able to meet the needs of pupils with complex presentations. The Tavistock is trialling one of the Green Paper pilot projects and, with its model, making the case for the new school services to be run by CAMHS, so that, when cases are urgent, risky, and complex, they can be transferred into clinics or hospitals in a timely way.

"In a way things have come full circle", says Biddy Youell, "Child Guidance Clinics were started as an educational initiative and then education and health drifted apart, with child psychotherapists and CAMHS firmly placed in the health sector and becoming rather split off from education. And, now, schools are to be the mental health hubs again." Something that has, regrettably, changed in recent years, she says, is teaching staff's freedom and ability to attend courses like the one she ran for many years, largely because of increasing workloads and decreasing funding for continuing professional development. "People say they really want to do courses and just can't", she says.

But, at the same time, child psychotherapists are now working more than ever in school-based projects, directly with children and families and also with staff. Youell says the thinking with staff, whether in the work around families or more formal work discussion groups, continues to be crucial: "It has a powerful impact. When teaching staff get the opportunity to talk about their work in an open ended way they find it is immensely relieving—the power of just sitting, thinking and talking. I think teaching is the most difficult job there is. You're under pressure from all sides and you have to work in such a tight system at the same time as trying to open up the world for children."

PART II

CHILD PSYCHOANALYTIC PSYCHOTHERAPY IN MAINSTREAM PRIMARY SCHOOL

CHAPTER FOUR

Early transitions:
Child psychotherapy in a school nursery

Kathryn Fenton & Anya Suschitzky

It is early in the school year, and parents and carers are preparing to leave their children at the school nursery. Some children are ready for the day: they say goodbye, hang up their coats, and turn to staff for help with finding an activity or joining their peer group. Others don't say goodbye: they plunge into something very busy or physically demanding, or they seem to go off into their own world, rather than notice their surroundings or the transition. Still other children are tearful and forlorn, anxiously clutching their parents' or carers' hands or attaching themselves to a teacher for the day. Home-time scenes are similarly varied. Some children become restless and charge past their parents/carers when they arrive to collect them; some wait anxiously at the door and are upset or withdrawn when it is their turn to leave; others come out of the classroom chatting or proudly displaying something they have made during the day.

These scenes of "hellos" and "goodbyes" bring the emotional experiences of nursery children to life in a visceral way. They highlight children's many different ways of managing transitions. Similarly, the variety of children's responses to the school toilets, lunches, assemblies, and playgrounds suggests the diversity and strength of feeling that are stirred in the nursery by the structures of the school day and the process of moving from the family into the school and wider community. It is important to consider how children's feelings must be amplified for parents and carers, and challenging for teachers, who are trying to manage a class of children with different needs while also remaining sensitive to the particular needs of an individual child and parents or carers in that moment. Schools with regular and direct access to a child psychoanalytic psychotherapist have an opportunity to think about such challenges and understand the difficulties faced by parents and carers, school staff, and young children, so that the children's emotional development, behaviour, and learning can be supported at this important first stage of their school lives.

As child psychoanalytic psychotherapists, we have offered a Child Mental Health Service (CAMHS) outreach service to nursery and reception classes in a mainstream primary school for more than 15 years. The school we are based in is located in an inner London Borough. It serves a diverse population with a strong mix of cultural, ethnic, and socioeconomic backgrounds.

The experience of writing this chapter has led us to reflect on what our training as child psychoanalytic psychotherapists enables us to offer in a context that is very different from the clinic in which we ordinarily work. We explore how the difference in the setting shapes and informs our clinical work with children and parents.

In the first instance, it might be helpful to outline the nature of "outreach" or "applied" work, as it is sometimes referred to. Essentially, this means that we are based within the nursery setting rather than in a clinic, from where we offer a wide range of therapeutic services tailored to the needs of the families and the school. We bring into the school our framework of psychoanalytic thinking and our understanding of ordinary and unusual emotional development from birth onwards. This is what underlies our work with parents, carers, young children, and their families as well as our consultations to school staff in order to facilitate as full an understanding as possible of whatever is causing concern.

The work includes offering supervision or consultation to school staff at all levels who are working directly or indirectly with children; undertaking detailed classroom observations of children in order to offer an evidenced, specialized perspective about why a child might be exhibiting a certain kind of behaviour or difficulty with relationships or learning; providing direct psychotherapeutic work, if appropriate; and working with colleagues on specialized assessments when there are concerns about potential neurodevelopmental issues. We meet with parents and carers individually or as couples, with parents and carers and children together, as well as seeing children singly. It is not unusual for a member of teaching or support staff to seek us out to request that we meet with a distressed parent and/or child without the formalities of a referral or any preparation beforehand, so flexibility, openness, and a willingness to work alongside school staff are crucial.

The agenda for early intervention

Research and developments in neuroscience (Schore, 2010) have given weight to the psychoanalytic-observation-based understanding that an infant's early social and emotional development is vital to their longer term healthy physical, social, and emotional development. Adverse experiences, such as trauma and neglect in the early years, have a direct, detrimental impact on the development of the brain and therefore influence the child's emotions, relationships, and cognitive functioning in later life. However, it has been widely recognized that early intervention and prevention are crucial and effective in terms of recovering brain function as well as providing opportunity for emotional, relational repair.

What do we mean by early intervention?

Early intervention means identifying and providing effective early support to children and young people who are at risk of poor outcomes. It works to reduce the risk factors and increase the protective factors in a child's life. (Early Intervention Foundation, 2020]

The 1001 Critical Days cross-party manifesto published in June 2014 highlighted the importance of acting early to enhance outcomes for children from conception to a child's second birthday (Leadsom, Field, Burstow, & Lucas, 2014). It acknowledged that this can be a very difficult period for parents, who may find it hard to provide the care and attention their infant needs. However, it can also be a chance to effect great change, as pregnancy and the birth of a baby are critical "windows of opportunity" when parents are especially receptive to offers of advice and support. The manifesto outlines the evidence base for acting early and highlights the importance of local services identifying and reaching families who need additional services.

The Early Intervention Foundation notes that capacity for change extends beyond the first 2 years of life and that intervention can improve children's life chances at any point during childhood and adolescence. There has therefore been a drive to intervene not only through universal services across early years' provision, but also through primary and secondary school services.

Indeed, the goals for the National Health Service, which are set out in the NHS Long Term Plan (NHS, 2019b), include significant investment in community-based interventions to promote the health and wellbeing of all infants, children, and families and to target those with the highest levels of need by offering specialist input early on. The Long Term Plan also advocates the delivery of mental health services in schools and

closer collaboration between different agencies such as health, education, and social care, and mental and physical health. The integration of
child psychotherapists with nursery staff and parents in a school, and
the offer of brief treatments and other preventative input to families and
professional networks, fulfils many elements of the Long Term Plan.
Identifying difficulties and working with families to understand the
issues in order to recognize when things are starting to go wrong allows
schools and CAMHS to support professional, family, and community
networks around the child and their parents or carers. In this way, child
psychotherapists working in schools are in a position to offer a timely
intervention at a pivotal stage in a child's development.

Parents and young children facing separation and other issues

We have noted how children attending nursery will have had different
experiences of being separated from their parents or carers. For some it
will be the first time they are left for any length of time without a primary
carer. Others may have been cared for by extended family members or
had experience of childcare settings from very early on, with a nanny,
in a nursery or a children's centre, or with a childminder.

For parents and carers every new separation can stir up powerful feelings linked to their own background and experience of being
parented. There may be worries and doubts, hopes and expectations
that parents know about, as well as feelings that it is more difficult to be
aware of—usually more confusing or complicated feelings. The ability
of parents and carers to be receptive and responsive to the emotional
experience communicated by their child is often dependent on their own
experience of having their feelings noticed and attended to.

"Clinginess", "separation anxiety", "regression", and "difficult or
challenging behaviour" are common and understandable issues that are
described in referrals received in a nursery and reception setting. The
factors at play behind these presenting behaviours are explored in chapter 1; here we discuss what is involved in working directly with families
and schools in addressing separation difficulties and other issues.

As CAMHS child psychoanalytic psychotherapists, meeting with
parents for the first time, gathering a family history as well as the child's
developmental history helps us to understand the context in which the
young child is living. Sometimes parents question why this might be
relevant when it is their child they are worried about, not themselves.
But these are important areas to explore in order to have a shared
understanding of the context of the difficulty, including how parents

and carers view it and respond to it. At this point it is not uncommon to be told, "I am worried that I don't know how to be a parent because of the way in which I was parented", or, "I didn't have a good experience growing up, so I am not sure that I am able to give my child what they need."

The nature of our work lends itself to time-limited interventions. We offer a five-session model to parents or carers and young children. We have found that a light-touch intervention in a familiar setting enables us to work with parents to help them to consider their own anxieties and, later, to make links between these and their concerns about their child. Sometimes we are able to think with parents or carers about potential further support available from the school or from external agencies. This is often sufficient to reduce anxiety, and over time we find that the situation has improved.

Other difficulties may be linked to life events, such as the birth or anticipation of the impending birth of a younger sibling, which has left the child feeling angry and displaced. In our experience these rivalrous feelings are ordinary and to be expected. However, young children do not have the emotional language to articulate their distress, and so it is often communicated in other ways, such as via challenging behaviour, toileting issues, sleeping or eating difficulties.

Jack

Suzie, the mother of Jack, aged 3 years, requested an appointment because he did not want to go to nursery and also refused to use the toilet and would only poo in his nappy. This was causing a lot of frustration and anxiety at home. When Suzie encouraged Jack to use the toilet, he would not poo, leaving her worried that he was in pain.

Jack had a younger sister, Lucy, aged 6 months. When I explored his reaction to her pregnancy with Lucy, Suzie reported that Jack was very fond of his younger sibling, but added, "He hates it when I am breastfeeding and tries to distract my attention away from her." She told me that when her partner held Lucy, Jack climbed onto his lap to try to get his attention. Jack told his mum that he hated nursery and complained when Suzie took Lucy with her to collect him at the end of the day. He was very angry on the way home. Suzie also described some of Jack's controlling behaviour and said that he had a tendency to boss her and her partner about.

Together we acknowledged the difficulty for Jack in having to accommodate his younger sibling (who also needed a lot of her parents' attention), after being the sole focus of their attention for so long, and the conflicted feelings and tensions that this could cause him. Suzie described her guilt at not having as much time for Jack as she used to have, although he was by no means neglected. On reflection, she felt that she had overcompensated by allowing Jack to be bossy all the time, which she would not have tolerated previously. Suzie felt emboldened and set about potty training with renewed confidence that she was not going to harm Jack by being more firm with him and not giving in to his demands. Several weeks later, Suzie returned to report that Jack was no longer using his nappy; he had starting pooing into the toilet and was feeling very proud of his new-found independence.

We use this illustration to highlight how a brief intervention, where a parent has the opportunity to reflect on their own anxieties, can quickly ameliorate a situation that might otherwise become increasingly difficult to manage, impacting on family dynamics and functioning.

Working to engage families and support complex needs

The needs of children in a school reflect those of the community of which the school is a part, so schools in under-resourced areas generally have a large number of families who are in receipt of several different services. Close links between a school and other agencies in the geographical area mean that staff can build on existing relationships with the local CAMHS. However, many children and families who need therapeutic help have complex family situations. For various reasons, perhaps linked to economic factors, parental physical or mental health difficulties or issues related to alcohol or substance misuse, some parents and carers are not able to support children's regular attendance at clinic appointments. Parents are at additional disadvantage when their child enters the nursery, because they often lose contact with integrated early years services and health visitors, who may have known the child since birth. If the family asks for help, or if the child's behaviour is a concern, it is likely that the school, not the CAMHS clinic, will be the context in which therapeutic work takes place.

Parents may seek support and advice from school in preference to seeing their GP or approaching a CAMHS service because of worries about social stigma and blame. In particular, families who have been involved in the Social Care system express worry that asking for help to understand or manage their child's behaviour might be taken as further evidence that they are unable to cope or that they are not good-enough parents. Collaborative working with a trusted teacher or SENCo at the school facilitates our engagement with families who are wary of contact with agencies and may be struggling to manage difficult and disturbing behaviour, as well as enabling children who are in emotional distress to access much-needed support.

In the school nursery, we accept referrals from school staff, and parents are also encouraged to self-refer. It is not unusual for a parent to request support to think through some of the worries they have about their child's development. These worries might be about common issues such as wetting, soiling, biting, eating difficulties, or tantrums. We think about the meaning of those behaviours in the context of the child's relationships and circumstances at home and at school. For example, if a family is contending with severe over-crowding at home and disruptive or dangerous neighbours, an understanding of the impact of the housing situation on the parents' emotional state can inform how we address difficulties in the child's behaviour and the parent–child relationship, and how we communicate with the professional network on the parents' behalf.

We often have referrals for children whose sibling has been diagnosed with a life-changing condition, such as a learning disability or a chronic or life-threatening illness. We try to help the family to digest events, and we give the parents an opportunity to focus on the referred child, who may be struggling with anxieties both about their sibling and about their own needs and emotions. Parents often feel anxious and overwhelmed by the demands on their time and emotional resources when a child is diagnosed, and this can make it difficult for them to notice the strengths in their parenting. Having a better understanding of their own feelings can restore a sense of agency, so they feel better equipped to work with nursery staff to support the referred child and more confident with the many professionals involved in the care of the sibling with complex needs. The clinical work of absorbing, untangling, coming to better understand, and communicating with parents about their own and their children's emotional states and the work of liaising, consulting, and building relationships in the professional system are inter-related aspects of our approach with families who have complex needs.

Liaison with social workers is a particularly important aspect of linking with external professionals, either when they have been involved with a family for a long time or when new safeguarding concerns arise at nursery and a referral is made. Our psychoanalytic perspective helps us think about the meaning—both overt and underlying—of the anxieties experienced by children and their parents as well as the risks, and helps us to convey this carefully to other professionals. We work closely with safeguarding leads in the school to coordinate our responses to the family and the network, as this can address anxieties and preserve trust at a time when the family's engagement with services may be in question.

Occasionally, our work with parents suggests that they might benefit from therapy in their own right. Parents may request help because of a traumatic bereavement, an ongoing conflict or relationship breakdown, or a long-standing mental health difficulty that needs specialist treatment. We liaise with GPs, make referrals, and support the transition to adult mental health specialists. At other times, parent–child sessions lead us to suspect that a parent has a history of unresolved trauma, which, without they themselves being aware of it, is playing a part in how they relate to their child and so is affecting how their child feels and behaves. This needs to be thought about carefully, especially if the parent has not spoken about their history or believes the focus of the work should be on the child. But while it is painful for parents to consider whether difficulties in their own background are being communicated to their child, it is usually a relief to understand the dynamics of intergenerational trauma and abuse and to find a way forward.

Uses of psychoanalytic observation in school

Observing a child in the nursery classroom can be a good way to think about a referral with parents and carers and teaching staff. Child psychotherapists pay particular attention to the emotional responses stirred in them while observing in detail how the child responds to ordinary life in the nursery, such as separating in the morning or preparing to leave at the end of the day, playing with toys, eating a snack, listening to a story, or going out into the playground. Thinking about the relationship between the child's experience and that of the observer—how the observer feels, what thoughts come to mind while observing—can bring us closer to the patterns of imaginative and emotional associations and connections in the child's mind, as well as offering clues about their day-to-day relationships and interactions with family, teachers, and other children.

Child psychotherapists undertake training in psychoanalytic observation through the weekly observation of a baby in their family from birth to 2 years, and the weekly observation of a nursery-age child for one year. Observers develop a capacity to adopt an unobtrusive, receptive stance in the face of everyday occurrences and intense emotions; and they learn to make sense of their observations through recording and discussing their experience using ordinary language. Observing and digesting the raw impact of interactions gives access to very early emotional states. Psychoanalytic observation offers a basis for an understanding of non-verbal communication and the feelings that lie behind what can be observed, which is fundamental to clinical work (Briggs, 2002; Miller, Rustin, Rustin, & Shuttleworth, 1989).

In primary schools, observations can be used for gathering information, feeding back and enriching discussions with the school and family, and supporting the system around the child (Malberg, Stafler, & Geater, 2012). Our position of being both within the school and having a role connected to, but outside, education has a parallel in our contribution through observation, which offers an inside/outside view to extend the perspectives of teachers and parents or carers. On hearing about an observation, families and professionals in the school often take up a more observational stance themselves, noticing their feelings about the child in a new way or reflecting differently on events about which they have previously felt only troubled or stuck. We learn from the process of discussing the detail of what has been observed about the impact of the child's difficulties, which helps us make more sense of the observation and referral.

Observations are also a chance to bring professionals and families together. Because the observed detail conveys curiosity about interactions that are familiar—and visible—to the family and professionals in the school, an observation can invite fresh thoughts and ideas about what is happening. The teacher might feel more acknowledged and appreciated through talking to a sympathetic witness about their challenges with a child. Hearing feedback on the observation can help a worried parent or carer to notice links between the child's behaviour at home and at school, or to make new connections between the child's past and present. Being in a position to make a contribution in this way can develop trust and support the family's engagement with the assessment.

Sometimes, communication between home and school comes under strain due to the extent of a child's disturbance, the complexity of the family situation, or concerns about safeguarding. Teachers or parents and carers may feel blamed or on opposing sides of a discussion. Anxieties about the child may run high and can create pressure to act before there has been time to identify where, and what, the problems are (Music, 2007). An observation that conveys the value of following the detail and sequence of what happens carefully and respectfully, even in the heat of the moment, can get things back on track and can become a basis for renewed, thoughtful cooperation. Taking time to think about the details of a child's day at school can be therapeutic in its own right: children respond well when they know the adults are thinking about them. Strategies might also emerge from the discussion, such as moving a child to a different carpet space, or giving them special jobs to do; or a specialist assessment might be arranged. Psychoanalytic observation can help everyone to pool their emotional and practical resources and work together to face and try to understand the anxieties and so enable planning ahead.

Lola: using an observation during brief work

> Lola, a white British girl aged 3 years, was the younger of two siblings in foster care with Diane and Jo. She was referred half-way through the school year because she was distressed at nursery and would not eat or play with other children. At home she was clingy, a picky eater, and had tantrums. Her brother, Kai, had a diagnosis of attention deficit hyperactivity disorder (ADHD), and the teacher thought Diane needed additional support.

> At the first appointment I learned that Lola had been born prematurely. She was in hospital and then temporary fostering before going to Diane and Jo when she was 12 months old. On-going medical treatment and Jo's overnight shift-work added to Lola and her foster carers' difficulties. The evenings were particularly challenging, because Lola and Kai were unsettled and Diane gave in to their demands to stay up late, but then felt impatient and tired. We discussed Diane's "goodbye" routine with Lola at school, and Diane remembered that Lola had recently brought home a box had she made at nursery and placed it carefully on the kitchen table. Diane seemed glad to think of Lola making a connection between home and school in this way, and she gave permission for an observation. The following is a summary:

> Lola's uniform was baggy, making her look very small. She was wearing a necklace of coloured buttons and was threading some other buttons onto string. She made eye contact right away, as if she knew I was there for her. She put the buttons on her head, like a crown, but they fell off, and she left them. A child approached, and Lola put a button attached to string into her pocket and walked away.

> The teacher gave Lola a box of raisins, and she put it in her pocket and went into the playground. The teacher took Lola to a bench in the sun, and she sat and ate, looking at me. There was a tree nearby, and she leaned back so the tree obscured her view of me, and she smiled when she leaned forward and saw me again. She did this repeatedly. She also put her box of raisins down where I could not see it, and then lifted it up again. Both these things reminded me of playing hide and seek, and I felt the pleasure of finding Lola and being found by her.

She climbed into a tunnel on the climbing frame. A boy got in from the opposite end and nudged Lola. Lola shuddered, backed out, and went to sit with the teacher. Then she crawled under the tunnel, where the boy was still sitting, and turned to me with her finger to her lips, as if we had a secret.

She went indoors and took the button on the string from her pocket. She played with it like a yo-yo. When it was time to tidy up, she went back and forth between me and the playground gate. Some other children were sitting on a bench near the gate, and she pointed at them and caught my eye, as if she wanted me to do something.

This observation shows Lola struggling to join the world of the nursery, where she must share the adults and the play equipment with other children. It suggests that she navigates the challenges by making herself feel special. She makes a crown, suggesting an idea of being a queen; she communicates her pleasure in being kept in mind by giving the observer the pleasure of being found in peek-a-boo; and she gets the teacher to feed her and give her a comfortable place to sit. The tunnel may have felt like a special, secret place for her. When the boy comes in, Lola seems anxious, as if he is felt to be intruding or as if she has lost the special-ness of the place, and she goes to sit underneath. Through her glances and gestures she conveys an idea of a secret alliance with the observer. Perhaps the observer's similar ethnicity and sameness of gender lend themselves to Lola retreating into a feeling of a special, secret connection at a point when, faced with another, different child, she is suddenly unsettled and unsure. Later, when there is no place for Lola by the gate, she again looks to the observer for support.

The observation also suggests that Lola is working hard to share Diane and tolerate the separation by keeping connected with her in her mind. She joins the two ends of the string in a necklace, perhaps representing a secure connection; she keeps things she values safely in her pocket; she plays peek-a-boo, communicating her pleasure at being found; and she drops and retrieves the button so it repeatedly comes and goes. Freud (1920g) described how his young grandson, when left by his mother, made a cotton reel disappear and reappear in a similar way. Freud realized that when children play like this, they change a passive loss into an active rejection, thereby gaining a feeling of con-trol and managing the emotional pain and aggression associated with separation. Discussing Freud's paper in the context of children who have been deprived of dependable care, Alvarez (2012) suggests that the "cotton-reel game" can also be a way of exploring hope and the qualities of people who want to come back and do so in an interested, attentive way. These are helpful contexts for understanding Lola, whose traumatic birth, medical interventions, and early separations are likely to have prevented her from developing a feeling of being reasonably consistently cared for and loved. Perhaps this early lack of security leads her to seek to control her relationships with her peers by keeping away. But she makes the most of her contact with the adults, and she seems imaginatively to hold onto a feeling of connection with Diane through joining up the ends of the necklace, keeping precious things in her pocket, and playing peek-a-boo with the observer.

When I discussed my observation with Lola's teacher, he noted that it was sometimes hard to stand up to Lola, but that she would accept compromises—for example, to sit next to him rather than on his lap. He also mentioned that, after her first session with me, Diane had felt upset and guilty about Lola's separation difficulties. I was not sure how to understand this, but thought I might not have talked sufficiently about Diane's work in helping Lola to recover and move forward after her traumatic start in life.

At her next session, Diane told me that Lola was now eating better but still did not play with other children. I responded that in my observation Lola did not seem ready for the unpredictability of the playground and wanted to know the adults were on hand when needed, but she also played peek-a-boo, which suggested that she was engaging with the feelings associated with separation and on her way to being more able to tolerate these and was starting to trust in the process.

Diane seemed to feel understood and appreciated. She spoke about Lola's recent visit to the neighbours, where she played with children her age and ate all her tea. Diane seemed hopeful that Lola was gaining confidence, but she was concerned about Lola's insistence on staying up late and wanting to sleep with her when Jo was away. I suggested Lola might be protesting about being outside other people's relationships and that, given her early history, she might need extra help when she felt worried or vulnerable. This seemed to open things up. Diane described Lola's jealousy when Kai and his friends went to the park. And recently, after seeing photographs of events in the family that had occurred before she had arrived, Lola had messed up Kai's bedroom and broken one of his toys. We discussed Lola's struggle to accept being small or not knowing things, and Diane thought about how she could give Lola and Kai individual attention and separate bedtimes, as well as keeping time in the evenings for herself.

This observation, and the liaison and feedback that followed, got a straightforward conversation going in a complex case. It helped Diane to feel valued rather than blamed and guilty, which meant that she could think more freely, and in her own way. And it helped us all to understand

Lola's development and how we could support her next steps. The following week, I asked Diane about her impressions of the work so far. She spoke about her continuing frustration but also requested further sessions. She and I made plans to include Lola in some of our meetings and to consider individual psychotherapy for her in the future.

Consultation

As already mentioned, one of the tasks of the child psychotherapist working in a nursery school setting is to provide psychoanalytically informed consultation to school staff as well as to parents.

In her book, *The Learning Relationship: Psychoanalytic Thinking in Education*, Biddy Youell (2006) reflects on the "therapeutic potential of relationships between pupils and teachers". She is careful to point out that "teachers are not, nor should they be 'therapists' but their relationships with the children they teach have enormous reparative as well as developmental potential" (p. 2). Indeed, school staff face a highly complex task. They have to prepare lessons, often for quite large and diverse groups of children with mixed abilities, where there might not be a shared first language. We have observed first-hand the challenges school staff face in having to balance these demands with the pressures of curriculum delivery. They have to meet targets and assessment requirements alongside having to contain children's challenging behaviour, and they have to manage their own anxiety and sense of helplessness about being in close contact with children who are living in adverse circumstances, such as extreme poverty or exposure to intergenerational trauma.

In order to withstand the demands made on them, school staff also need support. CAMHS child psychotherapists in schools offer a confidential, neutral space in order to give school staff the opportunity to think individually, and in groups when appropriate, about the powerful feelings that some children evoke in them and to reflect on and explore their emotional responses to different situations.

Staff sometimes ask to meet to discuss particular anxieties about how or why a child might be very challenging and disruptive in the classroom and elicit different responses in them as a staff group, which can be divisive and impact on their functioning as a team. Permission to be curious about this together, without fear of judgement, can help to illuminate difficulties and develop a deeper understanding about a child's communication-through-behaviour, including its impact on staff, generating ideas about this can be managed within the classroom setting.

On other occasions consultation and support has been requested to help school staff manage emotionally painful situations.

The deputy head asked if I would meet with a group of reception staff to think about how best they could support Tom, aged 4 years, to return to school after the very sudden and unexpected death of his mother.

Tom

> I met with Tom's class teacher and several teaching assistants. They reflected on their shocked response to the news of mother's death, and I became acutely aware of their strong desire to be supportive alongside a sense of paralysis about how they could help in such traumatic circumstances. Questions and anxieties were explored about how they should "be" with Tom. Should they bring up the issue of his mother's death? What if he talked about her or asked them questions? How should they respond? What would be the right thing to say?

> I spoke to a sense of feeling overwhelmed, which was met with some relief. We were able to think about how Tom might be feeling overwhelmed with feelings for which he had no name. We also thought about how the familiarity and routine of school could help to ground Tom, whose life had been turned so cruelly upside down by circumstances beyond anyone's control. We considered how important it was for Tom's teachers and teaching assistants to remain open and curious and be available to him, signalling that they were able to tolerate his anxiety and upset in a way that was appropriate to his developmental age and level of understanding.

The opportunity for the staff to share their emotional responses and anxieties about saying the "right" thing or the "wrong" thing in what were already extremely painful circumstances enabled them to start to process their own sense of shock and recover a capacity to think. They acknowledged that although they were not therapists, they could play an important part in supporting Tom, while remaining mindful of the boundaries and limitations of their roles. Tom's teacher agreed to make contact with his father to plan a gradual return to school at a pace he would be able to manage. Later, she let me know that initially, and understandably, Tom became very upset at separating from his father at the beginning of the day, but he was also pleased to see his friends and take part in the familiar routine of the school timetable and was reassured when his father came to collect him at home time.

Jake: parent–child work

Jake is a 4-year-old boy of mixed-race heritage. His mother, Alisha, is White British and his father, Chris, is Black British. He was referred by his teacher, who was concerned about his behaviour in class. She described how he did not listen, struggled to make eye contact, and often hit children and adults. Jake's father had also asked the school for help because he was having difficulty managing the boy's behaviour at home.

I arranged to meet with Jake's father at the school to hear a bit more about his concerns and to gather some background history. He said that Alisha had fallen pregnant quite quickly after the couple had met. She had experienced mental health difficulties and issues with substance abuse in her adolescence. She was taking medication at the time of Jake's birth, so had not been able to breastfeed him, which had been upsetting for them both. Chris said that Alisha had been extremely low and anxious and was subsequently diagnosed with post-natal depression, so he had undertaken a lot of Jake's care in the early weeks, while Alisha had struggled to bond with him.

Chris said that they had initially lived with Alisha's mother, but this arrangement could not be sustained because maternal grandmother was experiencing a lot of physical health difficulties. They found a flat and lived together with Jake for six months, but the relationship became strained, and the couple separated when Jake was 2½ years old. Jake lived with Alisha at this time, and Chris kept in contact with Alisha and saw Jake regularly. However, Alisha experienced a relapse of her mental health difficulties and struggled to cope with Jake as he grew older. Social Care became involved with the family due to concerns that Alisha was unable to manage, and the couple agreed that Jake would go and live with Chris, who gave up his job to care for Jake, then aged 3 years.

Chris said that Jake saw Alisha regularly, but he worried about how confusing this must feel for him. He said that Jake looked forward to seeing his mum but became very distressed when it was time to say goodbye, and Chris wondered if it would be better if Jake did not see her at all. Jake had struggled to settle in nursery, and staff had difficulties managing his behaviour. Chris said he thought that he gave in too much to Jake because he felt guilty about him not living with his mum.

Asked about his own experience of growing up, Chris said that his parents had separated when he was young. His father was an alcoholic, and social services had also been involved with their family because he and his brother had been physically chastised by their father.

Chris became annoyed with me and stressed that he did not think his own experience had anything to do with Jake's difficulties. I became acutely aware of my own identity, a white professional woman asking quite personal questions, and how this might be experienced as intrusive and potentially judgemental by Chris. I remembered that he had referred to me rather deferentially as a doctor when I had first made contact with him, and although I had explained to him that I was not a doctor, I was mindful of a possible experience of power imbalance between us. I wondered whether what I had described as an assessment had been perceived by him as an assessment of his capacities as a parent, which had stirred something in him about his experience of professionals as a child, rather than as an opportunity for us to think together about whether what I was able to offer might be helpful to him and to Jake.

I explored with Chris whether he experienced my curiosity about their difficulties as being judgemental of his situation and wondered how we could work together to try to understand something about what was going on for Jake.

Chris softened and said that he had been a lot like Jake when he was younger: he was hyperactive, did not always listen, and he got into a lot of trouble at primary school and later, in his teenage years. He said that he did not want this for Jake. Chris wondered whether perhaps his own mother should have taken him for some help, like Jake was having.

We thought about Jake's experience of starting school and starting to develop a sense of himself in relation to the other children, who were also from diverse backgrounds, and how he might make sense of this in relation to his own identity. Chris was interested in Jake's experience, reflecting that Jake was sometimes curious about his skin tone, comparing it to Chris's and to his mother's.

He added that Jake seemed sad and emotional and would lash out when he was upset, so Chris felt that he needed to keep him busy to cheer him up. He talked about the pressure he felt to keep Jake occupied and "use up his energy", so that that he didn't get bored at home, because that was when the trouble started.

He added that Jake could also be quite controlling, wanting only to do what *he* wanted to do, and said that he struggled to compromise with him. He described how exhausting it felt to care for Jake at times.

We thought about what might be most helpful, and Chris agreed when I suggested that I observe Jake in his classroom and then see them together.

I undertook a classroom observation of Jake: he was a small boy, slim in stature with dark curly hair, light brown skin and dark brown eyes.

Jake was neatly dressed in his school uniform. He sat with the other children on the carpet listening to the teacher reading a story. He found it difficult to wait his turn and seemed desperate to have his voice heard, frequently calling out and putting up his hand and waving it about impatiently to elicit the teacher's attention.

He seemed to want be helpful to other children, for example, helping them to find cutting shapes and different coloured playdoh for their creations, but this seemed overpowering at times, and I had the impression that they found him intrusive and wanted some distance from him. I was reminded of how Chris had described feeling worn out by him.

Jake spent a long time moulding playdoh and announced that he was making a cake, which he showed to me and several other children nearby. They moved away, and Jake called to ask if they were his friends, and one of them said, "No!" Jake looked sad and returned to his cake-making.

When I spoke with Jake's teacher at the end of the observation, she said that he seemed older than his years and sometimes took himself off without letting adults know where he was.

I shared my observation with Chris, who was understandably concerned and very worried about how isolated and in need of attention Jake seemed in spite of his difficult behaviour.

I suggested that I spend some time on my own with Jake in order to get more of an idea about how he related to others and gain a better understanding of what was going on inside him.

I met Jake and Chris together to talk about the sessions. Jake remembered me from the classroom but seemed shy; he climbed onto Chris's lap and snuggled into him, suddenly coming across as very little, talking in a baby-like voice. Chris seemed rather embarrassed, telling Jake that he was a big boy now and didn't need so many cuddles. At other times Jake became more aggressive towards Chris, for example, demanding that Chris bring him his favourite chocolate bar when he collected him after school "or else", wagging his finger in warning at Chris, who seemed unsure about how to respond.

First session

Jake came willingly with me to the room for his first session. He set about keenly exploring the box of simple toys that I had provided for him. He pointed to his tie, saying, "I've got a tie, that makes me a big boy." I said that he felt grown up in his uniform, and he agreed.

He seemed appropriately curious about me and spent time cutting up playdoh and making various cakes for me, saying it was like the one that he had made previously when I had been in the classroom. I said that he had noticed me in the classroom and wanted to check that I had remembered him, and he nodded. He talked about his parents and what food he liked and seemed to want me to know about his family. He spent time drawing and writing out his name and also trying to spell mine, asking for help to do this. He appeared to enjoy being the focus of my attention, and I noted that he was able to draw for a sustained period of time, checking in with me as if to reassure himself that I was still there watching him.

Second session

In the second session he took my hand as we left his classroom and opened the box eagerly, looking for the playdoh. He said that he saw his mum on the weekend and had been bought presents by both his parents; he always gets presents. He looked fleetingly in his box and then looked disappointed and shouted angrily, "There's no playdoh, stupid!" He looked again and found it nestled at the bottom. I talked to him about how he seemed so ready to be disappointed when he thought that I had not taken care of the playdoh. He said he thought it was gone and returned his attention to the playdoh and appeared pleased that I remembered the cake he had made the previous week.

Jake drew a large volcano with huge plumes of dark purple and black smoke coming out of it. I commented on how much care he was taking with his drawing and he nodded. His drawing became more intense as he pressed the crayons hard against the paper and agreed when I suggested that he might have some angry feelings that poured out of him at times just like the smoke coming out of the volcano.

He said that he got angry and hit kids in the class and got into trouble with the teacher. Sometimes his daddy makes him have time out if he hits at home.

Jake asked my name again and spent time trying to write it, checking that he had spelt it correctly. He gave the impression that he was keen to let me know that he could be a good boy. I said that it felt important to him that I knew that although he had angry feelings inside, he was also a nice boy who wanted to take care of people, and he nodded.

Last session

Jake marched over to the bin, took off the top section, and placed it around his waist, telling me that he was a Superhero. I said that he didn't have to think about being a little boy if he was a Superhero. Jake put the bottom section of the bin on his head and made loud angry roaring noises, saying, "I'm a baddie!" and then took it off his head saying, "I'm a goodie!" He put it back on and peeped out from under it. Jake was alert and attentive when

> I talked to him about a Jake that had loud angry roaring feelings and one that liked making playdoh cakes. He appeared to be taking in what I was saying, but then he said, "Go away stupid . . . go way . . . you're stupid!"

The session appeared to put Jake in touch with more vulnerable feelings that felt difficult to tolerate, so I was the one who was made to feel small and stupid.

In a follow-up meeting with Chris, I was able to share my observations and growing understanding of Jake's struggle to be a good boy while simultaneously feeling overwhelmed by powerful feelings over which he felt he had no control, which exploded out of him at times in the form of hitting.

By working together with Chris and the school, we were able to piece something together about Jake's emotional experience. We explored how it appeared to feel difficult for Jake to feel held in mind by adults and by other children, and how this sometimes compelled him to force his way into others' minds in a rather intrusive way, which was affecting his learning and relationships.

Jake's teacher, Chis, and I met together to think about what might be most helpful. Although initially ambivalent because of his own childhood experience, Chris agreed to a referral to Social Care, so that he could access some parenting support to help him feel more confident about establishing appropriate boundaries with Jake.

Chris agreed that Jake could continue to meet with me for sessions at school so that we could explore more of his feelings together in order to try to better understand them. Over time, Chris became more curious about understanding Jake's behaviour and spent more time playing and talking with him at home. He felt that their relationship had improved a little. Jake's teacher reported that his behaviour had settled in class and there were fewer incidents, although he continued to require a lot of individual attention.

As child psychotherapists, we are often asked by teachers, other professionals, and parents to provide strategies in order to help them to manage difficult or worrying behaviour that a particular child might be exhibiting. My intention in this vignette has been to demonstrate how we use our observational and clinical skills to reflect on our own experience of being with a child in order to share some of our understanding about their emotional experience, which may be contributing to the particular difficulties.

In Jake's case, we can see that he had experienced a very difficult start in life. He had endured several transitions and had not had an experience of feeling sufficiently held in his mother's mind because of her mental health difficulties. As a result, he felt compelled, at times, to force his way intrusively into others' minds uninvited. I was able to share my experience of being with Jake to think together with Chris and Jake's class teacher about what might help him to feel more able to be a 4-year-old boy rather than a super-hero, less frightened of his powerful feelings, and so less likely to rely on a bossy and more omnipotent way of alleviating his anxiety.

Conclusion

Our intention in this chapter has been to illustrate the different ways in which our training as child psychotherapists enables us to apply psychoanalytic thinking and understanding to our work in a school nursery, and to support school staff, children, and parents with a wide range of presenting difficulties.

You will see from the brief vignettes that we have shared that the work is diverse and wide-ranging. It requires us to be open, flexible, and creative as well as to engage and collaborate with a range of agencies and professional networks. We offer brief, time-limited interventions with parents and children with ordinary developmental issues or worries. This can provide relief quickly and reduce stress on family dynamics. Some families are referred on for specialist support—for example, children with neurodevelopmental difficulties. On other occasions the difficulties are more entrenched and not as easily resolved. We might need to do a great deal of multi-agency collaboration and sensitive work, with high levels of complexity and risk, alongside school staff before parents are ready to start to engage with a more direct therapeutic intervention. We might also discover that the therapeutic needs of the family are beyond those that can be met by one child psychotherapist working in a school. However, having built up an initial relationship with the family in the familiar environment of the school, we are then well placed to function for them as a bridge to the CAMHS clinic, where they can work with ourselves and/or colleagues in a multidisciplinary team.

Our work in the school nursery has given us an important, privileged role in identifying needs at an early stage and offering interventions at a crucial period in children's lives, thereby supporting them to move onto a more hopeful developmental trajectory. Our experience illuminates the variety of ways in which a brief intervention based on psychoanalytic thinking can help staff, parents, and other professionals consider the meaning and emotional impact of a child's difficulties, and understand this within a developmental context. This can help to alleviate the pressure to find quick and dramatic solutions, such as a change of class or school, and it can open up more time and space for creative collaborations between the child, their family, school, and wider context. We have also found that parents and young people who have had a positive experience of accessing support early on are more likely to be able to notice when or if things are starting to go awry again. Having had the experience of their difficulties being tolerated and understood at nursery, they feel empowered to seek support again when they need it, which is, in itself, a sign that they are developing resilience and a capacity to help themselves.

CHAPTER FIVE

Children's group psychotherapy in a mainstream primary school

Marta Cioeta

In this chapter I present an innovative form of group psychotherapy with children in a primary school. After providing a brief overview of the technical and theoretical framework underpinning group psychotherapy with children and exploring the reasons for undertaking this in schools, I give an account of the group therapy as it unfolded. In this work, a child group psychotherapy frame of reference was used in conjunction with Mindfulness technique and drawing-led activities. This account of group therapy brings to light the richness of integrating different approaches, especially when working in outreach.

Children's psychotherapy groups: an overview

Child psychotherapists have been providing children's psychotherapy groups in clinics and schools for a long time. It was actually in primary schools that Tavistock students first did group work with children (Reid, Fry, & Rhode, 1977), and soon after this the Tavistock model of children's group psychotherapy was developed and formalized by Susan Reid (1987, 1999).

At the core of Reid's model is the view that group participants will bring to the group their strengths as well as the most disturbed, denied, and unwanted parts of themselves. For each child, the different aspects of their personalities will become more accepted and integrated as the group work progresses. "What starts out each time as a number of

DOI: 10.4324/9781003185925-8

individuals, moves towards the experience of THE GROUP as a psychological whole, with some modification of self-centred behaviour in recognition of the needs, wishes and feelings of others." In short, for Reid, "becoming a group is the therapy" (Reid, 1999, pp. 257).

By not focusing on structured activities, group psychotherapy allows for children's emotional experiences to manifest at their own pace. Reid views groups as offering children the possibility of being together and seeing how they react to each other and to the adult therapists. This is paralleled by the group therapists' capacity for acceptance and their focus on trying to follow and understand the meaning of any type of communication within the group. The children themselves notice and comment on what happens, and the multiple perspectives multiply the opportunities for helpful change.

Children's group psychotherapy is challenging for therapists to sustain because of the intense anxieties activated in a group situation, promoting powerful anti-developmental, anti-thinking, and anti-group processes, which threaten the survival of the group (Canham, 2002; Reid, 1999; Wood, 1993; Wood & Argent, 2009). In particular, Hamish Canham (2002) talks of a gang state of mind versus a group state of mind. In the former, destructive parts of the personality gather up to keep hostage those parts of the personality that would otherwise be in contact with vulnerability, dependence, and not knowing. When a group is in the grip of a gang state of mind, there is no space for concern and thinking, and the children are more prone to verbal and physical violence, while rejecting the adults' support and boundaries in favour of the idea that they can be self-sufficient and strong in their gang status. Group state of mind functioning, in contrast, is able to allow difference, dependence, and vulnerability to be acknowledged and accepted: knowledge about oneself and others can be reached and maintained, and the therapists' authority and parental roles are valued. These two ways of functioning fluctuate rapidly in groups, making "knowing each other and [our] selves . . . the central task" of child group psychotherapy (Canham, 2002, p. 124).

Why children's group therapy in schools?

The many-faceted educational, emotional, and social learning that takes place in primary schools happens in a variety of group settings, such as in class, in smaller learning groups, or at playtime. Schools know all about the potential for groups to maximize change and development in order for learning to happen. Children need to navigate and master all sorts of social situations during and beyond their school life. This makes it easy for schools to see the likely benefits of group therapy, which privileges a focus on social interaction between children and adults, including paying attention to the possible unintentional meanings of what is said and done. The beneficial impact of group therapy can extend to the whole school as the group members make progress in their school social life and learning.

In addition, school children with complex and varied emotional needs, often with traumatic histories and from vulnerable and marginalized families, might not be able to access ordinary CAMHS clinics for group therapy. This is due to a number of reasons, such as difficult family circumstances, parental worries about stigma and blame, or concern about involvement with agencies.

The inner-city school setting, with its diverse communities, helps in the establishment of what Reid called heterogeneous groups (Reid, 1999). Such groups, normally with a maximum of five children, are set up to work with the differences between children in terms of problems, personalities, gender, ages, race, and ethnicity. In so doing, the group has within itself the possibility of rapidly mobilizing a variety of strengths and difficulties, facilitating group exploration of feelings and thoughts through identification with or differentiation from others.

There are inevitable challenges that need to be considered when thinking about group therapy in schools. The school as the host institution needs to be supportive of the group therapy, not only in terms of providing a reasonably suitable room, but also in terms of making mental space for it and keeping it in the mind of the institution at various levels across the school, from management to teachers and assistants. It is really a collective effort, which requires child psychotherapists to have fully established themselves and their service in the school first, with a firm trust in their work already consolidated. Inevitably, as group processes generate heightened emotions in the children, tensions in the group can spill out into the school corridors, requiring support and cooperation between school and therapists in order to be managed.

For parents and carers, the offer of group therapy to their children in school is often well received compared to a recommendation for individual psychotherapy. There may be several reasons for this. Group work is seen as less stigmatizing of an individual child, and the idea of helping children in a group setting with two adults, resembling a family unit within the school community, can have an immediate positive resonance for families from community-based cultures. In addition, parents and carers with experiences of marginalization, who have a limited sense of belonging, might view the offer of group therapy for their children within school as a particularly inclusive gesture on the part of the school. A particular family comes to mind: a very isolated and overwhelmed grandmother, who had adopted her grandchildren, saw the recommendation of sibling group therapy as an unexpected act of acceptance of all her children from our service and the school, which was even more meaningful due to an intergenerational family history of displacement and abandonment.

"'Til we find our place"

This is an account of a children's psychotherapy group, which brought together techniques from child group psychotherapy, Mindfulness, and picture-led activities. The group was run in an inner-city primary school where a child psychotherapy outreach service had been working for many years, and where other groups had been run before.

The five children were from the infant and junior classes (Year 2 to Year 6), and presented with emotional and behavioural issues. They were all struggling with social relationships with peers and adults, linked to highly reactive and challenging or withdrawn and inhibited behaviours. The two boys and three girls came from different ethnic backgrounds and had suffered significant trauma and/or neglect. Parental experiences of displacement and mental health difficulties were also a common feature.

The group ran weekly for over two terms and was co-run by a colleague child psychotherapist—whom I will call Emilie—and myself. Before the group started, there was a period of meeting the children and their parents and doing classroom observations to assess the children's needs and work out whether a group or another treatment approach would be the most helpful.

The children

The youngest child in the group was Aziz, a 7-year-old in Year 2. He had suffered traumatic and protracted exposure to domestic violence. There was a long history of involvement with social services, and his mother had had limited engagement with CAMHS. Aziz struggled to regulate his feelings and would easily lose his temper in an explosive way with other children. When we observed him in the classroom, he was noticeably easily provoked and unable to modulate his frustration or excitement, turning his behaviour into something potentially hurtful to others, even if not necessary intentionally. In class he was often seen crawling around on the floor. When we met Aziz with his mother, he appeared very subdued—different from the boy we had observed in class. He had lots of questions about the group, seeming to respond to the idea in a lively way.

Helen was 8 years old, in Year 3, and the youngest of the girls. She was described by her teacher as a rather "switched-off" child at school, lacking in liveliness and often becoming cut-off, her learning lagging behind. Helen was not responsive, and her neutral demeanour made her become rather invisible to other children; she was, indeed, lacking friends. Her mother, who looked after Helen and her brothers, told us that she had been struggling with mental health issues and was now trying to get back to work. She accepted Helen's referral but took time to meet with us initially, remaining involved with us occasionally as the group progressed.

Miguel, the other boy in the group, was 9 years old and in Year 4. When he was observed in class, he displayed low-key disruptive behaviour, whispering and giggling with other children, yet trying to stay on task and learn. His parents were refugees from a war-torn country, where both had witnessed atrocities and lost their families in the conflict. Mother had been the more resilient of the two parents, while father had been suffering from mental ill health for years, needing ongoing therapeutic support and living a shielded life. Miguel was described as caring and respectful towards his parents as well as to the adults in school.

Aisha, a 10-year-old in Year 5, had for a long time been having difficulties with her reactive behaviour towards children and adults. Aisha's parents had split up, and her mother found it hard to manage her children's response to the separation. Aisha's mother had mild learning difficulties and needed her own mother for support. The referral to our service was accepted, though previous school offers of referrals to children's clinics had been turned down by the mother. Aisha appeared bright and keen to join the group when we met with her and her mother.

The oldest child was Nima, an 11-year-old girl in Year 6, for whom group work had been recommended following an Educational Psychologist's report, where her learning needs were understood as stemming from social and emotional difficulties rather than specific learning difficulties. Nima's parents were refugees who had arrived in the UK after a perilous journey. They had separated recently, and Nima's mother shared with us that she felt depressed and lonely. She told us that Nima was caring towards an elderly relative.

With regard to the group therapists, it is worth saying that since I had been working in the school for a number of years, I was well-established in school life and was a known face for the children in the group. My colleague, Emilie, was new to the school, although not new to school group work. Another important aspect of who we were is the fact that we are both white, as were two of the children in the group, and not from the UK, as were the parents of three of the children.

Unfortunately, due to limited clinical resources, we were not able to run a parents' group parallel to the children's group, but parents were offered regular review meetings, which they mostly attended.

Time and place and other boundaries

Child psychotherapy groups are run with set boundaries in terms of time and location. The school offered us a room in a part of the school away from the main corridors, which provided reasonable privacy. Given that we had children from most of the classes, we decided to run the group in the afternoon, when the majority of them would not miss out on particularly relevant lessons. The group was to run for one hour weekly during term time until the summer holidays. We had talked with all the children and their parents about the time-limited nature of the group.

Emilie and I gathered various toys, from baby dolls to pots and pans, a doctor's kit, dressing up clothes and hats, blankets, toy phones, foam balls, teddies, play-dough, stationery, paper, and a folder for each child.

Ordinary boundaries and the requirement for children and therapists to respect each other and keep safe, including avoiding any form of physical or verbal attack, had been explained beforehand, as was confidentiality.

Stormy beginnings

Despite all the preparation and assessment before the group started, its beginning was complicated by unplanned absences, ending up with the first sessions not being attended by one of the children. This uncertain start flooded the group and the therapists with tension and anxiety, as the extract below shows.

From the second session

> Emilie and I reminded the children that next week another child, a girl new to the group, would join us. The whole group first ignored us, then, as a response, the two baby dolls were found and played with by Nima and Aisha, who fed and cleaned the babies. Meanwhile, the two boys tried to open the locked cupboard. They peeped through the small gap between the cupboard doors, complaining that there were, "More toys and playdough inside!", which they could not get to! Emilie and I talked about their feelings at the idea of someone new joining the group and suggested that there

was a sense that there was not enough to go around for everybody, and that the new baby might take up a lot of the attention. The babies in Nima and Aisha's game then became unwell, "Their temperature is a thousand degrees!!" said Aisha, alarmed, and she invited one of the therapists to play doctors with her. We talked about excitement rising today at the news of the new arrival, like with a new baby. "All of this has made the room very hot!" we said. The boys settled themselves around the dolls and got interested in the babies, playing at checking and feeding them. This activity focused the group on the idea that doctors needed to be at hand, and we pointed to a connection with an idea of us as therapists being needed to help them and their question about whether we could help them enough.

The thought of another child joining the group triggered interest in the baby dolls and a worry about resources being scarce. Pressing questions about the state and survival of the group led to the children feeling that doctors and carers should be at hand!

The worries shown in this vignette reoccurred in subsequent sessions: anxieties about being unwell as a group, about dread of an unknown child who might join them and whom they might want to throw out, and fear of what would then happen to them, were communicated in various ways. For instance, when eventually the newcomer, Helen, did arrive, all the children dressed up and performed a play where an intruder who had entered the Queen's palace was discovered and immediately thrown out by the Queen, played by Aisha. It was notable how quickly this play was organized and staged, with none of the children challenging who would be the King or Queen: Aisha, who played the Queen, was the child whom the group had given the status of group leader.

Parallel to these enactments, the children developed stronger bonds, linking up either in pairs or as a whole cohesive group-body, which we, the two therapists, were not part of. The children gave the impression that something meaningful was happening between them, like when they sang the song "Who Will Buy?" together, from the musical *Oliver!*. However, the more they appeared united, the more we, the therapists, found ourselves feeling cut off and excluded from them, as if looking at a shop window, with the things inside remaining totally out of reach. Emilie and I realized that in the film the boy Oliver sings this particular song in a moment of pleasurable respite, when he wakes in the comfortable home of a wealthy family, having been rescued from the pickpocket gang. We thought the group sang this song together at a moment of intense excitement, in the face of feeling that there was not enough of what they needed, perhaps expressing an emotional flight into a highly idealized state, albeit precarious and limited. They felt like Oliver, trying to hold onto a "wonderful feeling", which made him "fly high as the sky" in the midst of his miseries.

Questions, fears, and tensions about resources, survival, and potential newcomers do ordinarily occur in group work and are part of the process of becoming and being a group. However, for our group these worries became very real, due to unforeseen events. Unfortunately, Aisha suddenly had to move school because of safety concerns for her family. This event catalysed and heightened the group's preoccupations in such a way as to bring the group almost to the brink of break-up and failure, polarizing the children in extreme states of excitement and defiance in opposition to each other or to the therapists. The therapists were cast in the role of repressive boundary-setters, like an idea of punitive police or severe judges ready to throw people out. The dread of being excluded forever from the group became terribly tangible and fuelled more and more the group's paranoid feelings, which they tried to counteract by becoming the attackers, creating a vicious circle of more paranoia and anxiety.

The emotional temperature in the sessions grew steadily, while less and less talking and thinking between the children and the therapists took place. The children's initial inquisitiveness, thinking about the group's reason for being, wanting to investigate what kind of therapists they'd got, and their acknowledgement of their need for help and treatment—"The group is for troubles with children", Miguel had suggested, echoed by Aisha talking of the need to be cured, like when someone fractures a bone—had long gone. Instead, the group tried to cope with anxiety through taking on tougher, more powerful roles or displaying increasingly challenging behaviour. Their pretend games became more overtly aggressive. The group played at shooting and killing, and direct physical and verbal attacks between the children started to appear. Safety boundaries were crossed. It is also important to mention that during this time there had been a series of shootings in the local area, and the children would have been aware of this. Because of this, shooting and killing had an immediate, shared, powerful meaning for this group of children.

Issues of difference and sameness were present and enacted in significant ways. When in a state of heightened anxiety, the group tended to act as an undifferentiated unit, as though feeling or being perceived as different could expose intolerably a group member's vulnerability. It was often Emilie and I, with our odd accents and unfamiliar names, who were to know what it was like to be mocked and attacked for our differences when a highly anxious state of mind predominated.

My colleague and I felt ourselves become more and more muted and dejected, and our comments seemed to fall on deaf ears. Our thinking together languished, and we felt apart and disconnected. We tried to use a more structured approach with a ten-point temperature chart, which could visually show the children how their behaviour escalated and guide them, then, to de-escalate. The children contributed to making the chart, all sitting at the table, discussing calm and less calm behaviours in the group and the feelings attached to these. We agreed as a group that if the temperature went above five, they would need to try to get seated at the table. Although this exercise helped them to focus on what had happened in the group and the variety of their feelings towards each other and the therapists, it did not restrain them from turning to verbal and physical attacking responses. A gang state of mind (Canham, 2002) had set in, dominating the group's life, as the following vignette illustrates.

From the ninth session

All the children started the session by pushing the boundaries, from opening the door to knocking at the window to get attention or trying to force open the room cupboard, which was locked. After having acknowledged that their attacks might be in response to their worries about the difficult session we'd had last week, Nima attempted to make a new calendar. Helen, however, rapidly scribbled out her own name, with the intention of doing the same to the other children's names. Helen stopped doing this when she was reminded that it was not up to her to delete the other children's names.

The group remained unsettled. After briefly playing with the ball, often hitting each other hard and giggling, Helen bashed the dustbin rhythmically, then very loudly, in an attacking way, as if wanting to break it, and then joined Nima, who had started to open the door. The girls laughed at what Emilie and I had written on the sign placed on the door, pointing out spelling mistakes, which were not there. We were ridiculed and made to feel like bad writers. We asked the children to come and sit at the table, where only Miguel had been sitting for a while. However, Helen and Nima, who had previously joined up to denigrate the therapists, rapidly got into a tussle, and in a flash one of them hit the other on the back, who started crying.

In this vignette, we see clearly Nima's faint attempt to change the group state of mind through trying to make a new calendar: we were indeed approaching a school break, and an earlier calendar had been ruined by the group, so Nima's idea was an attempt to restore some thinking about where the group was. However, this glimpse of meaningful and thoughtful activity was short-lived. Not-thinking and acting-out stances took over.

During this period, it was noticeable how the more reactive children like Aziz and Aisha led the way in what started as playful and quickly became over-excited activities, like playing football or dressing up. Children who had earlier been described as more caring started taking on group liaison roles in relation to the adults, especially Miguel, who was mindful and respectful of the therapists, at times in a touching way, and Nima, who was attracted by the doctor's kit and looking after the ill babies. When the group was more in the grip of a gang state of mind, Helen and Nima, who behaved in a placid and socially inhibited manner outside the group, joined in with the challenging or attacking behaviour, as illustrated in the vignette above. After Aisha had left the group, Helen, in particular, was the one who took on the role of provoking and stirring up the other children, making the group spiral up combatively, which either divided the children into opposing factions or glued them together against Emilie and me. At moments, however, Aziz, Miguel, and Nima would open up and talk about their country of origin or their family. While this was the start of something different emerging in the group and a sign that there was a wish to use the group differently and move away from the gang that they tended to turn into, for other children this information and talking was still experienced as provocative, as they were not yet ready to talk about themselves or their own families.

In the face of this worrying and challenging situation, Emilie and I decided to discuss with school and parents the children's level of acting out in order to think about how to proceed while keeping the group sessions safe. It was not easy for the parents to hear about the group situation, as they had hoped the group would deal more easily with their children's difficulties. We were able to discuss how divided the children were in terms of how they presented at school and at home and in the group, especially those children who were generally subdued and inhibited and whose level of aggression and anger was not usually shown. We were also able to think with some parents about the traumas their families had suffered, which had remained unprocessed and were possibly resonating for their children in the emotionally heightened environment of the group, especially in relation to loss.

We all agreed that a member of the School Management Team would be available in their office if we needed a child to come out of the group to calm down. Running therapy groups in schools often requires a robust working together with school staff when there are particularly difficult group dynamics. In a clinic there is the option of working with the support of the child's parents or carers, who might be needed to stay outside the therapy room or in the waiting room in case a child cannot manage the group session, but in a school therapists have to work with the school staff to support the therapeutic process.

At this point the school told Emilie and me that the children were doing a bit better in their classes and with their peers. They had also started to look for each other at playtime. This gave us confidence in the importance of the group continuing, and, with the support of supervision, further creative thinking together took place. We decided that we needed to draw on additional clinical tools to help the children manage their strong feelings and reduce their acting out.

Finding a place

The additional thinking provided by the supervision of an experienced child psychotherapist colleague, who had run many groups, allowed us to think outside the box and integrate other methodologies with child group psychoanalytic technique for this group. We thought that the unstructured framework, combined with unanticipated external events, unbalanced the dynamics to such an extent that the anxieties and acting out had become stuck.

Emilie and I also realized how the group had driven us apart. We found that we had taken up polarized views, either being overly compassionate and allowing too much space for the children's acting out or becoming more rigid and stern. We had become an ineffective working pair, unable to shift the gang state of mind that had set in. When a group is in the grip of a gang state of mind, attacks on the therapist couple are particularly intense, generating an inability for the therapists to join up and trust in the value of working together. The therapist pair has come to represent unwanted feelings of need and dependence linked to an idea of parents, while the gang formation offers powerful feelings of pseudo-independence and lack of need. Hamish Canham suggests that: "Allowing that they [the therapists] do have something to offer would mean an acknowledgment of dependency linked to a feeling of being deprived of something they [the children] want" (2002, p. 122). Canham adds that the group or gang mentality sets in according to how much the group is capable of knowing and owning how needy and vulnerable they are, and the degree to which others are made to have these feelings instead.

Canham also thinks that the combination of *anxiety, deprivation,* and *abuse* may significantly reduce the possibility of holding on to benign feelings in relation to need of, and dependence on, parents or adults, which then potentially impinges on the ability to know, own, and bear emotional pain (Canham, 2002). We knew that the majority of the children in our group had experienced, at least, emotional abuse and deprivation. Their actual experiences of adults who did not meet their needs with ordinary good-enough care or could not protect them from emotional harm was likely to have generated or exacerbated their tendency to impulsive and attacking responses, where locating and pushing unwanted feelings into others was prominent. The attempt to get rid of unwanted feelings or thoughts fuelled the children's actions and words when they were in attack mode. Added to this, the actual absences and losses experienced in the initial life of the group and the perceived strong working bond between my colleague and me intensely provoked and angered the children. In their eyes, we had not managed to run the group properly; we had not held on to all its children. We were perceived as not-good parents, and so we could not be trusted.

The group situation clearly highlighted the children's significant underlying preoccupations, but exploration with the children about what was happening and the anxieties at play was not possible while the atmosphere remained so fraught.

Using more structured approaches within children's group therapy had not been tried before by Emilie and me, although both of us were familiar with the new interventions and had used them in larger group settings. We were entering unchartered territory, but we saw that the group needed to feel safer and we trusted that this represented an important decision in terms of regaining the capacity to work together as a therapist couple.

We introduced Mindfulness technique to help the children to notice and reduce their intense emotional arousal, alongside a picture-led activity about issues they showed they were struggling with, such as peer problems and separation. Mindfulness, used extensively in schools with classes of children and recommended for some adult mental health difficulties, provides the opportunity to focus on the here and now of bodily sensation as well as on thoughts and feelings. It guides towards taking notice of oneself, while limiting reactiveness to external and internal stimuli. The idea is that this makes it possible to let go of the pull to become entangled in emotions or thoughts and what is happening in the environment.

The picture-led activity worked by giving the children images to elicit stories around emotionally challenging group situations. The children were asked first to talk about the pictures and then to draw what they thought would happen next. I had devised this activity when working with whole primary school classes. The activity had been used successfully as a semi-structured intervention to allow children to respond as a class group to a troubling scenario that was emotionally alive for all of them, like transitioning to a new school phase, losing an important adult, or struggling to share the class teacher. Figure 5.1 shows an example of the pictures used.

FIGURE 5.1   Picture used in group work.

Introducing these techniques was carefully thought through. We wanted to keep our psychoanalytic perspective, and we debated how different Mindfulness was from the psychoanalytic approach, which supports the child to recognize and own their disowned feelings and thoughts. What the two approaches have in common is careful attention to changes in the person, including openness to things happening within one's own mind. Mindfulness seeks to secure an inner balance, whereas psychoanalysis seeks to extend awareness and understanding of emotional states to make emotional life more manageable.

These technical changes were introduced to the children's group a third of the way into the therapy and were received with interest by the school and generally experienced as helpful by the children themselves, as the vignette below shows.

From the fifteenth session

Three children attended today, Miguel, Nima, and Aziz. They immediately noticed the different set-up and showed curiosity, looking at the drawing materials on the table. Aziz then, for the first time, noticed the colour of Emilie's eyes, and all three children commented on their own eye colour, carefully discerning the different shades of brown eyes. Emilie and I commented on how they were noticing things about the room and about us all today and invited them to sit at the table. I talked about the previous session, which had been very difficult for everybody. Emilie and I talked about how the group had become overexcited, and things got out of hand and became unsafe. So we had decided to introduce an exercise where we would learn to stop, disengage, and become quiet. We said that this was like an experiment for our group. We told the children how the "quiet time" would work, that everyone would sit down quietly with their eyes shut for two minutes, noticing what we could hear around us and spending some time with ourselves.

Miguel shut his eyes first, while Aziz and Nima remained seated but giggled during the first attempt. "How peaceful!" Miguel said, and, "Let's do this again!" Aziz begged. We had a few more goes at quiet time in this session, concentrating on our breathing and inviting the children to find a place they could sit and feel comfortable in. The two boys tried out various places to be. First they lay down on the blanket, and then they made a tent with chairs and a blanket, which they went under during quiet time. A lively conversation followed. The children said they felt "relaxed", and Nima was curious about what would happen next.

I showed them the picture of a big bird feeding chicks in the nest, where one chick gets squashed and pushed by the others. The children talked about the scene. They thought the birds were "hungry" and that one of them was "left out". Nima showed disgust at the sight of the worm and did not want to draw. Aziz drew the strongest chick being given the worm, while Miguel drew the hurt chick being given the worm.

This exercise signalled the start of a shift: the Mindfulness exercise brought with it the idea of each child having an individual place within the group. This helped to start to untie the strong bonds of the gang state of mind, which had not allowed the individual children to operate separately and independently. In the following months the children found or created various places for themselves, like beds on the floor, under and on top of the tables, and bunk beds made with the chairs. The task of securing a place and acquiring a sense of belonging had become meaningful for this group, after their struggles with intense survival anxieties. For a while they made signs with their names to stick on the places they had used for quiet time. The calendar acquired a new-found use: rather than being the butt of destructive attacks, the names of the children present started to be written on the day of the sessions, like a sort of group register, where the children could claim their entitlement to be in the group.

In the vignette above, we see the children being curious, noticing for the first time our and their different eye colours. This step towards knowing about themselves and others was significant and was shown more and more in the following months. For instance, they wanted to know about how their names were spelt, they talked about their countries of origin and families, as well as about things happening to them in school outside the group. They were sharing that they could know what they had in common and where they were different, while keeping the group in mind.

During this phase, their feelings could also be known and communicated in reasonably manageable ways. At the announcement of the approaching Easter break, Nima wrote on the table that she hated the therapists! The group anger, which Nima expressed, could now be named and linked with the approaching break. The children's working through and consequent ability to modulate their anger continued, supported by their growing capacity to see how their anger was triggered in relation to actual or threatened loss, either of group members or, due to holidays, of sessions.

It was also in this period, during one of the picture-led activities about a teddy left out by other teddies who were playing a ball game, that Helen started to sing the song "Circle of Life", from *The Lion King*. On this occasion, nobody joined in or derided her: the children allowed the song to capture the atmosphere in the group. In fact, the song is about realizing how all creatures find their place in the circle of life eventually, and how various and troubled the paths of life can be. After Aisha left the group, Helen had been the one who had become particularly challenging, often attacking the other children and leading the ganging-up acting out. Now she was letting us know that the children knew they had a place and felt safe in the group, despite the challenges they faced, including their own destructiveness.

The helpful changes in the group were sometimes still interwoven with challenging behaviours, though these were now more limited in duration and tended to involve no more than two children. With the aid of the pictures, we were able to approach the issue of physical aggression from another angle. Most of the children now talked about being "scared" when describing a picture involving bullying. This was the first time fear was mentioned by them, and it showed how far they had moved from the strident and unconcerned group in a gang state of mind.

The ending of the group

The approaching end of the group inevitably brought further anxieties about loss, and some defensive aggression came to the fore again—like waves after a storm, bringing back old debris. However, thinking together as a group continued, and with only a few weeks left, the talking about the lost member of the group intensified again. The children talked among themselves, wondering about the reasons for Aisha's departure from the group and asking about a new person possibly replacing her. The conversation moved to other losses they had had in their lives, like when their parents had spent time away from them.

As the end of the group came near, the group state of mind, as Canham (2002) called it, was sustained, as the vignettes below show.

From the penultimate session

At the start of the session, the first three children who rushed into the room began playing Hide and Seek, wanting to be found. They enjoyed playing together. When we had all arrived, Helen looked at the calendar and coloured in today's date, looking at me intently. We talked about the ending and the group's awareness of this. The children listened, and then they decided to play a new game they had never played before: "Charlie, Charlie, are you there?" They turned the lights in the room on and off. They explained to us that it was a game about a ghost. Emilie and I reflected out loud about their need to check the ghostly presence, linked to the end that was now upon us all. They talked about next year, and about Nima leaving the school. Nima asked if the group would carry on for the three remaining children. They all wished for the group to continue, and Nima said she would visit next year. We talked about the sadness in the room today and their questions about what would happen when the group finished.

From the last session

After Helen had shown me that her finger was better today, Aziz told the group that Emilie and I had met him and his mother earlier for a review. Emilie underlined how safe the children now felt to share things in the group. We wondered if they would like to talk about the long journey of our group, which had met for eight months. Aziz told us about the review meeting with his mother, and maybe we could review our work? We acknowledged how much the group had changed, from the initial intense struggles and fights. The children responded by playing a sort of game where they wrote messages to each other about liking someone in the group and signing with someone else's name. Then they passed the messages to each other. At first they showed some embarrassment about what they had written. Then they wrote on one of the notes that they liked the therapists! Emilie and I talked about how we had noticed a shift from the initial fears, upsets, and strong feelings between them. They all listened carefully. The boys then set off to prepare their Minecraft houses, while the girls kept writing and drawing quietly. A sense of calm and purposefulness was shared for a while.

As the end of the session neared, Nima started to sing, "See You Again" (by Wiz Khalifa), soon followed by Helen, while Miguel joined in rapping the song. The song had a beautiful melody, and the lyrics were about there being hope in relationships—the characters in the song have come a long way since they started, and their memories will help when they are apart. The song also acknowledged the importance of families. Emilie and I were moved and surprised by their touching singing and by how they had come together. We talked about this, and how the song, which was about ending, brought them together in a creative way. As the session ended, all but Miguel decided to take their folders with them. He decided to leave his folder with us so that we could remember the group. They then said their goodbyes to us as we took them back to their classes.

Both extracts show the group being creative, playful, and thoughtful in the face of the approaching ending. The children were in touch with their feelings and their vulnerabilities, including Helen telling us about her finger getting better, and they could speak up individually as well as for the group. They were able to admit their liking and appreciation for each other and for the therapists, accepting accompanying feelings of longing, dependence, and loss.

There was no group ganging-up aimed at breaking up the relationships between the children and us. Rather, there was a sense that we had all eventually managed to become a group (Reid, 1999).

Final reflections

Running groups in schools, as described here, is challenging and testing for therapists. It is not a solitary endeavour, but one that requires strong cooperation with schools, parents, and experienced colleagues in order to bring about change.

In this chapter I described how creatively we needed to work, including integrating other techniques, in the face of children's significant acting out and aggression. At the end of the group, all the children were seen to have changed in school, either becoming more alive and confident in class or more able to modulate their feelings when learning or playing. The group therapy allowed them to bring to the fore powerful and destructive feelings, as well as their need to belong and to be accepted by other children and adults, while acknowledging their histories and vulnerabilities.

The impact on this group of losses and absences was remarkable, as was the way the children responded to difference. Loss and difference, as described here, are issues that need to be held in mind not only when doing group work, but generally when working in schools where a high proportion of families have histories of displacement and trauma, as well as experiences of marginalization. As this group progressed, more thinking and knowledge about loss as well as the different aspects of themselves and others could be borne, tolerated, and explored, enriching the group and us.

CHAPTER SIX

Parents' experience
of a child psychotherapy outreach service:
Isha and Sheikh

Interview by Milly Jenkins

Mohamed was 9 years old and in Year 5 when his school referred him to the Tavistock Outreach in Primary Schools (TOPS) service, concerned about the intensity of his anger and distress and that his disruptive behaviour was becoming increasingly hard to understand and manage. His parents, Isha and Sheikh, were worried too, at a loss to know what was wrong but unsure whether a referral to the in-school service would be helpful.

Originally from Sierra Leone, the couple had been living in London for some time when Mohamed and his siblings were born. Although settled in the community around the school, they were living in inadequate housing and having to adapt to a different kind of family life in the UK, with less freedom and little support from wider family.

Here, Isha and Sheikh and the school's lead therapist, Marta Cioeta, talk—with an interpreter—about their two years of working together: their uncertainty about the referral, getting started with weekly therapeutic sessions for Mohamed and fortnightly parent sessions for themselves, and the impact a child psychotherapy approach had on the family over time.

* * *

Isha: Mohamed was always angry, and when he got angry, he would kick chairs, doors, walls. Whatever was in front of him, he'd

     DOI: 10.4324/9781003185925-9

throw it. He would shake, too, really shake, when he was angry. I remember one day school phoning to say he was very stressed and angry, that they'd taken him into another room, where he'd upturned chairs and pulled down posters. They called me in to see what he'd done.

We didn't know why he was so angry. He was doing this at home, too, and it had been going on for three years. He had also been wetting the bed. We wondered if it was something about school, if he was unhappy and uncomfortable there. But we didn't know for sure. We had been to the GP, and he had been sent for an MRI scan, but the hospital couldn't find anything wrong. We felt so confused, especially as this was our first baby.

When the school said they wanted to refer him to a therapy service, we asked ourselves—what has *happened* to this child? We felt doubtful about whether he would like the sessions, if they would be fun or helpful for him. We worried it could make things worse. We also worried about someone we didn't know getting involved in our lives, if it would be good for Mohamed or the family. But we knew it was affecting his education, and the school were complaining about him all the time. In the end, I thought: "We'll just try it and see, give it one or two months and, if it gets worse, we will stop, I will keep my child."

Marta: Mohamed had been struggling for some time, but the referral came with a peak in his difficulties. He could become extremely upset and distressed over ordinary changes, running around the school, putting himself at risk. There was a sense of this being an angry boy but also a scared boy. The school were struggling to understand and contain his behaviour. They were concerned that sometimes his reactions were quite unpredictable and intense, to the extent that they were worried about his mental health and needed help from our team to support him and staff. Isha and Sheikh were very worried, too, and aware that these problems were getting in the way of his learning.

Sheikh: Yes, the school often had to take him out of class, so he was missing lots of his education. At first we were sent to a clinic, and it was good there, but it was better for us to have meetings at the school. It was closer to home, easier, and it felt more comfortable.

Marta: That's right—the family were initially referred to CAMHS, and that referral got routed to the Tavistock Clinic's Refugee Team. They went there with Mohamed for an initial assessment, but the team and family decided it would work better for them to be seen in school, so I joined a meeting at the clinic to help with that transition. Back at school, I began an assessment, meeting with Isha and Sheikh.

Sheikh: We came every week at first, both of us.

Marta: Yes, it was important to see both of you, to begin to get a picture of the family and a sense of what was needed. An interpreter joined us, and fortunately she was able to keep working with us for those two years. Indeed, she is here with us today. We have been lucky to have her. After a series of exploratory sessions, an assistant therapist began to see Mohamed for weekly therapeutic sessions. I continued to see Isha and Sheikh for fortnightly parent sessions. The assistant therapist worked with Mohamed throughout year 5 and became very attuned to his anxieties. When she left, I saw him for individual work in Year 6, as well as seeing his parents. We also worked closely with his teacher and, initially, when things were still difficult, had regular joint meetings with Isha and Sheikh and the school's senior leadership team.

Isha: When I first saw Marta, I was feeling so worried—I couldn't really think about anything else, I couldn't laugh or have fun. It was very difficult for Mohamed to talk to us, to say anything, so it was hard for us to understand what was making him angry.

Marta: I remember we talked about an image of a volcano, something hot and explosive, and how everybody panicked when the volcano started to heat up. We began thinking about what Mohamed might be feeling and how it made others feel and act in response. We also, slowly, began to think about the family, their history and origins, talking and trying to put the pieces together. I think that was the journey we went on, and Isha and Sheikh were willing to come along, to share their memories— sometimes very painful, sometimes happy—and to make links.

Isha: All this helped—to share everything together, about our family, our past, and how we are now. I told Marta about my father and sister, how I was when I was young. We talked about Mohamed not eating my food, going to the neighbours' to eat dinner. They were very poor, so I used to cook and take the food there without him knowing! Talking about it, I remembered I had been like that, that I hadn't liked my mum's food, and that I also went to my neighbours' house to eat.

Marta: Yes, this was one of the issues we talked about in our sessions— Mohamed not eating Isha's food—and we tried to figure out what it was like for her, when she was young. Little by little, memories started to come back about how Isha had been a bit like Mohamed. We thought a lot about the history of the family and began to make connections with what was happening with Mohamed now.

We also talked about very ordinary feelings Mohamed had about his position in the family, being the first-born child in a growing family, how much he wanted to be a good boy, but how hard he had found the arrival of new babies. It can be difficult for parents to think about the impact of that, but Isha and Sheikh began talking to him in a more open way about what was going on for him in the family. We began to get a sense, too, of Mohamed feeling he somehow had to be the "grandfather" in the family, that he was carrying a lot on his shoulders. All the talking his parents did with him made him realize he didn't have to be so big, that it was okay to be a boy.

Isha: He began to talk more, to be less embarrassed to say what he was thinking. When I was pregnant, he started asking lots of questions about when he was a baby. When I gave birth to my daughter, or when I changed her nappies, he asked: "Did you do that for me, too? Did you give me milk? Did you breastfeed me? Did you take me to the GP when I was sick?" Sitting next to me, asking a lot of questions, all day, all the time! He wanted me to have another baby, and for it to be a boy this time, so he could see if I was different with boys.

Marta: Yes, he had lots of questions about when he was little. Isha and Sheikh began to share their memories with him, and I think that was very important for him, to see that of course mummy and daddy remembered baby Mohamed very well, that there was still a space for baby Mohamed in their minds.

Isha: Things got easier, and we began to understand more about what was good for him, what was bad, what made him angry and what we could do. But change did not come quickly; it did not come straightaway. He began to slow down. He stopped shaking. He still kicked doors and walls but it lessened, week by week, month by month.

Sheikh: He became calmer, less angry, and by Year 6 things were better, and school could see that, too. He got a lot from the therapy, a lot of experience.

Marta: Mohamed started to trust that adults could link up and work together, his parents and teachers. There was a noticeable shift in Year 6. He began to have friends and to really enjoy his friendships. The unpredictable behaviour was not there any more, so he had space to learn and get ready for SATS. He was worried about those, as they approached, but he was more confident that he had something inside him that could help him not get too worried or angry, and the school could see that improvement. We also did lots of work around transition to secondary school, thinking with Mohamed and his parents about how it might feel to leave this place he had been in for so many years, that felt so familiar, as well as about the positives of secondary school. We helped him to make bridges in his mind to a new school that might also become a good, familiar place.

Another important part of our work was about becoming more familiar with our different cultures. We talked a lot about cultural differences, how different it is in London. It was a major realization for Isha and Sheikh to see how constrained the lives of their children would be here, compared to how their childhoods had been. It's hard to adjust to that level. Also, to adjust to a different kind of parenting when you live in a very small home without different generations of family, without a large community. We thought about the loss of their country and also about them having more of a sense of belonging in this country.

Isha: Seeing a therapist from a different country, language, was not a barrier, but with our cultures, it's different. But that was helpful to think about, too. Our children are living in both cultures, so they need them to be in parallel. There is more freedom and safety where we grew up, children can play outside from 2 years old, it's very natural to do that, to play with neighbours. Here, everyone stays in their home, and even a big 13-year-old boy needs to be taken to places. Also, problems with children get managed differently.

Sheikh: There, you are in a community all the time, surrounded by family and neighbours who help. If there is an issue, an uncle, aunty, or grandparent will take children to stay with them in a different village for a while. They might go to a farm where they can play, eat fruit, have a different experience, and feel some relief from their problems; they have a chance to change their habits and behaviour.

Isha: Back when he was throwing and kicking, I didn't think he could get better, that things would improve. You wouldn't believe how much he has changed. But that change came step by step, slowly, slowly. Since he went to secondary school, there have been no complaints, and, a few years in, he is doing well; he has just been picked to go on a special trip because he is one of the best students.

Sheikh: It is easier at home, too. He helps around the house. He is good with his siblings, too, and has a sense of his place in the family. He did not need a referral to a new service when he left primary school and has not needed further help. Our younger son is now seen by the TOPS service, and we know we can ask Marta for advice about getting help for Mohamed if he ever needs it again.

Isha: I now tell friends . . .

Sheikh: And she has lots of friends!

Isha: . . . I say: "If you are experiencing something like this, just tell the school, tell the GP." I tell them we had that experience, and things did change. But if you don't get help, your child will not reach his goals. As soon as our other son started having difficulties, I told the school straightaway.

Marta: Isha has supported other parents in her community to use our service, including a friend whose family is now seen at CAMHS. So perhaps something else that changed is this family's sense of agency—it has grown massively. They have been writing to their MP about housing, and it now looks as if they will get a new home.

Isha: Mohamed still talks about his therapists, asks if they are still here, talks about what they did together and the toys that were in the room. He likes talking, a lot. And he loves my food. He says: "Mum, *you* are the chef."

Acknowledgement

Isha and Sheikh, Mohamed's parents, have given permission for this interview to be published.

CHAPTER SEVEN

"I just thought I'm doing something wrong if she needs therapy": A grandmother's experience

Mel Serlin

For many children, the relationship with grandparents is a special one, with grandparents playing an important role in their lives as "sources of wisdom, stability and family identity, as well as babysitters, mediators, friends and listeners" (Downie, Hay, Horner, Wichmann, & Hislop, 2010, p. 8). For some children, this relationship becomes crucial when parents are unable to look after them safely and grandparents agree to care for them instead. In the case of children who have suffered neglect and/or abuse while in the care of their parents, this arrangement, known as kinship care, enables them to remain living within their families, but at a safer distance from the issues afflicting their parents' lives. These issues, such as mental illness, addiction, domestic violence, and imprisonment, are usually a symptom of more longstanding difficulties—a complex interplay of individual, familial, social, and environmental factors that have impacted on the psychological health of the parents. These often have their roots in traumatic events and painful experiences of loss within the family over several generations. It is not uncommon, for example, to find that kinship carers were once looked after by grandparents themselves.

Although many of the early experiences of children living in kinship care will be the same as that of those who are adopted or placed with non-relative foster carers, the particular situation of children being separated from their parents but continuing to live within their family system can bring specific benefits and challenges for all members of the family.

DOI: 10.4324/9781003185925-10

In some cases, support is needed to help children and families heal from difficult experiences in the past, understand changing roles and relationships in the present, and strengthen their capacity for new, different possibilities in the future. However, many studies have highlighted that gaining access to clinical services is not always easy for kinship families, especially those who are not in receipt of local authority support (Wade, Sinclair, Stuttard, & Simmonds, 2014). This may be due to limitations on public services, as well as reticence on the part of carers, who are reluctant to seek help from professional agencies due to feelings of worry, guilt, or shame, and fear that they will be judged or blamed.

In this chapter, the complexities of grandparental kinship care are explored, giving an example via the perspective of one grandmother who sought therapeutic help for her granddaughter through her primary school. In this case, the school were able, through their partnership with a local charity, to provide child psychotherapy sessions on-site for those children and families who needed this type of support. The details of this family's circumstances and the therapeutic intervention provided were gathered through individual interviews with the grandmother, the school's Special Educational Needs Coordinator (SENCo), and the child's therapist, as part of a doctoral research study investigating the experiences of children in kinship care. Their contributions and perspectives help to highlight the value of psychoanalytic psychotherapy for children living in kinship care and the benefits of this being available within schools, where carers may feel more willing and able to access external support.

Kinship care

> Where a child cannot remain living with his or her parents, the local authority should identify and prioritise suitable family and friends placements, if appropriate.
>
> [DfE, 2014, p. 11]

In the UK, around 180,000 children who are unable to live with their birth parents are cared for instead by members of their extended family (Wijedasa, 2017). This arrangement is sometimes the outcome of social care involvement; it may be a legally binding agreement made by a court, such as a Special Guardianship Order, or, as in the majority of cases, it is a private arrangement reached informally within families to prevent involvement by children's services.

Where children have been legally removed from the care of their parents for their own protection, local authorities are duty-bound by the Children Act 1989 to explore other potential caregivers from within their family as a first priority (DfE, 2014). This requirement reflects the understanding that, in most cases, enabling children to stay within their family of origin and maintain ties to their cultural heritage and identity will be most beneficial for their psychological wellbeing and development.

Alongside the wish to support children to have the best outcomes possible, the high financial cost of looking after children in foster or residential placements provides a further incentive (inevitably heightened during times of austerity) for local authorities to identify family members who can take on the long-term care of children in need of permanent homes. Since their introduction in 2005, statistical data show a steady rise in the use of Special Guardianship Orders, under which a relative can be granted parental responsibility for a child until the age of 18—with increasing numbers of children leaving the care system under this legal order (Wilkinson & Bowyer, 2017, p. 53). Although in many respects this is a positive development, reports investigating the use of Special Guardianship Orders have highlighted the need for caution, given the "relatively high rates of [placement] breakdown . . . within two years of the order being made" (Wilkinson & Bowyer, 2017, p. 75). The importance of careful assessment, preparation, and support for kinship carers is emphasized, particularly in circumstances where relatives did not have a close prior relationship with the child (Wade et al., 2014, p. 52).

While there are many benefits to children being looked after by family members, kinship care can also present significant challenges to both children and carers, with researchers (Nandy & Selwyn, 2013) and family rights groups (Kinship Care Alliance, 2019) raising concern that many kinship families live in poverty and deprivation.

Grandparents

> "You do things differently than you did the first time, and you know what to look for as well. You know, problems you can see coming before . . . things are just different, I don't know . . . it's more fun as well, in a way."
>
> [Eileen, Grandmother]

In the UK, the majority of kinship carers are grandparents (Wijedasa, 2017). A survey conducted by the charity Grandparents Plus (2017) found that many looked after their grandchildren while coping with a range of challenges. These included being a single carer, raising two or more children, having a disability or long-term health condition, and also caring for disabled/elderly relatives. For many, the strain of managing these demands was exacerbated by insufficient household income, with carers often having reduced their work hours or left employment in order to care for their grandchildren (Grandparents Plus, 2017, p. 5).

For grandparents, motivated by the desire to support their child and prevent grandchildren from growing up in local authority care, coping with the demands of looking after children at an older age is often not easy. Alongside their wish to help, carers may feel angry with their child for the harm caused to their grandchildren, and frustration at parents' inability to change the behaviours, which resulted in the need for them to provide alternative care.

Within the wider family, there may be different views on why the parents' difficulties occurred, who is to blame, and how best to respond. Where varied perspectives are articulated by different family members, this may give a voice to the grandparent's own feelings of conflict and underlying anxieties about the factors that had contributed to their child's difficulties. This might include the ways in which their own experiences of being parented had shaped the parental care that they provided. There may also be feelings of regret and ideas of what they would do differently now, with the benefit of hindsight and experience.

These different perspectives can sometimes become a source of tension within families and pose a challenge to grandparents who are trying to manage the dual task of being a parent to their child (and support their child's position as a parent), while also protecting the welfare of their grandchildren. These roles may at times feel in conflict with each other. This tension often emerges most visibly around the responsibility on carers to manage contact arrangements between grandchildren and their parents. For most grandparents, these quite exceptional challenges are mitigated by the feelings of enjoyment and reward that come with looking after grandchildren and supporting their development.

Parents

"We had to put the phone on loudspeaker, because she was asking her to meet her and 'don't tell your nan' and things like that."

[Eileen, Grandmother]

For parents concerned about their children being taken into local authority care, there may be enormous relief and feelings of gratitude when grandparents agree to look after them. Keeping their children within the family, particularly as an informal caregiving arrangement, may give parents hope that they will, in time, be able to have their children returned to them, and grandparents, too, may have this in mind as a longer-term goal. Where children's services are involved, there is some evidence (Holtan, Ronning, Handegard, & Sourander, 2005) that, compared to non-relative foster care, parents are less likely to contest a kinship placement. This can have a positive impact on children's capacity to settle into their new home and make progress, without the worry that building a relationship with their new caregiver could be experienced as being disloyal to their parents.

Parents may also struggle with feelings of guilt, in relation both to their children and to their parents for looking after them. However, this can often be mixed with feelings of anger and blame, if their parents are felt to have played a part in the development of their own difficulties. This may be due to issues in the relationship with, or between, their parents that affected them as children, such as marital conflict, domestic violence, and alcoholism. In a study by Barnard (2003), in which interviews were conducted with parents whose drug use affected the care of their children, it was found that a "high proportion of parents reported dysfunctional family backgrounds" and many "spoke of difficult childhoods" with "family homes marked by conflict and violence" (Barnard, 2003, p. 295).

In this situation, parents may feel resentful, excluded, and at times even jealous of seeing a loving caregiving relationship developing between their children and parents—whose circumstances may now be very different from when they were children. Such feelings, along with worries about being replaced as parental figures in the minds of their children, could lead to attempts to undermine the grandparents' authority and enjoyment, by creating conflict in the relationship between kinship carers and their children.

Children

> All the young people felt that they were encouraged by their kinship carers to go to school more regularly and to do well at school . . . kinship carers appeared to be instilling in young people a feeling of self-belief and supporting them in striving towards their aspirations and ambitions. Almost all the young people were able to identify career ambitions, many of which were professional in nature.
>
> [Burgess, Rossvoll, Wallace, & Daniel, 2010, p. 303]

For many children, kinship care provides a loving, safe, and long-term home environment. For children whose needs were neglected while in the care of their parents, or who lived in homes where adult behaviour could be chaotic and unpredictable, the ordinary routine of life within a kinship home can provide a welcome experience of stability. In studies investigating children's experiences of kinship care, this often includes the value placed by carers on regular school attendance and achievement, which in some children's experience may have previously been lacking (Aldgate & McIntosh, 2006; Burgess et al., 2010).

Compared to children placed with non-relative foster carers, living with grandparents often increases the opportunity for children to have ongoing contact with their wider family network and spend time with members of their extended family in an ordinary way (Pitcher, 2002). This can help to support children's feeling of belonging and sense of identity.

However, adjusting to life within a kinship home can also present new challenges. For some children, moving to a kinship home means relocating to a new area and school, leaving children missing the familiarity of their local area and friends. For those whose kinship carers live within the same community, the lack of distance from their parents' home, the likelihood of chance encounters with them, and local knowledge of their family circumstances may be difficult for children to manage and make it difficult for them to settle in their new home. They may also be confronted by seeing parents forming new relationships and creating new families.

Within the home, children may struggle to adapt to new boundaries and expectations. Where carers are older or in poor health, children can feel worried about who will look after them in the future. Many children share their kinship home with their siblings, which may be a source of support, but this is not always the case. In larger sibling groups, children of varied ages and needs may be separated between different kinship, foster, and adoptive homes. In interviews with children in kinship care in Scotland, Aldgate and McIntosh (2006) found that out of 24 children who had siblings, only 3 lived with all of them, although most were in contact with siblings living elsewhere (p. 71).

As for all children who have been removed from parental care for their protection, children in kinship care may be struggling to understand their past experiences with and separation from their parents (and siblings). A common misconception is that where children have remained within family networks, this means that they will know all about their family history and why parents were unable to care for them. This is often not the case. In a study involving 80 carers and children living in informal kinship care, Farmer, Selwyn, and Meakings (2013) found that, "one in five children had unanswered questions about why they had not been able to stay with their parents or were troubled by events that they did not understand" (p. 28). Similarly, Aldgate and McIntosh (2006) found that out of 30 children, "almost a third had no sense of personal history about the significant transition they had experienced, often at an early age" (p. 40). These findings suggest that while it might be easy to presume that children in kinship care have been told about their individual and family histories, by virtue of the very complex nature of family difficulties this can make it hard for carers to discuss these details openly, due to worry about the powerful feelings that might be evoked in both carer and child if they did.

There may also be a belief within the family that, in the absence of good-enough parental care, the ongoing presence and caregiving provided by extended family members throughout a child's early life will have mitigated the impact of their separation from their parents. Although this may be true to some extent, this way of thinking could also enable the significance of the loss of the child's parents to be unwittingly minimized or denied, leaving children unable to articulate their feelings of loss and abandonment by their parents. Where children have been removed from parental care and placed with relatives, social workers may also not have provided children with details of their early life story to the extent that they would for those placed in non-relative foster or adoptive homes, particularly at times when local authority resources are overstretched.

Access to Children's Mental Health Services

> There were two commonly recurring worries . . . wild, destructive behaviour, which the grandparents could neither understand nor manage; and a child who is somehow "too good" or "adult in their understanding". In these cases . . . grandparents found themselves wondering whether this young person (most often a girl) was a "time bomb waiting to go off". This was often connected with the question, "What if she turns out like her mother?"
>
> [Pitcher, 2002, p. 10]

Coping with all of these experiences, and the feelings they provoke, can be confusing and distressing for children. This can result in behaviours that are challenging for carers to manage and understand, putting kinship relationships under strain. Without appropriate support, difficulties can intensify, along with carers' worries about where this behaviour will lead. Such concerns may increase as children approach adolescence.

However, carers may often feel reluctant to approach professionals for support. There may be concerns about sharing private family difficulties with statutory agencies and a wish to keep these out of sight. Such feelings may be heightened where informal kinship arrangements have been made to prevent involvement from children's services.

In the case of families who have had previous involvement with social care, sometimes across more than one generation, there may already have been contact with a large number of professionals. Where this has resulted in children being removed from their parents' care, there can often be residual feelings of mistrust and a sense of little differentiation between different agencies and roles, preventing families from turning back to professionals for support. Carers may also feel worried about how their need for help will be perceived and where this could lead, especially where children have been formally placed in their care. In interviews with over 30 sets of grandparental carers, Pitcher (2002) found that worries of this kind could be a significant barrier to accessing support.

> For many, there was a high level of anxiety that if they appeared in any way "demanding" of help, social services would judge that they could not manage and would place the child elsewhere. This led to reluctance to ask for too much practical help at a time when it was desperately needed. [Pitcher, 2002, p. 8]

The idea of needing support from mental health services may well provoke additional worries. For families where parental mental illness has been a contributing factor in the need to remove children from their parents, it may be very painful to consider the idea of mental health provision being needed for young children when they have been living in alternative care. This may stir up all sorts of very uncomfortable questions and concerns: Does it mean that mental health difficulties are hereditary and inevitable? If a child is showing signs of emotional disturbance, does this mean that someone is to blame or suggest that the caregiving they are receiving is lacking in some way? What impact would receiving mental health support have on the child's sense of identity and self-esteem? Would children worry that there is something wrong with them and feel different from their peers? If help were permitted, what is it that mental health professionals would see? Would services understand the family's situation and provide the right sort of support to meet their needs?

For many families, a lot of work may be needed to help overcome such concerns. The time and effort this takes is beyond the scope of many services that do not have the resources to invest in helping families to engage. When families do attend CAMHS clinics, often the types of short-term medical treatment models available, driven by cost-efficiency objectives, are gravely insufficient to contend with the level of complexity and distress surrounding children with a history of maltreatment.

> Too often Child and Adolescent Mental Health Services (CAMHS) are organized around diagnosis-led clinics, leading to fragmentation of service provision and dissatisfaction amongst users. . . . Caregivers, whether looking after children in fostering, kinship care or adoptive placements sense that the difficulties the children experience are not adequately recognized and poorly described by the usual diagnoses, such as ADHD or conduct disorder. The treatment may be similarly narrowly focused. The experience of caregivers is therefore one of fragmentation and of being poorly understood. [DeJong, 2010, p. 596]

Without access to the type of help and understanding that they need, this can have a negative impact on children's capacity to learn and on their relationships in school. Aldgate and McIntosh (2006) found that contact with parents was a key factor affecting children's ability to function well in school. For some, this resulted in a decreased capacity to concentrate in class, while others struggled to regulate their behaviour after seeing parents. An inflammation of physical conditions, such as eczema, was also recognized as a visible sign of increased emotional strain (p. 67).

In families where there is reluctance to seek professional support or attend mental health clinics, the presentation of these difficulties in school can help to facilitate opportunities for intervention. Where children have remained within their local area, schools may have known the family for more than one generation. This longstanding relationship with teaching staff can help carers to feel safer to trust their advice, and they may subsequently be more willing to engage with a school-based clinical service than with a referral to an external agency.

Given their experiences of relational trauma in their early years, separation from parents, and the complex nature of their current family circumstances, it is important that clinical work with children and their kinship carers takes into consideration how these different experiences affect children's ability to understand their feelings and relate to others. Through the use of the therapy relationship, psychoanalytic psychotherapy enables children to discover more about themselves and the way they experience others. Through their actions, drawing, play, and talking, children's feelings are communicated to and absorbed by the therapist, so they can be looked at, carefully and at the child's own pace, by child and therapist together. The therapist's task is to observe the varied ways that children respond to them and their own emotional states in response to what children say and do, as a way of gathering together important information needed to develop an understanding of the less rational aspects of a child's anxieties and emotional conflicts. Through this process, children have the opportunity for confusing and painful feelings to become better understood, thereby lessening the need for troubled feelings to be expressed through troubling behaviour. An example of this is shown in the story of 8-year-old Kayla, who received child psychotherapy sessions in her primary school.

Family story

Kayla, Dylan, and Eileen

Kayla came to live with her maternal grandmother, Eileen, when she was 3 years old. Her brother Dylan, who was four years older, initially lived with them too. Social care had been involved with the family when Dylan was an infant, due to concerns about alcohol use and domestic violence between his parents. Eileen, a single grandparent, lived nearby. Despite suffering from a range of long-standing health complaints, she tried to help out where she could by offering to babysit Dylan in her home.

When Dylan was 2, his parents' relationship ended. His father left the family home and did not have any further involvement with his son. Within the home, things appeared to settle down for a while. When Dylan was 3, his mother entered a new relationship, and Kayla was born the following year. During Kayla's infancy, Eileen began to have concerns again. She suspected that her daughter had been introduced to drugs and worried about the influence of this new relationship on her daughter's capacity to provide care for her children:

> Eileen: She was taking Kayla out, and she'd come back and she smelt really not nice, she wasn't bathing her and, you know, that sort of stuff.... So there was lots and lots of stuff with the social worker ... I agreed to have Kayla if she wanted to go out for a couple of hours ... and she'd go out and not come back for days, and things like that, so, yeah, that how all started...

Both children were eventually placed full-time in Eileen's care. Over the next few years, both children attended school regularly and had fortnightly contact with their mother. Kayla's father disengaged from the family. Kayla looked up to her older brother, who had always been protective over her. However, as he approached adolescence, Dylan's behaviour began to change. He became more withdrawn, lacked patience with his sister, and started behaving in an aggressive way towards her in the home. This distressed Kayla who was keen to please him, and Eileen worried about Dylan becoming isolated and needing more male figures in his life. After much deliberation, it was agreed that Dylan would go to stay with his aunt and uncle, who had two teenage sons. Upon completion of his primary education, Dylan transitioned to the secondary school that his cousins attended, resulting in Kayla no longer seeing her brother every day.

Relationship between home, school, and therapy service: Angie

Angie, the Special Educational Needs Coordinator (SENCo) at Kayla's primary school, was a longstanding senior member of staff. She already knew Kayla's brother and had a good understanding of her early years when Kayla joined in the Reception class.

> Angie: We already knew about the family when Kayla started school, because Grandma Eileen was very open. She wanted the school to know all the background of the children and was actually very keen to always stand and talk about things. So it was very common, first thing in the morning, when the children would line up to go into school, that Eileen and I would have quite a long discussion about what had been going on generally. So, we were aware of the background of the family.

This relationship was a crucial source of support for Eileen, who initially felt quite isolated in her role as a grandparental carer, until, later, she was introduced to a support group for kinship carers.

> Eileen: The first year you get a social worker coming, I think maybe three times in the year, after that you don't see a soul, so if there's any problems you've not really got anybody to talk to, so yeah, I found that quite hard.

As well as being an important support for Eileen, her openness with Angie enabled the school to ensure that timely and appropriate support was put in place for Kayla.

> Angie: Eileen was quite concerned about her . . . she said that she had advice from when she was born that because of the drugs that mum had been taking, that might have affected her. So we were always aware

that because of that there could be issues over her concentration. We didn't know about her development, you know, whether that would be an issue. She was quite slow to pick up her reading and writing, so she was flagged up for that and had quite a number of academic skills support systems in place all through Key Stage One, to ensure that she was keeping up with her peers.

In her first few years of primary school, Kayla was found to be a quiet girl who did what was asked of her and never behaved in a way that would require her to come to anyone's attention. Angie recognized that within the busy school environment and alongside children whose emotional needs were much more prominent, it would have been easy for Kayla to slip out of people's minds. Consequently, she made sure to keep an eye on Kayla's progress.

> Angie: At termly meetings, if Kayla's name wasn't mentioned, I would bring up with her class teacher, "Everything okay? Has she said anything?"

During her fourth year in the school, when Kayla was 7, they noticed that her behaviour was starting to change. Although she continued to be respectful in her interactions with teachers, she began getting into disputes with her peers, particularly in the playground, and she seemed to be finding it hard to share and take turns. Angie talked with Eileen to see if there was anything different going on at home, which might help to explain this change.

> Angie: We spoke to Eileen about it, and yes, there was things going on, like mum wanted to see her children but then wouldn't turn up. It was agreed that she would come at a certain time after school, or on a Sunday, and then just wouldn't turn up, and that caused the children quite a lot of upset. So it was those sorts of things that were going on.

Eileen confirmed she had also started to notice a change in Kayla's behaviour at home, particularly since her brother had gone to stay with their aunt and uncle. She often complained that things "were not fair", that her Nan was too strict, and her friends' parents let them do things that she didn't let her do. "She would scream and shout and bang doors and refuse to come out of her room." Eileen was concerned at the emergence of "these teenage behaviours" occurring at such an early age.

With Eileen's consent, Angie brought these concerns to the attention of Zoe, who led the Child Psychotherapy Service that operated within the school. Due to the complexity of Kayla's family circumstances and the serious nature of her early years' experiences, Zoe agreed that Angie should make a referral for Kayla, to see if they could help her with the feelings that were causing her to become so angry and distressed. Eileen was pleased when Angie advised her that the service would be able to offer her an assessment.

> *Angie:* Eileen could see the benefits of it, you know, she didn't have to take her anywhere else, it was there, on site. She was concerned about her getting very emotional, upset, angry, and getting into conflict with her peers, so she wanted her to have support for that.

Child Psychotherapy Service: Zoe and Alicia

Eileen was initially invited to meet with Zoe, the lead child psychotherapist in the school. Through their discussions, a fuller picture of the likely reasons for Kayla's upset and struggle with feelings of unfairness began to emerge. Eileen shared that they had recently learned that her daughter was now in a new relationship and was pregnant, expecting a girl. This explained why she had not attended contact sessions lately, as she had not yet wanted this news to be known. Eileen and Zoe thought together about how hearing this information might have felt for Kayla, and the sorts of worries it could bring. Would her mother lose interest in her, now that she was expecting a new little girl? Would her mother and new partner be allowed to keep this child, and if so, where would Kayla fit into this new family? Would the baby be safe in her mother's care, and if not, who would look after her little sister?

Eileen supported the idea of Kayla having an assessment with one of the therapists to get a better understanding of the worries that were troubling her. It was agreed they would meet again the following week, to discuss the idea with Kayla and introduce her to a therapist called Alicia.

When they met, Alicia noticed that Kayla was initially pleased to be offered some individual sessions in school.

> *Alicia:* It was explained that she'd have it, and I remember that she went, "Just me?" She seemed quite excited at the thought that it would be just for her.

Kayla was advised that she would meet with Alicia once a week, for three weeks, once she returned from the coming school holiday. When they met for the first session, Kayla came prepared with a list she had written over the holidays, of the things she wanted Alicia to know about her—such as what she liked to do and the things that she was good at.

Alicia: She had to wait to come to me, and she'd written this list . . . she said she didn't want to forget, she wanted to remember things that she wanted me to know, which was really poignant.

Alicia found Kayla to be a calm, polite, and appealing child, who was keen to make use of the drawing materials available to her in the therapy room to show Alicia all her positive qualities and skills.

Alicia: She'd like to show me things she could do. In the very first session she told me she liked drawing and could do mirror writing. She could do beautiful mirror writing and seemed to be very good at art. She was very careful and could make things very neat. But she didn't really talk about herself, and my feeling was, at another time she might well do.

From her experience of Kayla in the assessment sessions, Alicia considered how important it was to Kayla that adults experienced her as a friendly and likeable child. Although she did not display any of the challenging behaviours that had led to the referral, Alicia wondered whether her very careful play was a way of trying to keep in check some unusually powerful feelings. She felt that Kayla would need more regular sessions before she would be ready to allow Alicia to see any of the more upsetting feelings that she was holding about herself and others. At the end of the assessment, Alicia recommended that Kayla be offered weekly sessions, to give her a space within which to explore the underlying feelings that troubled her. Kayla seemed really pleased to be offered this regular time with Alicia, and Eileen supported the idea too, keen for Kayla to receive any help available to her. Eileen was also offered some individual meetings of her own with Zoe, to support her in her role as Kayla's primary carer.

Having therapy in school: Eileen

Once the weekly sessions started, other feelings about her granddaughter needing therapeutic help emerged. For Eileen, this was triggered by the fact that Alicia would collect Kayla from her classroom, to take her to the room where her therapy sessions were held.

Researcher: What was it like for you having a child in therapy?
Eileen: To be quite honest, I found it embarrassing at first. Because she'd go to the classroom and take her out of the classroom, and everybody knows who it is and why she's . . .
Researcher: Why she's going?

Eileen: Mmm [nods].

Researcher: So you felt embarrassed on Kayla's behalf?

Eileen: Yeah, and for myself as well. I just thought I'm doing something wrong if she needs therapy.

Researcher: As if it reflected badly on you? That other people might think you're not being a good-enough parent?

Eileen: Well, I didn't care what anybody else thought. I felt like it.

Researcher: "I'm not doing well enough if she needs a therapist too?"

Eileen: Yeah.

Researcher: So for you, one thing was that it felt embarrassing. Were there any other feelings?

Eileen: No, just upset that I couldn't . . .

Researcher: Do it all?

Eileen: Yeah. But I don't feel like that any more.

Eileen was concerned that Kayla felt the same and wished that a member of school staff, such as the receptionist, could have collected her from her classroom instead.

Researcher: How do you think it was for Kayla, having therapy?

Eileen: She felt embarrassed. It's the same reason, the fact that the actual woman comes to the class.

Researcher: Because the other children in the school all know that's the therapist?

Eileen: Yeah, because there's quite a few kids in the school see somebody, so . . .

Researcher: So then it shows that she's having therapy?

Eileen: Mmm, I think that was the embarrassing part.

This arrangement seemed to stir similar worries in both Eileen and Kayla. Did it suggest they were lacking in some way? Was there something wrong with them? Had they not done well enough?

Alicia: She [Eileen] wasn't sure about the work, she said that she [Kayla] was a bit concerned that children that went for therapy were often quite sort of disturbed and . . . perhaps children who were seen to have quite a lot of behaviour problems. I tried to say there were all kinds of reasons why . . .

As a result of these concerns about collecting her from class, Alicia explored with Zoe whether a different arrangement might be made to spare Kayla these feelings. However, after careful thinking, it was agreed that it was important that the same arrangement applied for Kayla as for all other children receiving therapy in the school. This was not just for practical reasons (as it would be hard for there to always be a member of school staff available to collect her), but also because an important piece of information about Kayla's feelings had now been brought to light. Rather than helping her to avoid this difficult feeling (which would not help her in the longer term), it needed to be explored within her therapy to understand better why it troubled her to the extent that it did—as not all children felt this way.

Through her experience of Kayla in the sessions, Alicia came to understand how, for Kayla, standing out from others or feeling different from her peers was really difficult. This was something she had always worked hard to avoid—for example, by keeping her head down in school and never behaving in a way that would attract attention. This seemed to be linked at a deeper level with more upsetting feelings about not living with her mother like other children did and appeared to be driving some of the rivalrous behaviour with friends in school, who, Kayla felt, had more than she. As a consequence of recent changes in her family life, these difficult feelings had gained in strength and were now too powerful for Kayla to manage quietly inside herself in the way she'd always done before. Now her upset and anger were bursting out at home and in school, and this was creating an additional source of worry for her, as she didn't want to be thought of as a child who was badly behaved.

Eileen's wish to protect her granddaughter from feeling subjected to standing out from others and exposed to feelings of embarrassment also appeared to be connected to the relationship with Kayla's mother, with whom there had been some difficult past experiences during their family contact time. On occasion, it had appeared to Eileen that her daughter may have been under the influence of drugs when she met up with them in their local community.

Eileen:	Once in a while she's loud, she's really, really loud. She'll talk on the bus about anything, and everybody's listening and everybody's looking and we all sort of wanna just die, really it's horrible.
Researcher:	It's embarrassing.
Eileen:	And she can't see it. . . . Things like that, it is embarrassing, it really is.

Eileen's view was that her daughter's difficulties had begun when she was a teenager. That she was keen to be liked, and this made her susceptible to being used by others, particularly male figures who might have negative intentions and take advantage of her willingness to please. Eileen worried that, much like her mother, Kayla could also be vulnerable to unhelpful influences, which could potentially lead her astray.

> *Eileen:* She's really, really easily led by naughty, really naughty kids. When they went on an activity camp, this one girl, whatever she wanted Kayla to do, she would do it, and that is really worrying, because that's how you end up getting in big problems, stealing and drugs and stuff. And hopefully she wouldn't but . . . I don't know.

Eileen was keen for Kayla to receive therapeutic help while she was young, in the hope that in adolescence she would be more emotionally equipped and not have to follow in her mother's footsteps.

Child psychotherapy treatment: Alicia

Like many children referred for psychotherapy, Alicia found Kayla to be a child who wasn't yet able to talk directly about her family experiences and relationships, as much of what she had lived through as a young child had been confusing and difficult for her to comprehend. However, in the sessions, through her drawings, play, and ways of relating to her therapist, Alicia noticed that certain themes were expressed frequently and that there was a pattern to the way in which Kayla related to her. By exploring these, Alicia was able to understand more about the ways Kayla had made sense of her experiences and help her with some of the difficult feelings this had left her with.

> *Alicia:* Winning—to be the winner, it came up all the time, right at the beginning and all the way through. She liked to play games, she'd make up rules very often and would enjoy singing, "I'm the champion" and making me be the loser. But then, if she missed something, it would very quickly become: "Why am I a loser? Why did that happen?" I thought about what the meaning was for her of losing—for a child who has lost out in some very significant ways. I also think the feeling of needing to be good enough was really important for this child. She had a need to show me she could do things, and she was good at this and good at that, and although—I mean, any child can enjoy showing you—it seemed to be more of an urgency; a really strong feeling attached to the idea that she had to be good at things.

Alicia learned, through feedback meetings with Eileen, that these same feelings had been affecting Kayla's progress in school, as her desire to do well could sometimes inhibit her from getting on with her work, out of worry that it wouldn't be good enough.

> Alicia: At the first review, Eileen mentioned that Kayla had handed in a project—she was pleased, because that had been a concern for her, that Kayla wouldn't sit and do her homework, she'd leave it too late, and then it was hard to get it finished. I thought this may have been largely the result of anxiety about not managing to do it well enough.

It appeared to Alicia that the loss of her mother as her primary caregiver and the absence of her father had left Kayla with all sorts of worries about why they hadn't looked after her properly or fought to be able to keep her. Was there something about her that had caused her parents to turn away? Had she been a difficult baby to manage? Was she not an appealing enough child to keep their interest?

In her sessions, feelings of being forgotten and left out in the cold were present in Kayla's play, enabling some of these themes to be explored with her therapist in a safe and manageable way.

> Alicia: She played a lot with this teddy. The teddy started being hidden in the fridge and got forgotten one time and then it was freezing—it became something that died. That was quite remarkable to me, that this teddy froze to death and, right near the end, was a dead body, which was quite shocking. So, this teddy, that was kind of loved and in the end was abandoned, is interesting really about, you know, her.

It was possible to trace the origin of these feelings back to a very early time in her life when Kayla had experienced neglect. Now, as she was growing older, gaining greater awareness about the world and faced with new challenges (such as her mother's new pregnancy and her brother moving out of the kinship home), these unresolved anxieties about the impact she has on the people she loves seemed to be surfacing again. In their review meeting, Eileen confirmed that questions of this nature had recently been occupying Kayla's mind.

> Alicia: She said Kayla had asked her about her mother, and how she [Kayla] was as a baby. I think she was coming to that age where children begin to make links and work out and be curious. It made me think she's probably wondering why? Was I too difficult, why?

In discussion with Zoe, Alicia thought about how Kayla seemed to relate to her as though she were someone fragile who needed protecting, not an adult who would be able to manage being on the receiving end of her more aggressive feelings.

> Alicia: She presents as someone that doesn't want to make too many waves in case you wouldn't manage, and that might result in her being somewhere where she doesn't want to be.

Reflecting on her experience of Kayla in this way helped Alicia to see how Kayla might be left feeling very anxious about the relationship with her grandmother, who had brought her up from an early age and on whom she was dependent. Her concerns would likely have been heightened by the fact that Eileen was older and suffered from several health complaints, which were related to stress. Alicia could see how worrying it must have been for Kayla to allow herself to externalize her anger and upset, out of concern about further burdening her grandmother, and where this could potentially lead. What if she were too much for her grandmother to manage? Providing Kayla with a regular confidential space in which she could be supported to explore her angrier feelings without worry that this might upset her grandmother or jeopardize her friendships in school was an important aspect of the work.

Clinical outcomes: Eileen, Angie, Alicia

Kayla's sessions lasted for three terms, and Eileen met with Zoe and Alicia each term to review her progress. Sometimes in these meetings, Eileen raised concern about whether attending sessions for a year in school was a long time. But then, when they thought together about how longstanding and troubling the situation had been, it made sense that to untangle the emotional impact of such difficult early experiences and attend to the very deep emotional wounds left behind would require some time. By the end of the therapy, Eileen confirmed that there had been a marked improvement.

> Eileen: She started getting a lot calmer. She didn't bang doors any more and all that sort of thing—yeah it was a big difference.

The school also reported positive developments.

> Angie: It took a couple of terms before everybody thought, "Oh, Kayla's not been upset lately." And she was quite happy in the playground. She'd quite happily go off with the others and have much happier playtimes and then that impacted on how she was back in class.

Certainly, she settled down in school. Her ability to concentrate and to write improved. Her grades improved. Eileen was really, really pleased about that, that she did a lot of catching up between Years 4 and 5. It was a combination, we felt, of the therapy and the fact that she was maturing, as well, because she grew physically, and actually emotionally she grew. She became able to really concentrate to a much higher degree in class and actually challenge herself—whereas before she'd been very uncomfortable about being out of her comfort zone with any work that was presented to her. So I think that the psychotherapy intervention certainly was very beneficial. I think obviously we all had to recognize that it was a situation that wasn't going to resolve itself very easily . . . that it was a situation that she had to live with. That things were not going to change, but trying to build up some sort of resilience and understanding that it wasn't because her mother didn't love her, or she wasn't lovable, it wasn't her fault, and actually coping with having an absent mother.

The fact that this intervention had been available to Kayla and her grandmother in her primary school was also recognized as being crucial to her gaining access to the help she needed.

Angie: I think it was absolutely the right thing to do, to make the referral. I mean, there is no doubt that it had a very positive effect on the family. I think had the psychotherapy service not been there, it would have been tricky. Because we could have made a CAMHS referral, but I doubt Eileen would have taken her there, because she had so much on her plate that to try to get her to a clinic, I don't think that would have worked. So, actually, I'm not sure they would have had the same outcome without the service being available in the school. You know, I can very clearly say that, I think.

It was agreed by all that this intervention had been worth while. The sessions had helped to free up Kayla's state of mind, enabling her to be better able to learn in class and enjoy easier relationships with her peers. However, it was understood that due to the ongoing challenges in her family life, Kayla may require some further support in future, when navigating her way through adolescence.

Alicia: We noted at the end of the treatment that she was a vulnerable child, and as she grows and tries to make sense of all of this, she would certainly need an eye kept on her about which way that might take her.

Conclusion

"There were a number of families at our school where children were in foster care and had social services involvement. But there were 'these' families—as it happens, in each case, there was social services involvement—but they were not put on any sort of data to be tracked and monitored. Because local authorities have responsibility for children in care, to really monitor and supervise. And whenever an educational psychologist would come in to do a planning meeting, always on their agenda was, 'I need to identify the children who are in care and I need to track their progress and emotional needs.' But when we said, what about children living with grandparents, they said, 'Oh, right, well they're not on our list, are there any issues?' And invariably there were."

(Angie, SENCo)

This child's story highlights many of the difficulties that children, parents, and grandparents often face, as the challenges they encounter in the present are navigated under the shadow of traumatic family experiences in the past. Yet despite their level of need and vulnerability, children in kinship care are often overlooked by public sector services, whose limited resources are directed towards those children for whom they have a clear duty of care (e.g. due to a legal responsibility or mental health diagnosis). This was highlighted during the COVID-19 pandemic, when the worrying circumstances of children living in grandparental care made headlines (Turner, 2020), as a result of their dependency on caregivers who, by virtue of their age and often pre-existing health conditions, became an at-risk group who needed to self-isolate, thereby putting additional pressure on already disadvantaged households (Ashley, Johnston, & Hall, 2020).

Where families struggle to access appropriate support, either due to systemic failures to see and respond to the needs of this population or families' own fears about seeking professional help, the likelihood of children being able to make different choices and create new pathways for themselves in the future is reduced. Through Kayla's story, we can see how being able to access timely and appropriate support in primary school was an effective way of reaching a child and family who would otherwise have not made it to a CAMHS clinic to receive the help they needed.

Kayla was fortunate to have a child psychotherapy service based in her school, with clinicians trained in working with children who have suffered emotional trauma and have complex needs. The family was supported by an experienced Special Educational Needs Coordinator, who saw Kayla's disputes with her peers as a communication of distress and was receptive to listening to her grandmother's explanation and concerns. She kept a watchful eye over Kayla's development and was active in ensuring that appropriate academic and psychological support was put in place for her in school. Above all, Kayla had a grandmother who was able to put her trust in the SENCo and share details about their family situation and who was keen for her granddaughter to receive the help she needed. This linking up between home, school, and therapy was central to securing access to and the effectiveness of the therapeutic intervention.

Despite these benefits, delivering clinical work in schools can present many challenges, including the concerns about exposure raised by Kayla and her grandmother. Understandably, some children may prefer their difficulties to be attended to outside school, so as to keep this aspect of their lives separate and enable them to protect their sense of identity in school. However, providing therapy in schools can help to change the feelings of embarrassment, shame, and fear that exist around mental health, through the development of a culture in which different forms of learning are valued and integrated within the school. This includes learning about one's emotional world and ways of relating to others. It is only by normalizing the idea that having some help to make sense of troubling feelings is something we all need at times when life is hard, that the stigma around mental health can be dispelled.

CHAPTER EIGHT

Conversations across education and mental health in a mainstream primary school

Interview by Milly Jenkins

Tavistock Outreach in Primary Schools (now an extended service called TOPS with Families) is a child psychotherapy service that has been working in Camden primary schools for nearly 20 years. It currently works in eight schools across the borough. Each school has a lead therapist and two assistant therapists who provide an in-school assessment and therapy service one day a week. The schools pay an annual fee for this, and the project is supported by charitable grants.

The TOPS team work closely with staff in the schools, meeting regularly with a member of the senior leadership team—often the inclusion manager or deputy head—as well as liaising and consulting with teachers, teaching assistants, family support workers, learning mentors, and reception office staff. Most of the schools have long-standing, firmly established relationships with TOPS and have come to value having a flexible in-school service that can work in partnership with CAMHS and specialist assessment services and that can join multi-agency networks of professionals working with families. The wider TOPS team also includes an adult therapist who works with parents wanting support in their own right, and an advocacy worker, linked to Mind in Camden, who helps parents with a range of issues; both can work in the schools or alternative venues, if preferred by the parent.

Here, Marta Cioeta, who at the time of the interview was the TOPS project manager, talks with Georgina Harcourt-Brown, the deputy head of the school she is based in, and Tracey Duff, the school's family

DOI: 10.4324/9781003185925-11

support worker, about how they work together, the benefits of an in-school therapy service for children, families, and staff, and some of the challenges, too.

* * *

Georgina Harcourt-Brown (deputy head):   Marta and the assistant therapists are here one day a week, and that regularity, and the fact they're here from the start to the end of the day, is really important to us. As safeguarding lead, I'm sometimes dealing with quite high-level cases, often with families Marta and the team have done assessments with, so it's really helpful to have another professional, weekly and on-site, to talk to, someone available to have a conversation with. Personally, I feel the burden of responsibility worrying about a family. "Are they okay, what's going to happen, what do they need?" And when I make a referral to Marta, I know she is looking at all these things too, thinking: "What is happening with this child? How is that mother feeling? Is she coping. . . . What are we going to do?" So I get to share that burden.

Tracey Duff (family support worker):   I do lots of work in Early Years, sometimes with children, sometimes with parents, sometimes together—play sessions, parenting programmes, building relationships with them. I can get to a point with families on my caseload where I don't know where to go with them, and maybe lots of worrying, concerning things have come up in those sessions. So I might have a consultation with Marta to think about that. In talking about a child and a family, we might come to the conclusion that they need to see a clinician, so then it gets discussed in the Inclusion Team, and Georgina makes the referral.

Georgina: When we refer to TOPS, they start with an assessment to think about the issues at stake. Marta is very holistic in those assessments, so it's not just about the child, it's thinking about the family and everything around it, about the past, about other services involved, getting their understanding of the situation. It's a wide-ranging assessment. After that, if the child and family have ongoing treatment, it can be one-to-one therapeutic sessions for the child, often with parallel parent work sessions, or parent–child sessions, or group work, so there's flexibility in what they do. Marta and the assistants also have lots of conversations during the day with

staff about the children, and she offers individual consultations to some.

Marta Cioeta (lead therapist):   We meet every week to discuss families
the school is worried about. For a case to be referred to us,
it needs to have significant level of need and complexity.
Normally the children referred have already had a number
of interventions in the school; they will have had lots of support for learning or social skills, but things have not shifted.
Sometimes it might be a family where the school know there
is a particularly difficult home situation impacting on the
child's emotional development and learning. Sometimes it's
a family that has been involved with social services, and they
have recommended that the child be referred. But the over-
arching theme of cases referred to us is that they are families
that will not engage in clinical settings, so families that, even
if they're close to a Child and Adolescent Mental Health Service (CAMHS) clinic, will struggle to go and engage there or
haven't been able to in the past. Would you agree that's the
main criteria, Georgina?

Georgina: Yes, the cases we refer to TOPS are the tricky ones, where
there isn't a simple solution to be had. It might be families
where you are seeing difficulties with the child, but there
are also systemic issues, where parent or family work is
needed, and however many interventions you try in school,
they won't help, because there is a bigger issue. We might
refer children who are hurting themselves, having suicidal
thoughts or eating issues, a whole range of mental health
difficulties. But with the majority, they are children who are
struggling with emotional regulation. Their understanding
of their emotions is just not there. And when we meet with
the families, we can see that support around that is needed;
for the child to get help, but also for the parents to help
understand the child, to be able to put themselves in their
shoes. Sometimes they are parents who, for many reasons,
are not emotionally available or constant for their child.

The cases I refer to CAMHS, and the ones that go to TOPS,
can be quite similar. The decision might depend on waiting
times. But I tend to choose TOPS over CAMHS if I think
early intervention is needed, but the family will not turn up
at CAMHS and then it will get closed. CAMHS don't have
capacity to chase them with lots of phone calls if they don't
attend. Marta has a caseload of six families here, and, unlike

a CAMHS clinic getting dozens of referrals a week, she is able to call them and offer a time that suits, in a setting they already know. I think it's easier than getting a letter in the post asking you to go somewhere you don't know, at a time you maybe can't go. Being in school feels like it removes one of the barriers to accessing services.

It might be that some parents will go to CAMHS, but, out of the school setting, the child's problems might not seem that big a deal. But we know this is going to escalate. Or, it could be that the child is doing OK at school, there is nothing seriously concerning, but the parents are worried, and we know them well enough to know their concerns need to be taken seriously before things get worse.

These are often families with really complex social circumstances and histories. Housing is a major issue, with families living in damp, overcrowded, maybe temporary accommodation. Domestic abuse affects lots of families, and that's something TOPS can help with, supporting families with previous abuse and trauma, difficult childhood experiences, drug and alcohol problems. Or they might be refugees who have experienced horrific things. Housing issues can then compound all those other issues—the families are further unsettled, living transient lives that make it hard to access support for their other problems. They can't put down roots, and that's unsettling and scary.

Marta: There can be cases that aren't appropriate for us, say, where it is clear that a multidisciplinary CAMHS team is needed because the child needs to see a psychiatrist about medication. Or where risk is at a level where the family need a service available all week and during the holidays. There can also be cases where, before we see them, something else needs to happen first—an Educational Psychology assessment, or a specialist assessment for autism spectrum disorder (ASD)—so we can know more about the child. We work with a wide range of agencies, from the local learning support team to hospitals treating children with physical conditions.

We tend to get most referrals from Years 4, 5, and 6, when other interventions have already been tried, when the learning demands on children are increasing and issues in the classroom or with peers are becoming more prominent and harder to manage; also, as anxiety rises about how children will manage at secondary school. We are lucky in this service to be able to then see families quickly. If we have space, we can see most families within a week. If we are full, there is a wait. But if a family is in crisis, we can become immediately involved to assess the situation, maybe arrange for them to see a psychiatrist, help get a referral to CAMHS. So there is a rapid response, and that reduces anxiety for the family and the school.

Engaging hard-to-reach families

Tracey: Because we are working with families right from the start of school, we get to know them really well. I do home visits before children begin in Nursery and Reception, so we get real insight before they even reach us. That means if we need, later, to refer them to a mental health service, like TOPS, we can do it in quite a gentle, sympathetic way—because we know them.

Marta: One of the advantages of doing clinical work in schools is that you can start with a fair amount of history that families have shared with the school and have agreed to share with us in the referral. Sometimes families have been known to the school for generations. So we can start to build a picture in our minds before we have met them. If they then share further information with us, we do not share that with the school unless there are safeguarding concerns, and we make it very clear from the beginning that this room where we are meeting, in the school, is a private space, unless there is a concern about risk.

We have to be careful about those boundaries because some parents feel very worried about seeing us. Meeting with a psychotherapist can be alarming. But it helps that we are introduced via the school, that it's a familiar environment they're being seen in. Even so, there are still families who find it hard to trust us initially.

Tracey: I think it can be particularly hard for families with English as an Additional Language (EAL). They are not used to the UK school system and need it to be a friendly environment if they are going to engage. It's hard for refugee families, too.

Marta: Yes, with refugee families, where there is a cultural difference and sometimes a stigma attached to mental health, where admitting there are concerns about the child is not straightforward. Many of the parents are survivors who have put all their hope into the new generation. For it then to be said, "actually, your child needs support", breaks the bubble of hope they have. So we need to do a very gentle piece of work with these parents, because we need to keep those hopes alive. We work carefully to engage them and then slowly go a bit deeper into things that may have happened, that are very traumatic and are impacting on the new generation.

Normally, after families meet with us and start working with us, they engage well. In fact, nearly all the families referred to our service do. But there are parents who are not easy to engage, particularly those with social services involvement, where we are part of the Child Protection Plan, so it is a mandatory referral to us that the parents have to comply with. We are, of course, immediately associated with social workers, and they feel suspicious, don't see us as clinicians, so it takes time and determination to get their trust. In my experience it is really important for the main carer, normally the mother, to see that we value her input, her view. We need to reinforce "the good mother", what she is capable of giving to her child, so that anxiety reduces and she can begin to share things she is struggling with, with her child's behaviour. We need to work in a particular way to maximize engagement.

For many families it takes time to work with the level of trauma they have experienced. Fortunately in this service we have the luxury of being able to work with families as long as needed, and the schools and our funders are in agreement with that. There might be some families where a term of parent–child work is enough to bring a shift, or a few weeks of work helping a child with the transition to secondary school. We can do tailored interventions with clear endings. But then we have cases that last two or three years, with individual therapy and parallel parent work. We can take our time doing assessments, too, if that is needed, to really understand what help the family need. Luckily our schools understand that there is no such thing as a quick fix.

Working together—supporting each other

Marta: The school also understands that the work can be challenging for children and families, especially when we have recently started working with a family; things can become more intense for a while when the child and family begin to face the difficulties. For some children, their behaviour might deteriorate, and it takes careful joined-up working with the school to help understand why that might be, to support the school and contain the child.

Georgina: Yes, sometimes we need to support teachers, as well as the children, with managing the therapy. At the moment all our cases come and go quite easily from the classroom to their therapy sessions, but there have been times when children come out of sessions dysregulated, challenging, and not in any way ready to come back to class, maybe even refusing to come back. So then we get together and think about how to do things differently. Maybe they need to be seen in the last hour of school, so there aren't further learning demands on them afterwards. Or maybe in the hour before lunch, with a bit of time to decompress in the playground with a teaching assistant (TA), then eat and play and be able to come back to class calm. So we need to manage things creatively. I tend to think that if you have a child reacting strongly to therapy, it is another sign that they really need this support and that we need to support them with that.

Tracey: There is constant communication. When there are children and families I know Marta is working with, and difficult, or even small things, have been going on that week, we can talk to her when she comes in on Thursday morning, update her so she is not going in cold, and so the child is not going into a session with the therapist not knowing what has been going on. That is important.

Marta: It really helps when Tracey and Georgina tell us about things that have happened during the week, between sessions. The staff are excellent observers. And then, when we feed back—in general terms—that can then help the school put a particular incident or behaviour into a frame of reference and understanding. It becomes part of our shared formulation of that family rather than just an anxiety-provoking incident.

Georgina: I think informal conversations can make a big difference in helping teachers and TAs. When TOPS ask, "How's it been this week?", a teacher might initially say: "Fine." But then: "Actually, this happened . . ." That discussion can help the teacher keep the child more in mind, help them notice things that could have got lost in the mix, help them think about things a bit differently. If I feel a teacher has got stuck with a child, in a stand-off, or needs help to understand the child differently, I might arrange a supervision for them with Marta. It's a form of emotional support for staff. It's stressful, working in a big, busy school. Of course, TOPS also make more formal contributions, like Marta coming to reviews, Team Around the Family, and Child Protection meetings.

Tracey: Yes, Marta supports us in managing our work but also in managing our own emotions. You can be holding quite a lot, and, rather than feeling it is spilling out, you have somewhere to come and share that. I also do group work with older children, with another member of staff, like transition groups for Year 6, and we meet with Marta to think about what's going on in the group and, if we feel stuck, how we might approach it next time.

Georgina: I think staff value the support. You know, when you've got a child suddenly acting up and escalating and you're thinking, "Oh my goodness, why is this happening?", it can feel less of a burden when you get a chance to think about it with someone, to understand it a bit better. I think also, over the years, knowledge has filtered down from TOPS about how children push their feelings into others. In this school, staff understand that, for example, if you're a nursery teacher, you are dealing with little people with massive emotions and worries, and that makes it a stressful job. I think we are, anyway, a mindful and inclusive school, but TOPS contributes to that.

Another intervention TOPS has done here in the past is run work discussion groups where a group of staff meet regularly with the lead therapist to think each week about a different child, in general, or maybe about a particular morning or incident. I remember us thinking about a child who brought out strong feelings, in me and in others, of annoyance. She was always pushing and pushing, and it was just such a helpful place to think: "Why is this happening, why is she behaving like that?" We thought about her behaving like a little baby, how that could provoke feelings of irritation in staff, but also that she was telling us about her unmet needs. We thought about getting her to sit close to her teacher on the carpet, sometimes holding her hand, just little tweaks that brought a small shift and helped the teacher build a relationship with the child. They don't have to be ground-breaking ideas. A more cynical member of staff might say: "Well, what difference will that make?" But I think that kind of thinking has a powerful drip effect in the school. In recent years we haven't run that group because I'm so mindful of teachers' time, how much they have to do. For now it works better for teachers to have individual consultations with Marta if and when they need them.

Marta: It's good to hear staff find us supportive. But we always need to tread a fine line, because although it's helpful to do lots of liaison and consultation with staff, we need to be realistic and acknowledge that teachers' primary task is to teach and that they have very tight schedules. We need to respect that and not come in demanding their time. We need to make sure our service works in a way that relieves, not adds, pressure.

Tracey: Some teachers can be reluctant to work with TOPS because of time and the enormous pressure for high attainment that filters down from OFSTED and the government. Sometimes, if they haven't worked with therapists before, they're not sure how helpful it will be. I think it's hard for teachers who, when they qualify, might not realize that children don't always come to school ready to learn, that there might be lots of barriers to remove before they can learn. That can almost be a smack in the face for some of them; it's really deskilling to realize that having learnt to teach, you now have to learn a be a kind of mum or dad, containing all the emotions in the classroom, maybe even be a social worker, too. Some teachers just want to teach. For some there can be a hope that TOPS will give them a quick fix, an immediate solution or strategy, so they can get back to teaching.

Marta: I think it can be so painful for a teacher to sit down for a moment and really get to grips with a particular child and their predicament. Sometimes they would rather just keep going. So it's a matter of us letting them see that we are here to support them. It's like with the parents we work with, we have to go gently with teachers in order to build a relationship. But inevitably there are some teachers who are less welcoming of that support, more defensive, and we can't force that.

Georgina: No, and while it is so helpful if teachers try to understand why a child has come into the class angry and upset, we also need to acknowledge that it can test their patience and is an interruption when they're trying to teach a whole class. We have to get that balance. Of course it's important we provide emotional warmth in the classroom, but it's not always the right place to unpick what is going on for a child. That conversation might need to happen with Tracey, or a behaviour for learning mentor, or TOPS, because you might be opening a can of worms you can't then deal with in a class full of children. Also, when children are having a hard time, it's important they have consistency, routine—so as teachers we need to make sure normal life continues, that when a child is feeling all over the place, we're saying: "It's OK. We are still going to do maths." But it's good for us to know TOPS are in on Thursday, and we can think about it with them then.

A school—and home—for families

Tracey: I have been at this school for 26 years, and TOPS has been here for most of that time. I think we are very lucky to have their help, and it's quite scary to think about not having it. I don't think families would fall through the net, because we'd still be identifying them, but it would be very hard making sure they got the help they needed outside the school; if they didn't engage at a clinic, their needs would not get met.

Georgina: Yes, I've been here for more than 10 years and came from a school in a very different sort of area, a county outside London where as SENCo you only had maybe three complex children on your caseload, but you would be banging on people's doors to get help, with no services to work with. Here, the level of need is much, much higher, but the level of support is higher, too. We are lucky to be in this borough, and lucky to have TOPS. Our budgets have been significantly reduced in recent years and are now extremely tight. We have had to slim down some of our mental health support, but we have never come close to thinking we might stop TOPS. Whenever we meet to think about what we can do differently, what might be cheaper, we always say: "We need to keep this service, our children need it. This has a secure evidence base and we can see the benefits." Although we could spend the money on more TA time, when we weigh it up, we find there is a big impact day to day from the depth of support we get from TOPS.

Tracey: I think something we have learnt over the years is how much it helps to have services and interventions available in the school, as much as can be afforded. My role has really evolved in the years I have been here, and, as well as buying in services like TOPS, we now provide a lot more in-house, too, ourselves. Originally I was mostly signposting, scooping up parents and taking them to outside agencies to get support. But it wasn't empowering for them; they wouldn't go unless I went with them every week. So I did more training so we could offer courses and classes, helping the families here in the school.

We now have an adult learning centre in the playground, which I manage in partnership with a local adult learning college, offering English for Speakers of Other Languages, reading, and maths sessions, as well as sessions on supporting children with homework. We do coffee mornings with knitting, sewing, crocheting—a nice little group, predominately with refugee families. We sit in a little circle, and it's very contained, like being in a family, and what the parents produce is amazing. Sometimes they leave looking like they've been "fed", that they are full of these really lovely things they've done together.

Marta: And they tell me about what they do there and bring what they have done to show me! It's a community experience, and although it's not therapy as such, it's a therapeutic experience. Some parents are only able to use our service because they've already worked with Tracey and have become less isolated. Others might see us and then, after a while, they feel better, with more sense of agency, and it's not therapy they need any more but maybe an English course or something else Tracey can offer.

I think, for many of the families we work together with here, there is something about finding a home in the school. It's really striking how many times families, especially refugee families, compare the therapy room to their home, here or in their country of origin, talking about whether it's bigger or smaller. It's somehow symbolic and as if the room, and the school, help parents make a bridge from their past lives and experiences, that they are beginning to feel there might be a home for them, in the school and in the minds of all of us working with them.

PART III

CHILD PSYCHOANALYTIC PSYCHOTHERAPY
IN ALTERNATIVE EDUCATIONAL SETTINGS

CHAPTER NINE

Slow movements that create hope: psychotherapy with a boy diagnosed with ASD

Carlos Vasquez

In this chapter I describe my work as a child and adolescent psychoanalytic psychotherapist in a Special Educational Needs (SEN) school and discuss the psychotherapy of a 5-year-old boy with a diagnosis of autism.

The school

I work in an inner city Special Educational Needs School for children and adolescents 2–19 years of age. The learners (the school calls pupils "learners") have a range of conditions: learning disabilities, physical disabilities that are usually linked to learning disabilities, different severities of autistic spectrum disorder (ASD) and profound and multiple learning disabilities (PMLD).

Children with PMLD have a "severe learning disability and other disabilities that significantly affect their ability to communicate and be independent" (NHS, 2019c). Unable to use language or sign language, children with PMLD communicate via vocal noises, facial expressions, or behaviour (NHS, 2019a). In addition, physical movement is often severely restricted. Some children and young people with PMLD are fastened into a chair that can be reclined like a bed, so they can be moved around the school. They need other people to help fulfil their basic needs, such as toileting and eating. The health of children with PMLD can be extremely fragile. Some children have a short life-expectancy; some die while they are still attending school.

DOI: 10.4324/9781003185925-13

As well as being responsible for learning in school, the teaching class team feeds the children, physically moves them around the school, provides the required interactive stimulation, and makes sure medical recommendations are followed, coordinating with the family and medical staff. It can be highly challenging for these young people to communicate their emotional needs and experiences, especially because they are so dependent on others. It is equally challenging for families and teachers to work out what in the children's behaviour is a form of communication and what the meaning of the communication is. Families and school staff trying to engage with the children can find themselves feeling intense frustration and desperation. Perhaps in part these are their own feelings about the situation of their child or pupil and the difficulty of relating to them; in part the frustration and desperation could be understood as feelings they have been made to have through the way the child relates to them, outside language. This is not a rational, cognitive process, but it is an essential way of communicating for all pre-verbal children and for children who do not use words as they develop.

Children with a diagnosis of severe ASD are non-verbal and often very withdrawn, with episodes of extreme acting out. They tend to have normal mobility, and their physical health is not necessarily fragile. Children with ASD usually show more acting-out behaviour than children with PMLD, with a pronounced lack of impulse control, such as violent outbursts and sexualized behaviour. They are likely to make repetitive movements, such as rocking or flapping their hands, and can also hurt themselves, by banging their heads against a hard surface, for example. Although they are non-verbal, children with severe ASD do make vocalizations, often in a repetitive way. Much of the time they seem disconnected from the people around them and appear facially inexpressive, so it is difficult to read their emotional states.

At school, there are also children and young people with less severe ASD, and some of them do speak. However, these children may also be very withdrawn, make repetitive movements, struggle significantly with social interaction and with understanding social cues, and may show a rigid way of thinking.

As can be imagined, the school population's vulnerability is great. Children's life threatening or life-limiting conditions are highly stressful and traumatizing for their families. This also impacts on school staff, who have to face the worsening health of children who may die.

The institutional dynamics that this ongoing precariousness of health and life generates are particular: staff feel under constant pressure because of the frailty of the children. On a daily basis, school staff have to attend both to fragile children and to children who can be impulsively violent towards others.

School staff are often confronted with behaviour that can seem meaningless or extremely difficult to understand in terms of causal triggers. Children attacking their own bodies in extreme ways or flooding the toilets with water and urine can be disturbing, upsetting, and puzzling. These are just some of the issues clinicians working in the school try to help school staff to process. Some members of staff struggle to keep going, and at times there is a high staff turnover. Powerful feelings of hopelessness can emerge when working with children and young people with a severe disability, which clinicians also have to work through; this is discussed later in the chapter.

Being a child and adolescent psychoanalytic psychotherapist in a Special Educational Needs School

It has long been noticed by the school that their learners benefit from the input of mental health professionals, and a relationship with CAMHS has been sought. The local Specialist Disability CAMHS considers that it is much easier for families to access mental health support within the school, bearing in mind how overwhelming all the medical appointments they have to attend with their child can be. The relationship between the school and CAMHS works well.

The school also has a longstanding tradition of having child and adolescent psychoanalytic psychotherapists based within it. There are two specialist disabilities Child and Adolescent Mental Health Services (CAMHS) clinicians working in the school: a clinical psychologist colleague and myself.

Alongside the two in-school clinicians, other members of the CAMHS team come in to school for specific work: other clinicians may offer individual psychotherapy or a family assessment, for example. My colleague and I coordinate the mental health input and liaison between the school and CAMHS.

In my experience, children and adolescents attending this school usually express their emotional difficulties through acting-out behaviour or becoming more withdrawn: these are the most common presentations of mental health difficulties, and the school's main focus of concern. The school also prioritizes support for families and for school staff, who face huge emotional demands and want help with understanding the children's ways of relating and behaving.

There is a sense within the school that their learners can be helped to express their feelings in ways that are not so disruptive to others or to their own development. There is a hope that attending to psychological needs will make a difference to the level of learners' withdrawal and acting out, so they can make better use of the developmental opportunities presented by the school environment.

I think that child psychotherapists are useful in this context, because careful observation of behaviour, especially in relation to non-verbal communication, is paramount in our training. A particular expertise in observing the fine detail of non-verbal interaction and making sense of this is essential in work with children and young people with disabilities. I find that school staff value being supported to explore possible meaning in relation to what they notice about the minutiae of daily interactions with children who do not communicate in obvious ways. It can also be relieving for school staff to take seriously their own emotional responses to very challenging children, which helps with thinking about what might be conveyed to them by the children without language.

My role in the school is varied. I offer initial family assessment and specialist assessment following referral, and individual brief and longer-term psychotherapy with children who are often non-verbal or use few words. Parent(s)–child or family sessions are often the treatments of choice, especially to help parents notice some of the detail that can easily go unnoticed in interaction with their children, who can come across as disconnected and unresponsive much of the time. When working directly with a child, we also meet regularly with the school staff, so that there is a shared picture of concerns and change.

"Reflective spaces" are also offered to school staff. These can be group or individual spaces and are based on the Tavistock Work Discussion model. This model was developed by the Tavistock Clinic as a way of providing a psychoanalytic perspective to support the work of non-clinical professionals from a range of settings with children and young people (Rustin, 2008). Reflective spaces are an opportunity for members of school staff to present detailed accounts of interactions or situations arising with learners and families in the course of an ordinary working day. Usually staff bring work situations that they consider challenging or difficult. These situations are discussed in order to understand the different levels of communication, emotional dynamics, and psychological processes at play.

Situations in which children or adolescents have been violent to others is a common concern brought by staff. Another focus is the dynamic that develops between staff and parents, especially in PMLD classes, where anxieties in relation to death are high and the parents can be traumatized by their children's conditions. Parents can be highly anxious about whether members of school staff are properly able to take care of their children every moment of the day. Teachers find themselves under a lot of pressure dealing with parents' worried questions. Usually, these reflective spaces offer a wider understanding of parents' acute distress and consequent attitude, which can then elicit sympathy rather than defensiveness from teachers. At the same time, teachers' defensiveness can be acknowledged as understandable rather than criticized, which helps to sustain parent–teacher communication.

While reflective spaces have been appreciated by members of staff, it has been difficult, at times, to get groups started and keep them going. It is not surprising that there can be resistance to thinking about very painful events, such as the death of a learner. Sometimes the staff groups can feel provoked or additionally burdened by the idea that talking about their own raw, emotional states at work can be helpful. Over time, however, it has been noticed that the class-teams have become more reflective and thoughtful and less reactive in relation to emotional situations that emerge with learners.

There is regular liaison between the in-school specialist CAMHS clinicians and school staff, especially with the team in charge of monitoring learners' well-being. This partnership is fundamental to effective work with complex cases and includes attendance at school team meetings, care planning, safeguarding issues, and joint recommendations about additional resources needed.

Kevin's therapy at school

My work with Kevin, a 5-year-old boy, whom I saw for a year-and-a-half, gives a sense of child psychoanalytic psychotherapy in a special educational needs school.

Kevin is a non-verbal boy with a diagnosis of ASD. He had a difficult start in life, as he was born very prematurely. This meant that he had chronic health problems, with constant medical intervention, and had to go through surgery within his first month of life. His birth brought anxiety and distress to the family. For a while he had to be in a specialist unit for babies with extremely unstable health.

The birth of a child with fragile health can stir intense emotions, and this has a huge impact on parents. Parents have to navigate a situation fraught with anxiety. At this school, many parents have, like Kevin's parents, been through these overwhelmingly anxiety-provoking times at the beginning of their child's life.

Part of the reason psychotherapy in school was thought to be the right choice was because Kevin had to attend medical appointments in hospital regularly, as well as other appointments within school. As already described, the school hosted a multidisciplinary CAMHS disabilities team, which meant that Kevin could come to appointments with other clinicians, as needed. It would have been highly unlikely that the family could manage to bring Kevin to psychotherapy appointments at a clinic outside school.

In addition, children like Kevin find any kind of new experience or change in relationships extremely difficult. It is, of course, this difficulty with developing a capacity for relating and communicating that psychotherapy tries to help with. But feeling overwhelmed by contact with a new person who relates to them in a way they are not used to could lead a child with ASD to further entrenched withdrawal. School-based psychotherapy provides aspects of familiarity in the setting that can help a child with ASD slowly start to tolerate newness and strangeness. The sensitivity and receptiveness not only of parents but also of the school staff—encouraged by reflective discussion with the psychotherapist— whom a child with ASD meets through the school day, supports small shifts in the child's capacity to relate that emerge over time in psychotherapy.

Before I started seeing Kevin, he and his mother attended weekly parent–child sessions at the school with a child psychotherapist colleague from the specialist disability CAMHS. Kevin was referred initially because he came across as very withdrawn, and he struggled to separate from his mother. The parent–child sessions continued for a year, and it was then agreed that Kevin would benefit from once-weekly individual psychotherapy. It was thought that he might now need a space of his own—he had managed being separate from his mother with a little less difficulty during the parent–child work—in order to continue to develop his capacity to relate. This work had also helped Kevin's mother to feel more hopeful about his progress. When individual psychotherapy started, his mother attended fortnightly meetings with a child psychotherapist colleague to provide support and to have an opportunity to talk about how things were at home; to think about Kevin's emotional experience more widely and make links with his development in therapy and at school. The emotional implications of different health checks were also discussed in parent sessions. Kevin's parents were separated, and his mother was the parent most involved in Kevin's treatment.

At the start of therapy, Kevin's mother described him as someone who was "very guarded". He was cautious about approaching others and did not show a desire to connect straightforwardly, even though she felt he wanted to do so. The school staff thought he was worryingly withdrawn and sometimes passive in the face of attack from other children. In general, he came across as a sweet-natured boy, with an open, pleasant face. He is a white British boy, who usually wore his hair very short and was always rather neatly dressed. He enjoyed gymnastics and sometimes moved like a gymnast, making arches with his body. Initially, he gave the impression of being a happy boy, walking in a bouncy way, with a big smile. However, he could quickly become cut off, not acknowledging anyone else's presence. He could also be absolutely determined to make other people do what he wanted.

Weekly psychotherapy sessions for Kevin were punctuated by termly reviews with his mother that included teaching staff. I met regularly with his class teacher. Psychotherapy in school involved the professional network in continuous liaison in order to coordinate how we would manage were Kevin to run off on the way to the therapy room and to arrange the taking to and picking up from sessions by a member of staff. I also convened meetings with all the school staff who had regular contact with Kevin, to discuss the purpose of his psychotherapy and my approach. The class-team's understanding of why Kevin came out of class for therapy every week facilitated better communication between us. The termly reviews allowed us to exchange information about Kevin's difficulties and progress.

First stage of psychotherapy

Kevin started attending psychotherapy with his mother, as he still struggled to separate from her and come into the room by himself, as is often the case with children who have a diagnosis of ASD. Once in the room, he let us know clearly that he wanted to leave as soon as possible, going to the door and trying to open it and voicing, "Geet!" in a loud and desperate tone. His mother tried to engage him, and to begin with she brought some of his things from home to the sessions. A Thomas the Tank Engine book that he liked was put into his therapy toy box, and a sponge, which he liked to clean with.

In the first sessions, Kevin didn't want to have anything to do with me; he was painfully rejecting. His mother would sit him on her lap and read the Thomas the Tank Engine book, which he seemed to enjoy and be soothed by. At times, he curled into his mother's body and relaxed when she sang a nursery rhyme. Kevin's closeness to his mother was very strong, and mum told me that he would usually sleep in her bed.

His pronounced rejection of me can be seen in the following extract from the third session.

Session 3

We all sat down as we entered the room, but very soon Kevin went to the door and seemed to want to leave, lifting the blind and looking through the window.

Mum said to Kevin, "We aren't leaving yet." She unzipped his coat. Kevin walked around the room and looked at the dolls' house from afar but didn't focus on it. He looked around a bit more, went towards his mother, and said, "Geee." He went very close to mum and then looked at his jacket. Mum tried to take the jacket off for him, but he protested, and Mum said, "Oh, you want me to close your zipper." Mum closed his zipper, and Kevin went back to the door. As his mother didn't come with him, he took her coat and pulled it from the table. Mum picked up the coat and said that they weren't leaving yet. I said to Kevin in a lively way, "You've come in and you want to go right back out, don't want to be here."

Mum encouraged Kevin to use the felt pens, and he did so. He started scribbling. Once he'd done a bit with one colour, he moved to another colour. Mum seemed eager to keep him entertained so that he wouldn't lose the will to stay. I showed him some more colours to see if he was interested, and he picked one of them and continued scribbling. From time to time I commented that he liked to see the different colours, they were all different. Once he'd finished with all the colours, he seemed to lose interest and again wanted to leave. He went to his mother, tried to pull her up, and then went to the door.

At one point Kevin pulled Mum's coat from the sink counter, and the coat fell on the floor. Mum reiterated that they were not going to leave yet. Kevin complained saying, "Guuu!" in a loud and cross tone, scrunching up his face, showing annoyance. He climbed onto Mum's lap and sat there, looking sleepy, and I said that today Kevin wanted to be cosy on Mum's lap and was feeling sleepy. Kevin lay on her lap as if going to sleep. He sat up again. He grabbed his mother's hands, opening them and putting them back together, and I said that he wanted to open the doors.

Not long after this, he got up, came towards me, and looked at me very closely. I found myself moving my face back a bit, as he was so close. He grabbed my hands, his face right up to mine. He then grasped my ID badge (which is also a door fob), which was hanging from my neck. He tugged it and seemed to want me to open the door as he pulled me towards it. He opened the curtain. I followed him and said, "Where would you like to go out there?"

In this extract we can see how much effort needed to be made, especially by Kevin's mother, for him to stay in the room. Leaving seemed to be his overriding desire throughout the session. I started to understand, with mum and with the help of the parent worker, who had worked with mum and Kevin previously, that Kevin might be dealing with considerable loss in his transition to psychotherapy. He didn't have the parent–child clinician with him in the room any more. His repeated going to the door and looking outside may not only have been driven by his desire to leave the room and me, but also have indicated a question about where the other clinician had gone. It was the same room, but someone was missing, and instead there was someone new, and, clearly, he didn't want to be with me. He wanted what he had had before, and here I was, imposing change on him. I was very doubtful at this stage as to whether he would ever feel comfortable enough for us to work together one to one.

The parent-worker reminded mum that Kevin used to have a snack during the session, as it was snack time at school, and that missing this might add to his sense of loss. We agreed that mum would bring him a snack from now on, which Kevin enjoyed very much.

It is curious that after having close contact with his mother, sitting cosily on her lap, he approached me and initiated the only face-to-face contact in the session. Maybe there was something of him feeling that mum trusted me, because she had been talking to me calmly about the struggles of the previous night, that bridged the gap between the previous therapist and me and made him less anxious and so less rejecting of me, who was felt to be the source of his discomfort. He then went to the other extreme, coming so close that he seemed to want to get inside me. But wanting to get inside was followed immediately by wanting to get away. The new, different therapist-person left Kevin with no in-between position available to him. Perhaps he also wanted to get inside me to make me open the door with the badge he had noticed hanging from my neck. And was the close contact then suddenly too much for him? Or was my stepping back felt by him as a rejection, as if I had closed a door on him?

The pushing together and pulling apart of his mother's hands may have been an expression of his processing of the emotional distance between two people, including between the different potential pairs in the room. Perhaps him and his mother? Perhaps the potential pair that was him and me? There was a preoccupation with being extremely close and extremely separate in pair relationships that Kevin seemed to have been showing me through his behaviour, which may have been linked with him just starting to get to know me and not knowing where to put himself in relation to me. Kevin seemed mostly to orientate himself towards either mum or me, and his wish to be the one in control of the pairing was evident. However, he did seem able to allow a degree of connection between the third possible pair that was his mother and me; there did seem to be the beginning of tolerating a pairing that he did not always have to be central to.

Three months later, Kevin was less inclined to try to get away from the room and me and more likely to turn towards me, perhaps starting to claim and trust me. His mother and I agreed to see whether he would come to the room on his own, at least for part of the session, at some point soon.

Session in the fourth month of therapy

I was standing in the reception hall, and Mum came in with Kevin, holding his hand. I greeted them. Mum became distracted, looking elsewhere, and Kevin let go of his mother's hand and looked straight at me. To my surprise, he started to approach me, continuing to make direct eye contact.

I waved and said hello to him. In the middle of this (it may have been when I said, "Hello" to his mother) he stopped and looked at the wall, where there are pictures of staff and learners.

Kevin looked at the pictures for some time and then back at me. I waved hello to him again, and he walked over, stretching out his hands and arms towards me. I held my hands out towards him and he took my hand and started pulling me towards the door that leads to the therapy room. I said that we had to wait for mum. He pulled me insistently. We were very close to the door. I looked at mum, and we agreed with a nod that I would go with him on his own. I was aware of feeling both thrilled that he was venturing to come with me by himself and full of doubt and fear about how this might go.

As soon as we entered the corridor, he started to look a bit puzzled—I thought, about his mother not being there—and he stopped. But I continued walking and encouraged him to come with me into the room. He looked around—for his mother?—still puzzled, but hesitantly followed me into the room. Once in the room, he seemed to notice that his mother really wasn't there, and I wondered whether he also noticed that I did not have his usual chocolate snack with me. He looked around the room with a lost and panicky expression in his eyes, his mouth hanging open. He immediately took my hand and pulled me towards the door, wanting me to open it, saying in a commanding and slightly anxious tone, "Get! Get!"

I said, "Mummy will come in a moment", in as expressive tone of voice as possible, but he continued insisting, more anxious each time, so we went out of the room and went to get his mother.

Later, when both mum and Kevin were in the room, I suggested we could see whether Kevin could be on his own with me for fifteen minutes or so after the holidays. Mum agreed and said she could give me the chocolate snack beforehand to give to Kevin in the session. Kevin made some pro-testing sounds and looked at mum in an annoyed way. Mum said that he was complaining, and I said to both of them in an expressive way that he was protesting because she and I were talking too much, and he wanted to claim some attention for himself.

He looked at me, smiling, while eating the chocolate. He seemed happy and came towards me and rubbed my beard in a cheerful, close way, so close that I had to pull my face away slightly. I said that it seemed eating the chocolate sweetened the experience, and he felt happy and more comfortable to explore me, it made things feel better, and this encouraged him to explore and be curious about my beard.

After a little while he went and sat in my chair and then lifted his arms up in the air to me. I thought he expected me to lift him up and down, as I had done in previous sessions. He was very insistent about this, and I did lift him up from the chair and placed him back down, repeating this up and down movement a few times. When I stopped, mum engaged him in colouring. I joined in and started drawing a basic calendar, with images showing him and me not seeing each other next week because of half-term. I talked to Kevin about what I was drawing but found myself not finishing my sentence as I realized he wasn't paying much attention and I lost hope that my explanation would be registered.

Kevin started colouring, and I thought it was a good idea to do some col-ouring with him. I picked up the brown felt tip and started drawing squiggly shapes on a blank piece of paper. He looked at me as if surprised. He then stretched out his hand, holding the felt tip towards me, looking at me, con-veying the message that he wanted me to take the colour. I took the colour he handed me, and gave him the colour I was using. There was a sort of interactive moment, which he seemed to enjoy, where each of us was using the other's pen. Kevin had initiated this moment. He seemed to have a definite idea about the exchange of pens and to be greatly enjoying the interaction.

I announced that we had to start tidying up, as the session was about to finish. Kevin immediately protested and made fierce noises, almost cry-ing—with anger, I thought. I talked to him about how difficult he found the goodbye today. Mum said that he had been enjoying himself, and he didn't want to stop.

I said that it was very difficult to say goodbye, but we would see each other after half-term. He calmed down a bit but was still moody when the teacher came to collect him from the room. Mum explained to the teacher that Kevin had had a very good session but had found it difficult towards the end.

In this session, we can see how, four months after starting therapy, Kevin was more able to move towards me without so many reservations. However, he was still very cautious about being on his own with me and especially without his mother.

Kevin had started to enjoy moments of connection between us and to initiate interaction. There seemed to be some attempt to identify with someone else—exchanging the pens and using what I was using; and to invite someone else to see what it was like to be he—getting me to use what he had been using. This led to a more explicit wish to try out being in my position, to be the one in my chair for just a moment, then back to being a boy needing to be picked up, then another moment in my chair.

Instantly pleasurable experiences, such as eating the chocolate, seemed to ease the way for Kevin to explore the world with less fear, enabling him to explore my beard with his touch. Having come close to touch me, he could then increase contact, though this was entirely at his command. The increasing realization of someone being different from him and not following his will all the time also seemed to bring out more overt aggression. The rubbing of my beard may have included an element of wanting to rub out the evidence that we were not the same: not only that the words from my mouth were spoken in an unfamiliar accent, but that for him my beard rubbed it in that I was a man, while he was a boy. It is particularly emotionally painful for children with an ASD diagnosis to start to notice the differences between themselves and someone else, as I discuss later in the chapter.

Through working with Kevin and other children who do not communicate verbally, I have realized that increasingly I use the musicality of my voice, especially rhythm and tone, and the language of gesture and facial expression to communicate. This is very different from working with a child without an ASD diagnosis, who makes use of language in a more ordinary way, where I try to put my thoughts into words at the child's level, with timing and tone serving to modulate rather than determine meaning. In the extract above, when telling Kevin that his mother would be coming in a bit, I found myself speaking as if to a much younger child or an infant, exaggerating my expressiveness in order to meet his anxiety and match its level with my tone of voice.

I also notice that I am inclined to show that I have understood a non-verbal child's communication and to respond to this at an active level, like lifting Kevin up and down as though he were younger than 5, which I would be unlikely to do with a more ordinarily developing 5-year-old child. Susan Reid (1990) discusses adaptions to psychotherapy involved in work with a very developmentally delayed child who needed to be physically carried during sessions. As well as picking Kevin up, I started to play-act to amplify my words, performing a scene where I walked away from him and then came back, when trying to help him process his experience of a separation and differentiation, where both of us were separate beings with different wills, for example. Words alone were not enough. I had to evoke an emotional resonance in him through a visual or physical experience within the boundary of the session and the therapy room—rather like make-believe play with a more ordinarily communicating child.

Anne Alvarez (1992) has emphasized how important is not only the content but also the manner of what is communicated in work with children with an ASD diagnosis. What is the emphasis of the message? What is the tone? What is the rhythm? Alvarez not only gives weight to the use of gesture and tone in conveying meaning, but also highlights the value of liveliness in the therapist when a child is in a state of severe withdrawal. Alvarez calls this function *reclamation*—that is, a reclaiming by the psychotherapist of the child from their withdrawn state. She describes this in terms of the way in which parents reconnect with a baby who has disconnected emotionally in an ordinary way in day-to-day life.

Liveliness and ongoing effort to claim or reclaim connectedness with learners and help the learners to connect or reconnect with their environment also characterizes the school's approach: it is part of school culture. This is a helpful cultural context for clinicians working in the school, supporting adaptation to technique to meet the particular needs of the children and young people.

Liveliness in the therapist is linked to the appearance and disappearance of hope, which is a central feature in work with children with ASD or other pronounced disabilities. This is so for education staff working at an SEN school such as this, as well as for child psychotherapists and other clinicians.

The onset of hopelessness can be seen in the moment I was trying to explain the coming holidays to Kevin: when I saw his disconnection, I stopped trying. Repeated, insistent disconnection can make one feel that nothing communicated to the child is getting through, leaving a sense of pointlessness. Durban (2014) suggests that the therapist's feelings of hopelessness help in understanding the child's complex emotional experience, which is marked by particularly intense anxieties related to a crushing loss of hope in the contact with a lively other. Monitoring one's own feelings of hopelessness can point to the moment a child cuts off or becomes more profoundly withdrawn. This attention to moment-by-moment shifts in the psychotherapist's own state of mind can help with a technical change of gear in order to mobilize a reclaiming function.

One of Kevin's important developments at this stage was how he started showing his distress towards the end of the session, just when we were about to separate, with the separation in the excerpt above probably accentuated by the coming half term break. It can be difficult to see that separations, such as school holidays, have a big emotional impact on the children at the school; it is unclear how much they grasp what is happening in their environment when they mostly come across as disconnected. However, it is usually around holidays that children start acting out more frequently at school, and I think this can be understood as a communication linked to an emotional change in the school's atmosphere when everybody, including the staff, is getting ready to leave.

Slow changes in identification after one year of treatment

Over time, Kevin was able to come to the therapy room by himself. He grew clearer in his communication with me and began to show more of an explicit desire to interact. The following extract from a session one year after the beginning of therapy shows a small but significant change in the quality of interaction between us. Kevin seemed a little more able to be with me as someone separate, allowing me to have my own mind and will. This is in contrast to typical interactions with many children with ASD, who can behave as though another's body and mind are appendages, using someone else's hand, rather than their own, to do something, for example.

Session after one year of treatment

> Kevin moved his mouth, as if he was chewing something. He continued exploring the different things in his toy box and at one point moved across the room. When he looked towards me, I made a show of moving my own mouth as if eating something and said that today he wanted to get things in his mouth and eat. I said, gesticulating in an exaggerated way, that he seemed eager to come here, that actually he seemed eager to be with me in some way and was more connected and active.

> He walked to a chair and looked at me. I felt this was an intentional look, a connection. I said, "Hello Kevin", as if greeting him for the first time, and whistled a bit and repeated the "Hello Kevin." After a moment he put his lips together and made a similar shape to my mouth when whistling. He did this once and then stopped. He was sitting on the chair and stamped his feet, making a rhythmic sound, which reminded me of the rhythms he and I had made in previous sessions. I stamped my own feet in a different rhythm to his, and after some time he stamped his feet in what I thought

was the same rhythm as me. I was surprised by this and found myself enjoyed interacting with him. I felt he was acknowledging me as someone he could be with as a different person.

Kevin's awareness of a someone else separate from and different from him had grown. He was now very interested in taking up rhythms that I introduced. It seemed as if he was thinking, "There is someone else apart from me out there and I want to be like them." As discussed in chapter 1, processes of identification are crucial for development, and this is important for children with an ASD diagnosis. Developing curiosity and interest in someone else is a major step in starting to be less withdrawn.

It is usually thought that echolalia—echoing or exactly reproducing someone else's speech—is just a mindless and empty imitation of someone else, not a way of interacting meaningfully. This view is questioned by Donna Williams (1992), who has an ASD diagnosis and explains that her own echolalia was an attempt to relate to others. Williams describes how, as a girl with an ASD diagnosis, she used echolalia as a way of responding to someone else, something like, "I can interact with you." Following Williams, Maria Rhode (1999) considers that imitation can be a significant developmental achievement in relation to identifying with and communicating with another. I wondered whether Kevin's imitation of my whistling was an attempt to let me know that he felt that there was a connection between us. I think that my introduction of variation and a different way of communicating than he had expected gave him an experience of the difference and separateness that is necessary in order to experience a wish to connect. His capacity to notice and tolerate this difference and then do something with it in playful way was supported by the earlier miming of eating, where I followed his lead and commented on what was happening, both putting myself in his position and taking up an observational not-him position. The whistling and stamping played with feelings about not being the same and also seemed to be about the two of us communicating—an affirmation or even celebration of this. He showed me that he noticed and wanted to connect with me, perhaps fuelled by a desire to be like me.

Some weeks later, while I was talking about feelings to do with separation, Kevin started turning the lights on and off. I responded by waving at the lights and at him and saying, "Hello lights, hello Kevin!" When he turned them off, I said, "Bye bye lights, bye bye Kevin!" He was delighted with this and continued the turning the lights on and off game in subsequent sessions. He became increasingly aware of and more expressive in relation to gaps between sessions.

In the same session, he grabbed my glasses, placed them on his face, and then put them back on me. He repeated this several times. I thought he was showing his growing curiosity about others in the world; exploring the world through the eyes of another, identifying with me while seeming able to know about the difference between us, that my glasses and my way of seeing belonged to me.

Kevin began to manage greater differentiation and seemed more aware of who I was and where I belonged in the school, and where the teaching staff belonged. On our journey from the class to the psychotherapy room, he would come with his Teaching Assistant (TA) and me, until we were relatively close to the therapy room. Then he would turn to his TA and gently push her back in the direction of the classroom, as if saying, "You don't belong here, you belong back in the classroom." He would do the same to me at the end of the session. When his TA came to collect him, he would push me back towards the therapy room, as if saying, "You stay here, you belong here and not in other parts of the school." Although Kevin seemed rigid in his compartmentalization of the day and the people and spaces he encountered, this delineation did also seem to be a further step towards noticing differentiating details about people, what they did, and who they were to him. He began to look at me at the end of sessions, which he had not done before, as if acknowledging something of the pain of the goodbye, communicating sadness in his gaze.

In ordinary emotional development, being a child and noticing the differences between oneself and an adult is a process that can be fuelled by a desire to be like the adult in the future. However, for all children who want to grow up and accept that in the ordinary course of things they have to, this always entails painful acceptance of there being someone else more capable or more powerful than oneself. For a child with a significant disability, noticing the difference between oneself and others can be a particularly challenging task if it involves additionally painful acceptance of a greater gap than usual between one's own capacity and that of others, such as being able to talk or walk independently.

In Kevin's case, I think that the development of his capacity to differentiate between himself and me, his able-bodied adult male therapist, and between himself and others, allowed him to be in touch with feelings that enriched his relationships. This extension of emotional life brought him some new pain, as well as satisfaction. The sad gaze at the end of the session, which resonated with my own sadness, not only about the goodbye, seemed to be evidence of the expansion of his palette of feelings. At the same time, my increasing joy during Kevin's play seemed to indicate that I was with someone who could access a wider emotional range, making sessions more spontaneous and less repetitive. I think this may have been one of the important achievements in therapy, the broadening and enrichment of his emotional world and his less defensive stance in relation to difficult feelings, such as sadness.

Kevin's mother and teachers told me that he was far less withdrawn and correspondingly more explicit in showing his desire to connect. For other more ordinarily developing children this may seem like a small step; for a child with an ASD diagnosis, who is particularly withdrawn, this is a fundamentally significant step with a big impact on daily life at home and at school. It seemed that Kevin's anxieties about beginnings and endings or "hellos" and "goodbyes" were now less disabling at school. He was in a better position to make use of all the opportunities school could offer in terms of relationships and learning through relating with his teachers and peers (M. Rhode, personal communication, 2019).

Further progress towards the end of therapy

It is curious how towards the end of Kevin's psychotherapy with me, after one-and-a-half years, he started taking four wooden toy people with smiley faces out of his toy box. He would take hold of them at the beginning of the session, clutching them in one hand. He looked eagerly for each of these figures, until he found them all. I would point at one of them, and say, "Carlos", and then point at another one and say "Kevin", wondering out loud whether he was showing me something about what was on his mind, a major event happening between us: the ending of his therapy. In these last sessions I talked about the goodbye and, for the first time, Kevin started putting the wooden doll-figures inside the dolls' house. He placed them carefully, all lying together in a row in the corner of the dolls' house room. He then continued with the session as usual, climbing onto the different surfaces and trying out different sounds with his voice. I would reply by singing my thoughts back to him, and the communication was, at times, much more fluid as he responded with further sounds.

I found this development towards the end of treatment very encouraging. I thought it showed how Kevin seemed aware of the importance of feeling close to people and also some knowledge of separation; perhaps he was expressing a wish for people—him and me—to stay together. This was a pronounced change from being overly distant or intrusively close at the beginning of therapy. There was an idea of four people—his emotional world seemed to have extended beyond insistent pairing in which he had to be in control. Contact with other people seemed less anxiety-provoking for Kevin and so a little more manageable. This was, of course, particularly relevant because the end of therapy was imminent, which he probably sensed. (The treatment with me had to end because I was leaving the post. Kevin continued psychotherapy, however, with another clinician.)

In the last therapy review, Kevin's mother reported that he was not only less withdrawn, but that he had developed a close relationship with a younger cousin. He had been able to relate to his cousin in a communicative, responsive, and connected way, and when the cousin and her family moved away, he was able to show straightforwardly how upset and angry he was. Kevin seemed far less defended and guarded about letting emotional relationships have an impact on him and showing this. In the last meeting I had with the class-team, they told me that Kevin was more expressive and engaged with members of staff, making it easier for them to read his state of mind.

There is another aspect of Kevin's play in this last period of therapy that I want to highlight, which is his use of the inside space of the dolls' house. It seemed that Kevin could begin to think about things having an inner space, perhaps curious not only about the inside of a toy house but also about what goes on inside people's minds, including his own mind. Rhode (1999) and Maiello (2012) point out how vital a discovery this is for children with an ASD diagnosis: it becomes possible for them to feel that they can hold on to an idea or a feeling of another, and a feeling of a relationship with another, even if they are not actually together, and that others might also hold them in mind. For a child with ASD, this opens up the possibility of remembering and trusting that they will be remembered. It gives solidity to the emotional experience of relationships with others and within one's own mind, sometimes thought of as three-dimensionality (Meltzer, Bremner, Hoxter, Weddell, & Wittenberg, 1975), which is a major development from the flat literalness that is often associated with children with ASD.

Conclusion

In this chapter I have tried to convey how once-weekly psychoanalytic psychotherapy in school, accompanied by meetings for the parent with another clinician and supported by ongoing discussion with school staff, helped the development of a child who was extremely cut off and withdrawn. As Durban (2014) points out, it is easy to lose hope when progress is hard to notice, as is often the case with children who have a neurological condition such as ASD. I have only included a few of the very many moments in sessions where I felt the connection with Kevin was non-existent and I found myself feeling valueless and full of hopelessness. In general, in my work in this school, and particularly with children and young people like Kevin, I have noticed that there is usually more going on than is easily noticed or that the children easily let others notice. In my experience, children who are markedly withdrawn can be helped to emerge from these states a little, becoming more interested in being with others. This can be of enormous help for their future relationships. But, as Durban (2014) says, this is only possible if the psychotherapist is able to work through and try to understand their own feelings of hopelessness in contact with children such as Kevin.

Providing child psychoanalytic psychotherapy within a special school lends itself to the slow movement that children with ASD need in order to develop their capacity to relate. A gradual approach is anchored in the familiarity of the institutional setting, which forms part of the therapy setting. This allows for a bit-by-bit awareness of difference, which is necessary in order for a child with ASD to begin to tolerate wider and deeper emotional experiences, including separateness and separation. Working closely with school staff as well as family means that there is immediate and ongoing support for even the tiniest shifts in a child's capacity. When the relationship between psychotherapy, family, and school is working well enough, developments in the child can be met by developments in the family and school systems, promoting reality-based hope of contact with a lively other.

CHAPTER TEN

From exclusion to inclusion: developmental group work in a primary pupil referral unit

Fiona Henderson

W hen children as young as 5 are excluded from school and nursery, there needs to be an understanding of the distress they are communicating and a way to return to a positive developmental pathway. Children come into the primary pupil referral unit (PPRU) after years of trauma, neglect, family relationship difficulties, and parental addiction and mental health difficulties, followed by the experience of rejection and exclusion from mainstream school. The shared task for education and child psychoanalytic psychotherapy is to stop the cycle of blame and offer some hope that we can help to understand the meaning of children's behaviour, that absorbing, clarifying and managing complex feelings and presentations will allow change to happen.

Donald Winnicott (1963), a child psychoanalyst and paediatrician, said that the antisocial tendency is rooted in deprivation. Through the antisocial act, without being aware of it, the child attempts to stake a claim to recovery by mobilizing family and society to help mend environmental failures that have been forgotten. Antisocial behaviour represents a moment of hope in a child who is otherwise without hope. The PPRU seeks to provide a setting where there can be a hopeful working towards recovery.

At the PPRU, the return to a developmental path for these children emerges from a number of interventions involving teachers, parents, and the multidisciplinary team, all of whom provide consistency, flexibility, and communication at all levels. Child psychotherapy offers a particular point of view and way of working within this.

DOI: 10.4324/9781003185925-14

In this chapter, I first describe the PPRU setting, its aims and models of working. I then focus on the contribution of child psychoanalytic psychotherapy approaches to meeting the complex needs of the children and furthering the developmental aims of the Unit. Group work with children and staff is explored from a child psychotherapy perspective.

The primary pupil referral unit setting

The model of support at the PPRU was developed in partnership between Health and the Local Authority to reduce the number of children with complex needs placed in residential schools by meeting their needs locally in high-quality provision (D. Jones, personal communication, 2020). This means that the school functions both as a pupil referral unit (for children excluded from mainstream schools) and a special school (for children with the most severe social, emotional, and mental health needs). At the same time, an outreach team supports local authority schools to sustain mainstream placements of children with less severe needs, who might otherwise require alternative provision.

The children placed at the PPRU have complex needs related to a combination of factors, including historic and current experience of abuse and neglect, neurodevelopmental disorders (e.g. autism spectrum disorder, attention deficit hyperactivity disorder), and acquired mental health disorders (e.g. post-traumatic stress disorder), as well as family stressors, such as poverty and deprivation, parental mental health difficulties, substance abuse, learning difficulties, and issues related to domestic violence. Children may be on the edge of care or living in kinship arrangements; there may be ongoing court procedures, allegations, or safeguarding concerns; families may be struggling with political asylum claims, with trauma associated with seeking asylum, and with living in an unfamiliar country without knowledge of the language or systems. At any given time, many of our pupils will be designated as Children in Need or have a Child Protection Plan in place. Most, if not all, will have an Education, Health and Care Plan.

The PPRU is a well-resourced and centrally located school, part of a large campus, together with a mainstream primary school, an autism unit, and adult education provision. There are 20 children in the school, who present with a range of difficulties and with acute anxiety about change and development. The families usually feel strongly ambivalent about their child's move from mainstream school to a PPRU. Parents experience the stigma and social exclusion of the change of provision as well as the relief of finding a suitable school. Not surprisingly, working in the PPRU can be highly stressful for the staff.

The Unit provides specialist support not only for pupils but also for their families; not only in term-time but all year round. The school deploys a multidisciplinary team with expertise in the fields of clinical and educational psychology, speech and language therapy, occupational therapy, child psychoanalytic psychotherapy, systemic family therapy, and social work. This allows us to provide a single point of contact with professionals who are familiar to the children and their families. The children have an experience of being part of a relatively small group with a containing and consistent team of adults that maintains boundaries with high expectations and fosters thinking and talking rather than reacting, in order to work together in a well-functioning way.

This model enables the integration of specialisms to provide holistic assessment of how a range of factors interact to influence children's social and emotional development and to target interventions to meet their needs. Interventions may involve collaboration between different specialists and can take the form of work with families, individual children or parents, and groups of children or parents. This collaborative approach is reflected in the organization of the Campus within which we work, and our links with other agencies, which fosters the sharing of expertise and mutual support as well as maximizing opportunities for inclusion and partnership.

Links with CAMHS and agencies outside the school bring in family support workers and access to the extended CAMHS team, including family therapy and psychiatry. The school draws on external resources to facilitate assessments for ASD and ADHD as well as physical health with the school nurse. Families have been able to access home-based multi-systemic family work.

There is a strong emphasis on re-engaging children with learning and promoting their academic attainment. In general, after moving to the school, children show improvement in terms of their attendance, social interaction, emotional well-being, approach to learning, and academic progress. This chapter focuses on the contribution of child psychotherapy approaches in working towards these school objectives, particularly through involvement with staff reflective groups and leading psychotherapeutic groups with children.

The contribution of child psychoanalytic psychotherapy

The PPRU has a whole-school approach to children and families, and therapeutic approaches are embedded in all aspects of school life. The school's overall therapeutic aims are to assess difficulty, build concentration and focus, encourage academic skills and an interest in social activity, play, sport, music and physical skills, and support a move towards independence, including the capacity to develop self-esteem and confidence. Within this, child psychoanalytic psychotherapy brings a perspective and approach that is particularly helpful when difficulties are complex and the demands on education staff are great.

Claudia McLoughlin, a child psychoanalytic psychotherapist working in a Pupil Referral Unit, described the overlapping concentric rings of thoughtful, containing care around the children, their families, the staff group, and the service as a whole in its multi-agency context when education and psychotherapy are working effectively together (McLoughlin, 2010). This helps to define the complex and flexible approach needed from a child psychotherapy service in this setting.

At a whole-school level, child psychotherapists work closely with other multidisciplinary colleagues from occupational therapy, speech and language therapy, social work, and educational psychology, and with teachers, teaching assistants, and mentors in developing an integrated psychoanalytically informed mental health understanding. A child psychotherapy perspective is part of a multidisciplinary assessment and review for each child, collecting evidence from detailed classroom observation, individual or group therapy and involving discussion with the highly attuned, skilled, professional education staff. The collective sharing of information and observation continues in daily briefings, debriefings, and clear feedback of the formulation of children's presentation to the whole team, which includes consideration of the timing and capacity for reintegration to mainstream school.

In relation to education staff, child psychotherapists contribute to informal conversations in the classroom, playground, staff room, and corridors as teachers and teaching assistants deal with distressing, challenging situations. A more formal forum, the weekly reflective space, which the whole team attends, is facilitated jointly by a clinical psychologist and child psychotherapist and seeks to enhance understanding of what is happening with individual children.

Psychoanalytic developmental work with excluded children

The children in the PPRU have often had difficulties in managing social and emotional relationships and in being introduced to school learning at nursery and reception. They have sometimes been educated alone with one key worker, away from other children and unable to develop the skills to make friends, understand themselves, and know about their own or others' needs. They have an over-reliance on early behaviour in facing anxiety and change: the children often exhibit alarming acting out, with shouting, crying, and trashing the environment, which has previously been some sort of temporary solution for them in trying to be in control. The experience of being isolated from others due to their own aggression and disturbance leaves the children isolated from their class group.

Child psychotherapy offers a focus on the relationship between the emotional world and environmental context of the child. A developmental approach entails keeping in mind early childhood experiences and family dynamics, as evidenced in non-verbal ways through aggressive, hostile, and offensive behaviour, as well as language. This allows clinical intervention to be tailored to where a child is in terms of their emotional development and supports the school and family to manage daily difficulties that could become overwhelming.

My role allows me to be both an embedded member of the school team and an observer, bringing detailed observation from a psychoanalytic perspective to add to the team's formulation of ideas about a child's presentation and to draw attention to the importance of even very small developmental shifts.

In work with children, child psychotherapists offer assessment, brief or long-term individual therapy, group work, and the possibility of intensive psychotherapy for the most complex and challenging children. Work with a child is always accompanied by parallel work with parents or carers.

Children's group psychotherapy

For the most traumatized children in the PPRU, there is the opportunity for individual therapy, but all the children in the school participate in child psychotherapy small groups. It is work with groups that I focus on here.

As Susan Reid writes:

> The psychoanalytic therapy group explores relationships as they appear in the here and now of the group setting between members of the group, between individuals and the group leader or leaders, and between the group as a whole and the leaders. . . .
>
> The whole *raison d'être* of the therapy group, as in individual therapy, is meaning. An interest in meaning by all the members of the group is its aspiration. All communications, miscommunication and non-communications are treated as having significance and are therefore of interest to the therapist. The aim is that within the life of the group they will become of interest to the individual members and the group as a whole. [Reid, 1999, p. 253]

In the PPRU, I am often based in the classrooms. Classes are made up of relatively small numbers of children, who tend quickly to find a group identity with their teacher and other classroom-based staff. Children develop a relationship with the skilled teacher and feel contained by clear goals, targets for behaviour, and rewards and firm, consistent boundaries, with straightforward consequences. As well as being in a position to observe, together with colleagues I provide psychoanalytically informed group work in the classroom.

A typical psychotherapy group contains four or five children who have been moved from a range of primary schools in the borough. Children may have a history of having attacked staff and head teachers, and in some cases have been out of class since nursery. They may include some children who shout out, physically fight, snatch, and are highly distractible and provocative.

My aim with my fellow therapists and members of the class team is to allow some of the children's provocative, attacking, and offensive behaviour and language to happen in the group, so that it can be understood by the children and the staff as meaningful communication, promoting the children's capacity to understand themselves and others. The expectation is for the therapist and other staff to let the children find a way to communicate and interact with less external management than in lessons. There is a shared understanding that the children need to experience themselves as thoughtful, with positive skills and likeable personalities. For the children in the group, this is a process that starts with bodily expression and physicality and extends gradually to the capacity for language, play, playfulness, and humour and in being able to express feelings, thoughts, wishes, and beliefs.

During the psychotherapy group, members of the class staff team are also in the classroom. The challenge for the adults, including the therapists, is to resist the pressure to react instantly and to hold onto the mental/emotional functions of reflecting, reasoning, and linking. It is important for the children to feel that the therapist and staff team can survive attack and provocation. Some staff would rather not be present and struggle to tolerate the loosening of boundaries, while others have a capacity to tolerate, comment on, and try to understand what the children are communicating.

The children in each group have developed an attachment and a feeling of safety and predictability with their in-class support workers as well as with their teacher, and the introduction of a new pair of adults— the therapists—creates new anxiety. The idea that they draw what they want or negotiate how the group is organized feels like a test to them. The groups can generate a high level of emotion, including anger and competition, which can be difficult for the children and the adults.

Children who have not been socialized together or learned to recognize or manage their anger, frustration, and desire to be included benefit from these feelings and needs being attended to and thought about in the room. The children may seek the individual attention of the adults or may be highly sensitive about comments that are made. They are worried about their capacity to make and keep friends. There can be volatile exchanges leading to running out of the room or shouting and explosive rages.

The children are motivated because they want to be included in the group, and there is incentive to come back, join in, and gradually learn about the lives, interests, and minds of others. Within the group, the children can see the consequences and impact of their communications on others and notice their own responses to the other children. They begin to see, understand, and enjoy the personalities, weaknesses, and strengths of their peers.

I use drawing as a way of managing movement and activity, to anchor the children in an ordinary way, and to allow for non-verbal communication. They are asked to draw whatever they want. This can challenge them in terms of mobilizing their imagination and can activate a fear of lack of ability and of exposure to ridicule.

All the group members develop a memory of their own and others' struggle and development. The ground rules of psychotherapy, the regular, consistent times and the forming of shared group structures enable exploration of individual minds and group relationships. This exploration involves mapping a narrative of overcoming individual and group emotional difficulties and achieving developmental progress together, which in a group offers a powerful sense of achievement.

The classroom-based group work allows me to work with and contribute to an understanding of the complexities and development of most of the children in the Unit.

A young children's group

In the Young Group, the children are aged between 5 and 7 years. They usually lack the ability to experience and name feelings and states of mind, which would allow them to start to be able to play and to manage wishes and impulses rather than enacting them. When children are able to do this, they can begin to relate to other people as thinking and feeling as well.

Many of the children in the Young Group have limited language and extremely high anxiety with hyper-vigilance. They protect themselves from feeling intolerably vulnerable by pushing feelings of anxiety, threat, and alarm into others through their behaviour and language. Their shifts in behaviour can often appear to come out of nowhere, and the experience of the observers in the class can be that the switches of mood and mental states are random and meaningless.

Children with difficult early histories experience feelings as a threat of being overwhelmed and made helpless. They defend themselves by trying to impose rigid control on their environment, including their school and carers, and by denying and blanking out the experience of difference and separation. In this way they try to keep at bay their messy and desperate feelings and end up feeling both isolated and omnipotent.

The Young Group children need the capacity to structure and differentiate their emotional experience. This helps to prevent feeling overwhelmed and trapped in primitive magical thinking, which can embed a conviction that they are either very powerful or very bad. They need to learn to represent and symbolize their feelings and ideas through games, activities, and language, so they can begin to form the material of thinking and communication.

The Young Group, together with the class staff team, allows the child to feel secure enough to think. Limits are placed on enactment and aggression, and alternative ways of self-expression are developed. The children are encouraged to see the difference between fantasy and reality and to experience that the therapist and class staff team also know the difference. This helps them to begin to have genuine control over themselves and to be able to repair relationships; it allows them to acknowledge that they are young children rather than gangsters or powerful adults.

> The Young Group consists of five children, aged from 5 to 7 years. The children come in and settle down. One has been kept in for playtime and says, "Good, it's the group", and another child says, "Yes, it's home time." I say, "Yes, that's what you said last week. The group means it's home time." Another child says, "No, I like it—it's easy."

My co-worker and I represent outsiders to the children: outsiders who are going to ask them to express themselves with drawings and who will require some talk about their week, their ideas and thoughts, something potentially uncomfortable. One child seems pleased because the group signals the end of a playtime behaviour consequence, another child fast-forwards to home time, and yet another appears to like the group because it is easier than work. In different ways they let the therapists know they can resist the feelings stirred up by being in a group. The children rebuff our attempts to start this different sort of group. At the same time, they show us they are beginning to notice the reliability provided by the regular group time and structure. I am aware of the children's ambivalent feelings and encouraged that they are talking and saying what they think. Each small step towards trust and expressing themselves indicates incremental emotional change.

Although it is still early days in the life of the group, the consistency is acknowledged, the structure of the day is recognized, and the children are able to explore their responses.

> Jimmy, who has significant speech and language delay, is motivated to tell a long, detailed story about enjoying the game Roblox. He explains the game with words, drawings, and writing, using phonics and memory to write. The children are reminded to take turns and listen to each other. Jessie takes her jumper off and says how hot she is and goes to wash her hands and wipe her face. She embarks on a range of plausible activities in order to do her own thing, which appear reasonable but undermine the focus and purpose of the group. She then wants to go to the toilet, and I remind her about her going to the toilet last week having hidden a tin of Vaseline in her shoe and using it as lip gloss. I say that I think she can wait. My co-worker comments that walking with the Vaseline must have been difficult and uncomfortable.

Jessie acts out the wordless complexities of her individual needs. Through the use of her body, she tries bit by bit to take herself out of the group. She wants to put on a version of make-up, getting away from her own 6-year-old emotional needs. Simultaneously, she exploits the ordinary bodily requirements of a young child to see if the adults are engaged with her or distracted enough to let her leave. Her early experience of neglect has left her feeling safest when she is in control. Ordinary adult boundary-setting does not make her feel safe: rather, it makes the therapists seem unreasonable and unfair to her. In this situation, the task is to show that we understand her by providing structure to keep her in the group. This helps her to start to distinguish emotional communication that is reasonably straightforward from communication that is muddled or distorted.

> Larry and Peter get excited, drawing themselves and Roblox cars, and then become more excited making a drawing of pushing girls off a tower. Jessie, who has been distracted, leans over and invites Marie to come to play with her at a play space with her carer. Marie says that her parents would not allow this until she is 9, which is in two years' time. The rejected Jessie draws a large and extremely angry face, describing this as herself being mad with her carer, and then draws her carer as very small and thin. She starts to write down the names of the children in the group.

The boys have been aware of the attention focusing on Jessie and gang up excitedly to get their revenge on the girls. Jessie's offer to Marie partly attempts to build an alliance against the boys and partly tries to pull away from the group experience into a fantasy that she and Marie are already good friends, when in fact the girls have only a very precarious connection. Marie then feels that she must be very clear she wants nothing of this unreal overture of friendship. She feels she needs to bring her parents in as protection. Jessie expresses her anger and hurt effectively on paper. Perhaps the small, insignificant carer/adult in Jessie's picture is linked in her mind with a therapist–me: a picture that does have a carer–therapist–me in it, while the caring potential is belittled.

The experience of remaining in the group and of not having been able to split Marie and herself into a separate girls' group allows Jessie to begin to use the group for the help she really needs.

> Jessie says she has a problem, as she has baby dolls at home and wants to feed them. She moves her head from side to side, touching her shoulders. I ask the other children to listen and think about her problem. She says she has a packet of baby food, and her carer will not let her feed the baby, which has a hole for its mouth. The children listen, and Larry says that the doll is not real and it would break. Jessie says she has broken dolls before, like Baby Annabel. Peter leans back and thinks hard about how to play and feed the baby. I suggest that it is a pretend baby, and that this is the difference. Peter says that he goes to his cousin's house, and she has loads of dolls, which give him nightmares, and that he does not like their faces. He draws the faces. Marie draws a self-portrait, saying this is her with messy just-got-up-in-the-morning hair.

> Larry refers back to the earlier invitation from Jessie to Marie to come and play and says, "Maybe your parents don't have enough money", and Marie agrees that "You have to have enough to pay the bills." She says that her mother was cooking eggs, and the electric went off, and they had to go to the shop to turn the electric back on.

The children have begun to allow their hungry, messy, broken, baby selves and their nightmares a space to be thought about. They begin to listen, respond, and talk about their real-life concerns. Jessie is able to express her emerging need to understand her own baby feelings and early history, and the boys can then start to take her seriously. The children's real-life family experiences of not having enough money or resources and their real emotional experiences of not having had enough of what they need becomes group work.

The children have begun to trust that the adults in the group will be consistent and to feel that they represent a belief in the value of talking and expressing themselves. They make links with each other and the adults and want to take the risk of trying to develop a creative way to be together. They begin to see and differentiate the feelings and experiences in the group and to work out what is real and what is unreal.

> This group returns the following week, and my co-worker and I try to sum up the content of the last six weeks and to prepare for the half-term holiday. We talk about how the children were when we first knew them and how they have developed and changed.
>
> Larry asks if it is a two-week holiday, and I say no, that it is one week, and he says he likes the two-week holiday, and when is it.

The group shows their fragility as they become aware of the break. On behalf of the group, Larry voices the need to know what the structure is and to check whether the absence will be two weeks, one week, or possibly forever. Ordinary endings and returns are not manageable for the children, and they want not to need the group or the therapists and to be able to look after themselves.

> All the children appear agitated and distracted, and Marie, who is older and is seen as a leader, is quiet and noticeably less spontaneous and relaxed than in previous weeks. She seems to have withdrawn. I notice and make a comment about this. Marie denies this, and my co-worker says that she has been silent and not joining in the class. The children's anxiety increases. Larry excitedly draws Spiderman, and there is talk about playing the Spiderman video game, which is a sixteen rating, so he is not permitted to play. Jessie responds to the anxiety by drawing in an angry and destructive way. I notice she does not have her glasses on. The group appears to be in a state of near-collapse.

Marie has a powerful presence, and her withdrawal influences the children. It was her silence and bottling up of anger, followed by few, but extreme outbursts, that led to her exclusion from mainstream school. The impending holiday break from the group leads to regression to some of their previous ways of managing: excited enjoyment of unsuitable older-child games and retreat to repressed, wordless anger. The group's defences intensify: they try to be bigger and more powerful than they are, or silent and not able to see any more.

> I talk about the week's holiday break that is coming. There is a discussion about how the girls had been talking together well at playtime, and Jessie

says she had splashed Marie with a muddy puddle because Marie had not shared a bottle of bubbles. I ask about this, and Marie says she would not share and does not care. We talk about friendship, sharing, and revenge, and Marie answers in a clipped, brief way. Marie leaves the room to go home, and Jessie says, "Bye, I'll miss you." When the door closes, she says, "Actually, I won't miss her", which leads to more discussion about faking your feelings and not saying what you think and how difficult it is to trust.

This example of the Young Group focuses on the challenge of helping the children build trust with adults and peers in order for them to move from what they feel is the safest option of trying to control their own needs and environment. The move is from dependence on their own resources to a more developmentally helpful dependence on others, peers and adults, to help them learn and explore their feelings and experiences.

A year in the life of an older children's psychotherapy group

There is also a group for older children, between 7 and 9 years old, which runs through the school year with two therapists and other adults from the class available to facilitate and participate. I describe a group of four boys with a potent mix of personalities. The boys had complex histories and family arrangements. The themes linking them were exclusion from and idealization of the schools they had left behind, where, they felt, they were popular and had friends. The boys were lacking in confidence, with extreme anxiety about failing.

In school, the boys often joined together in denigrating the PPRU and in locating their difficulties in other children in the school (and in me during the group), who were then perceived as the problem. They often considered questions and comments from adults to be nosy, and they were suspicious of and defensive about all communication. Their differences in culture and background were usually not acknowledged or explored, though partly seen through their taste in clothes, video games, and food.

In the group, the children began to enjoy doing things together and to develop respect for each other's skills and curiosity about their differences. They found themselves starting to enjoy adults' interest and understanding. Over time, they became a little less defensive, and each child felt part of the group, until, as the year drew to its end, it was far harder for this to be sustained.

I describe briefly a year in the life of this children's psychotherapy group, presenting the development of the group dynamic rather than individual children. I explore anxiety, conflict, and the gradual emergence of new group capacities to express feelings and thoughts and to exercise care and concern for the group. I show the relationship between the group therapists and the children, including the way the therapists are seen and treated, and how this changes over time.

At the beginning of the school year, children in the older class who have not encountered a child psychotherapy approach before are initially surprised by the group boundaries, expectations, and ways of talking being different from the classroom activities they are used to. Usually they want to wait and see what happens.

> One child shouts at me and wears ear defenders, which he has been using in class, to partially block out and so tolerate or ignore my words. The children talk about their old school and their feeling of loss and tell each other about the great friends and good times they had there.

> In the new group, the children are motivated to be friends with others but do not know how. Some children can bear sitting at the same table, but others need to be able to leave the room with an adult or sit at another table and return when they feel calmer, when they will be welcomed back. It is common for some of these children to need to filter their experience with ear defenders. A child will sometimes be able to draw and begin to find a route in to talk about their life and family, while others find this too exposing and feel anxious about letting anyone know personal matters. Some children have no experience of being interested in other people or of listening: they communicate by relentlessly pointing out flaws in the others. The group also begins to cohere around excluding me as the therapist.

> As the group develops, there is more expression of fear and anger directed at me and my co-therapist, allowing us to experience what it is like to be excluded and feel hated.

> One child refuses to allow me to speak or listen to him. He says he is angry and frightened of me because I am old. Other children defend me, and he begins to experience that he is not able to control my function as the facilitator. This child walks out of the group in order to recover, for a moment perhaps a bit more in touch with the reality that he cannot manage his environment and relationships in this way. The child is easily upset and defeated by the other children but can focus on pushing his rage into me. There is the opportunity to observe the interplay between a quiet, subdued, undermining aspect of the child— and of the group—and a frightened and explosive aspect that attempts to resist the adults.

The children begin to understand that the two therapists will turn up at the same time every week, will be able to survive the group's attacks, and will remember what happened in the previous weeks. They will continue to remember the group's history and return to it and continue to be able to survive attacks.

Some of the staff team are in the group and can manage the need for children to take time out and return. They are able to allow more understanding of the group's need to express anger, noticing the changes and times when a more fluid, genuine communication begins to happen.

The children begin to build up a narrative of their time together and the development of their relationships in a more shared, authentic way with an exploration of the difficulties and vulnerabilities that have undermined their development. They notice that they miss other children when they are absent and that they miss the group when they cannot attend. It becomes possible to talk about and prepare for staff leaving and the acknowledgement of loss and affection allows more exploration of shared and different heritage, which had previously been too sensitive. One boy talks about the respect that people from his country have for old people, who are called aunty and uncle, and this seems linked to the beginnings of respect for me as the "too old" person. A child talks about their siblings and another boy expresses a longing for siblings that he would look after for his mother. A further discussion about each of their country's foods leads to an end-of-term party, arranged by the children, which includes food, music, and dancing for the adults and children.

In a group before the end of term and Christmas, the children are keen to draw and are more reluctant to talk about the previous week, or about how and if they want to mark the end of term or Christmas as a group. They all stay together, no one leaves, and all remain seated. One boy is gifted and spontaneous with his drawing, and he works with another boy, supporting each other. The other child is helped to write, draw, and express himself. The boys do not want to talk or reflect, but one of the group expresses his satisfaction at working together to get what they want, which is to draw rather than talk.

As the group progresses, the children develop their communicative skills, and tentative friendships form. The children also develop a group identity, initially to try to stop me talking, and feel proud that they can begin to find some agency as a group. At times, the children resort to a gang state of mind, which for this group is still valuable as a new and collective experience of building relationships, allowing for a group state of mind to develop (Canham, 2002).

The children begin to relate to what goes on in each other's minds. The angry child starts to identify with the creative child and can draw a volcano, which he has become fascinated with, as a topic. The children join together to stop me being the therapist. They ask why I always want to know what they are doing and tell me what a pain I am. The group agrees about how annoying I am. The group atmosphere changes as someone says how much they hate their lives. He gets drowned out by other group members making baby crying and toddler noises.

The volcano theme and the disaster theme continue in the following weeks. The children all begin to draw and to include the disaster imagery of each child in their own picture. This helps the group to find a space for different aspects of each other's personality and for an understanding of each other in an inclusive way, which starts to show a capacity for allowing change to happen.

Sometimes children must leave the Unit because of a decision about the education placement or a home situation. The group is able to help a child deal with this painful process, letting him use ear defenders, go out of the room and return, hold a soft toy, and sit away from the group in a quiet space. The group's ability to manage intimacy and emotional exposure is important.

The remaining children are able to feel they have played a part in caring for the child who left. This helps them accommodate painful feelings of loss of their friend, combined with relief that an extremely demanding group member has left, and guilt that the group has in some way excluded him. They return with excitement to the drawing and connection that had been made during the previous week; excitement perhaps protecting them from the more uncomfortable feelings.

The children continue to incorporate each other's images into their own work. The child with the volcano decides to draw himself rescuing the children in the group from the volcanic ash fallout. The children adapt their disaster pictures, now drawing adults involved in rescuing them with grappling hooks. I am included as the pilot of the helicopter containing all the other adults, rescuing the children from destruction.

The following week, when one child goes out of the group, another child draws a racing car with both of them in it together. The other children beg to be in his picture, and extra windows are drawn so that the whole group can be included.

Towards the end of this group's year, the children are able to draw and observe each other, to have ideas about how the others think and feel.

They begin to explore their own feelings and questions about life and families. As the group ends, with the group members moving to the newness and uncertainty of different classes, changes in structure, and relationships, old group behaviour reappears. This ordinary regression happens at the end of all group years and will continue to occur during emotionally demanding times, though the developmental work remains to be built on.

The reflective space for staff

As Monica Lanyado (2009) writes, staff who work in these settings are on the receiving end of ferocious, violent, disturbing behaviour, verbal and non-verbal. The work can be rewarding but also upsetting, frightening, and overwhelming. The staff experience needs to be attended to within the day-to-day functioning of the setting. If this does not happen, the staff can become unhelpfully defended against the impact of the children's communications. She considers that without the safeguard of the reflective space, staff can become exhausted and emotionally burnt out.

Lanyado points out that some of the defences that arise are essential for staff to continue to function: she cites the dark humour to be found in most humane caring organizations. However, emotional defences in organizations can be just as counterproductive, destructive, and resistant to change as in individuals.

In the PPRU, the impact of work with disturbed children and the differences in roles and expectations of professionals from education, health, social care, and CAMHS need consideration, through a different kind of working together.

The potential for division and taking polarized positions, for disowning one's own uncomfortable feelings and relating to others in such a way as to get others to feel the discomfort instead, is intensified when the pressure of being on the receiving end of violence, aggression, verbal abuse, and extended states of acting out is constant. The distress of witnessing and managing provocation combined with the task of educating the same provocative children can feel relentless and, at times, not possible to think about. The challenge of teaching, mentoring, or providing therapy to children who are distracted, disorganized, and dissociated can lead to feelings of being deskilled and a low sense of achievement in the staff team.

The PPRU clinical psychologist and child psychotherapist attempt to address some of this experience in the weekly reflective space, which takes place on a Friday afternoon. The whole team takes part, including the heads of school. This offers potential for the whole staff to listen and contribute. The reflective space can feel threatening, exposing, overly emotional, or irrelevant to its members some of the time. There can be a pull to make it into a business meeting, or a social and humorously bantering group, but the group does meet together to think about the important challenges and the meaning of the communications and relational interactions in the week.

There has been considerable discussion about how this group should run and whether it is really necessary, and what the task should be. The time is regular, and the group is consistent, although there are often child-related incidents and general exhaustion at the end of the day. The group is not a therapy group, and it is not designed to investigate staff team functioning, although I think that the coming together with some possibility of sharing and support can helpfully limit reactive group dynamics. The group has settled down to be a place to process the experience of the week without a set agenda—to communicate as a team. The focus of the group tends to be the impact of children on staff that week, and this can lead to different observations and seeing issues from differing perspectives. Developing a deeper understanding of complex issues then offers a greater capacity for reality-based hopefulness about outcomes.

The reflective group discussions allow for difficult conversations to take place in a safe-enough way. The tensions involved in managing the balance between tight boundaries with adult control and what can be perceived as a softer, empathic, and understanding-led approach has the potential both for dividing the team and for re-enacting emotional conflicts intrinsic to the child or family brought for discussion. The group is usually between 18 and 20 people. Some people do not speak and do not like silences, all want to go home, and there is the expectation that this group is a team requirement. The class teams come together with the PPRU heads and senior leadership, CAMHS clinicians, and other associated staff. The group can take some time to cohere, but with encouragement someone will begin to talk about an incident or a child.

Staff may bring issues relating to the connection between children's early history and their current behaviour. Discussion often centres on an example of a complex dilemma.

> A recent example was that of sexualized behaviour by a young child with a history of neglect and early sexual abuse. Staff brought their dilemmas: how to both keep the other children safe and avoid a heavily watchful approach, which could deny the child's need to play; how to manage the situation without positioning the child only as a perpetrator; how to keep in mind the child as a victim of pre-verbal trauma, which needed to be understood by the team and eventually by the child.

The child at the centre of this reflective space discussion was in intensive psychotherapy (three times weekly), and the child psychotherapist talked to the team in general terms about the type of play observed in the therapy room, showing how play could open up exploration and development of a narrative for the child of their early experiences. This discussion did not break confidentiality but offered the team a wider understanding of the complexity of the child's emotional state and of the value of the treatment. It also helped to sustain the team's continuing commitment to support the therapy, sometimes including accompanying the child to their session or sitting outside the therapy room to help manage the child's anxiety—valuable at both practical and emotional levels.

Issues relating to the impact of external factors on development are also brought for discussion:

In one group someone brought a perceptive observation of a child continually changing seats. This generated discussion about the child's emotional and behavioural deterioration, the slowing of developmental and learning progress, a return to a dissociated state, and a lack of engagement. The group talked about the difficult reality of kinship care, which was the child's home situation. They considered their task of working to improve a child's experience and noticing progress and the challenge of working with ongoing, complex extended family dynamics. To begin with, discussion focused on what happens to useful boundaries that have been maintained when safeguarding, social care, and court cases are happening, but that become less secure when the court cases are settled and care arrangements are established. The group talked about how the reality of increased contact with other family members can be unsettling for the kinship care placement. There was more serious talk about how hard it can be for Unit staff to build and sustain for several years positive relationships with children and families. This difficulty was described in relation to the reality of children's outcomes, including transition to secondary schools and school leaving, which are particularly challenging with a background of gangs and violence on the streets near the school. In this context, noticing children's progress and having faith in their capacity to develop was felt to be the main task.

In another reflective space, I was aware of an exhausted staff group at the end of Friday, in a transitional space between the intense, focused hard work of the school week and the coming release of the weekend:

I asked about a girl who was looking increasingly unwell: thin, greyish in skin colour, and with a vivid bruise caused by self-harm. The discussion focused on medication and its timings and the child's deterioration as the effect of the medication wore off. I became frustrated that the child, who had been in the school for a long time, was being talked about as a medication-only problem. I asked how she was emotionally, whether she had any friends, and whether she was interested in anything now.

The focus shifted to the child's improved behaviour since her arrival at the school. The reduction in her violent attacks on other children and staff and her growing capacity to learn seemed linked to the staff's increased understanding of her difficulties and family situation. The staff group talked about the chronic traumatic experience for children of living in households with domestic violence. They connected this to their experience of the highly anxious, hypervigilant girl and their own struggle to understand and develop a relationship with her while keeping her safe. The group noted that at this point in time the school and its staff were being blamed by the family and professional network for the child's ongoing difficulties. The discussion moved to the need for children to develop and move on and the difficulties for everyone—the family, the professional network, and school staff—of tolerating an impasse, with hostility, blame, and hopelessness getting passed around the system between parents, school, and health. A staff member suggested that the task was not to save the children or to create something miraculous: rather, that improving reading, writing, and maths and giving the children this advantage and keeping them in school was the brief. The group ended with the idea that hope needed to be maintained.

The Unit staff have to manage their feelings of attachment to the children as they begin to move on, especially when they have worked hard to better understand the complexity of parent/child relationships and other aspects of the child's life. Reflective groups may be used to talk about the Year 6 children who are making the transition to secondary school, some of whom have been in the school for a long time.

A group talked about two girls getting together to gang up on a boy by saying things quietly to him. Someone in the staff group said, "It's that Mean Girl's time." A class teacher said that one of the girls, Gemma, had told her that she was lonely and worried that the new school children will know she came from the PPRU and that she does not know how to behave. She had started her periods, had not been washing her hair, and had been smelly. Her class teacher was concerned that Gemma felt her body had let her down.

Another teacher talked about a boy who did not want his mother to take him to school until he is in Year 8, as she had suggested. There was a discussion about the progress this boy had made, although he was anxious about which mainstream school he would go to.

The therapists talked about a boy in the same class who gave them a heavy feeling when he said they were tricking him into doing Mindfulness and group work. He had told the therapists that they had no consent and were trying to use therapy by trickery. The child felt oppressed by the help that was offered.

The staff group reflected on these uncomfortable feelings, and then congratulations were offered to a family worker on her successful work with a parent. The group moved back to think about other Year 6 children. A child was considered to have done well in a difficult situation, and he had tried to support the boy who felt tricked by therapy by saying, "Therapy is not so bad, and what harm is there, and it is helpful." The group proposed setting up a peer support group for Year 6 children to talk about bodily changes. They talked about how to help the boy with the anxious mother and about the embarrassment of over-familiarity. There was a sensitive discussion about how to continue to support the children as they leave the relationships in the school.

A staff member talked about meeting a former pupil now working in a supermarket. She said he had told her he had passed his driving test now, and that he had not realized how far behind he was with school learning until he went to mainstream school. This idea of a continuing connection with pupils helped the staff group to think about the loss of the children they knew so well, whose futures they worried about. They felt heartened by a sense of the capacity the children did have to make use of their time at the school and the longer term impact that this experience could have.

This meeting ended with a discussion about a successful review of a child where the family worker had worked in a non-challenging but determined way over a lengthy period with complex parents, who were then able to feel less blamed. The whole staff team had been able to work together to reduce polarized division and the disowning and passing around of painful feelings in the child and family system.

Conclusion

The complex needs of children who are educated in the PPRU require a thoughtful and resilient multidisciplinary approach to meet the wide-ranging issues presented. This needs collaboration between education, health and social care, parents, and children to generate a return to positive development and achievement. The PPRU works with the complexities of behaviour and emotional presentation, which need to be met by resilience, consistency, imagination, and understanding. Child psychotherapy contributes to this task with regular, dependable child psychotherapy groups for children and through sharing the facilitation of the staff reflective space.

The groups all feature reluctance to come together to talk about feelings. The children and the adults, including the other facilitators and I, are aware that the serious work of thinking and talking has the potential for painful, poignant, angry, or aggressive feelings to arise at any point. There is a shared resistance to facing fears and conflicts, but the groups are brave and risk exposure, disagreement, and possible ridicule. The children's groups and the staff reflective group work to acknowledge loss and limitations in order to see what they have achieved and to realize how important incremental changes are.

CHAPTER ELEVEN

A parent's experience of child psychotherapy approaches in a primary pupil referral unit: Lena

Interview by Milly Jenkins

Alek was 7 years old and on the brink of permanent exclusion from his primary school when he moved to a pupil referral unit. He had been struggling since nursery, but his behaviour deteriorated seriously in the first few years of school, leaving both his parents and his teachers at crisis point by Year 2. He had been seen by CAMHS, but his angry and often violent outbursts continued.

Here, Alek's mother, Lena, returns to the unit to talk about that difficult time, the move to specialist school, and their experiences there, including the long-term individual and group psychotherapy the unit provided alongside specialist teaching, mental health, and social care assessments, and parent work. She is joined by Alek's long-term therapist, Fiona Henderson, who worked with him both individually and in groups.

Alek was one of the younger children at the unit; soon after he arrived, he was diagnosed with autistic spectrum disorder. He stayed until the end of Year 6, when he made a successful transition back to mainstream education, where he has remained.

Lena: hard times and transitions

Lena: Alek was a very angry little boy. He was like a rocket, just ploughing through life, not knowing his own strength. He couldn't understand or physically control his emotions and

DOI: 10.4324/9781003185925-15

feelings. We could see something was wrong early on and then at nursery, but it was when he got to Reception that he just went crackers, really. I thought he might have to go to a residential school, that he'd end up being taken off me. He was kicking, biting, spitting—me and the teachers. He couldn't cope, especially in groups, in the playground, with all the kids and noise, and he couldn't understand why he didn't think and feel the same as other children. He really wrestled with that. He was in so much mental pain, and it was heart-breaking, soul-destroying, to watch. I feel upset thinking about it now. Because there was the lovely side of him, wonderful and caring, but he just couldn't control himself.

At home he was bouncing off the walls. He had that much energy. I would sit in the park for hours, trying to get him to run if off. I couldn't take my eyes off him, because he was so unpredictable; any second something could happen. He could be a danger to himself or someone else. So I literally had to shadow him, and that meant he had no place to breathe. His older sister told me recently that she hated him then—hated coming home to the noise, the chaos, him destroying all her things in fits of rage and jealousy. Alek found it very hard to share me, and, sadly, that did lead to me and his father splitting up—or, at least, that was part of it.

You want your child to be happy, and he wasn't happy, so I was overcompensating, giving him all my attention, and our relationship got very tight. I think I got a bit obsessive, and we became quite dependent on each other. I didn't have a life outside him, and it was isolating. We couldn't do play dates, we couldn't go to parties. I was never, ever away from him. I couldn't get a babysitter, and if I did, they'd never come again. People do judge you. When you say that, people say: "You're paranoid. They're not judging you." But they are. When they see a kid go as crazy as Alek could, they're judging you.

I had been to the GP when he was little, because I was worried. He was a nice boy, but his behaviour wasn't showing that. I was told: "Wait till he's older." There was a lot of onus on milestones. "It's the terrible twos." Then: "He's coming out of the terrible twos later than most children. . . . He's adjusting to nursery. . . . He's adjusting to Reception." I said: "I'm telling you. It's not that simple. It's more complicated." We went to CAMHS for a while, about six sessions, but he was OK in a one-to-one situation, better with adults than children, quite charming. It was being in a group that he couldn't handle, and they didn't get to see that. We got some help at home from a family support worker, and he was really getting through to Alek, but then that got taken away: I was told we lived one street out of the right area for funding.

With budget cuts and the pressure to get perfect Ofsted reports, lots of schools just don't want to deal with these difficulties. These children are just an inconvenience. That's how I felt treated. I'd drop him off and be called back to get him five minutes later. It was getting to the point where that was four or five times a week. He didn't see the SENCo. He wasn't offered therapy. He had lots of exclusions. I knew permanent exclusion was coming, and I wanted him to believe that moving to a unit was a choice we had made, me and him, that it was a positive thing, that they hadn't made him go but that I'd taken him. So I begged the local authority to let him come here. If exclusion was going to happen, why drag it out? Why put him through more pain?

I was a broken woman when we arrived here. Most mothers are. Going to a supermarket was like Armageddon. Just getting a loaf of bread, you'd be thinking: "Oh my god. Get in and out as quick as you can." I remember being in a queue in a pound shop with Alek when he was 5 and an old man telling him not to suck his thumb and Alek saying to this 80-year-old: "I'm going to fucking do you." I remember thinking: "I'm *never* leaving the house again. I'll shop online." I wondered: "What the hell is going to happen to him in life?" He had no boundaries at all.

His morale and confidence was at zero when he came here. He sat under a table and screamed for the first week. There were lots of bigger kids, and I think he found that intimidating. I think he also felt ashamed: that this is where you come if you're bad. He was a handful. He could be violent, but he could also snap back to being charming, and when he's vulnerable, he's so loving. He's very cute to look at, so he can get away with a lot. But here there was nowhere to hide. They don't just say: "You're naughty." They say: "Well, let's find out why you're naughty." It felt like an environment where there were people with expertise and that they'd seen this a thousand times before.

Quite early on, they said they thought he might have ASD, high-functioning, and he got diagnosed at the local social communications assessment service. That was a long process, lots of appointments. They don't just say: "Yes, he's autistic." He has complex behavioural difficulties, and he now has quite a complex Education, Health and Care Plan. The diagnosis was a relief, I think, for everybody. There was a feeling of: "*Now* we've got something to work with."

But I felt scared at first, too, here. It's the fear of the unknown. There were things I found hard and disagreed with. I didn't like the quiet room. If he'd had a very bad episode—crying, screaming, kicking—he'd have to go in the quiet room, and he'd be so upset after, like broken, sweat pouring off him, and you'd think: "Hang on a minute, what the hell has been going on here?" But it had to be done, because whatever he was doing in there he had been doing to somebody outside the room.

Also, everyone has to do an assessment with the social worker when they arrive here, and you feel you're being watched. You wonder if there's going to be a blame game, if you need to withhold your thoughts and feelings because they'll be written down. You don't know if you can trust them and feel a bit paranoid. I didn't care about people gossiping about me in the playground at his old school, but I did care, when I came here, about whether they thought I was a bad parent. The best thing is when someone says: "No, you're not, you just need a bit of help." You think: "Thank God. I didn't think I was." So there was relief. Somebody saying: "It's OK. We're going to help you." Also, for the first time since he was born, I got some time to myself, because they don't call you to come and get him every day.

Lena and Fiona: the therapeutic process

Fiona: It was hard for Alek and Lena when they arrived. I think the children feel shame, just terrible about coming here. And parents do, too. Unfortunately everyone is starting with an experience of exclusion, and there can be a lack of trust, a feeling of being observed. I remember Alek in the early days screaming, piercing screaming, and him being violent. It was extreme and disturbing. He was a very articulate, clever boy, charming, but he could also be very personal and undermining. I think he was lonely. He wanted friends, but he just didn't know how to do it. He had no tolerance of others or the idea that anyone else had a right to their own thoughts, their own mind.

Lena: Yes, that stubbornness: "I'm right. You're wrong." Very strong in his convictions. And he would try to find a way in his head to never be at fault but would then get trapped in his own righteousness. And, because he's articulate, his language could be adult, and he could be very personal when he's angry. He really knows how to push people's buttons: "You're stupid. I don't care who you are and how much training you've got."

Fiona: So I saw him, from early on, for individual weekly therapy, and that continued throughout his time here.

Lena: I didn't have any doubts about him having therapy. I felt like we needed every bit of help we could get. He loved coming to see you.

Fiona: Well, he liked the attention, being able to talk about whatever most interested him, and he had lots of particular interests.

Lena: Sharks and dinosaurs! It's unbelievable what a sponge of information he was and is. I now know everything about dinosaurs. I could do them as my subject on Mastermind. And it's an art form, being able to look interested in dinosaurs for hours.

Fiona: Yes, what was charming was how interested he was in everything, but, like you are saying, it could be at some cost to the adult. But what happened, gradually, after lots and lots of him talking, was that he very slowly became more interested in me, in having a mutual relationship. I think he realized it was a problem and became interested in having relationships and not just talking about what *he* was interested in.

Lena: He also started coming to see Fiona with things that had happened, that were bothering him.

Fiona: Yes. But the real challenge for Alek was being in a group, and because of that, he and I had a very different experience in group therapy. He was really difficult with me there, so argumentative, so confrontational, relentless, very hard work, totally deskilling and impossible!

Lena: It must have been so hard for you. I don't know how you did it . . .

Fiona: Well, I believe in the process. And this happens a lot with children here—they love the attention of individual work, it suits them, but they feel very provoked by the group situation. So helping them with socialization is a real challenge, and Alek had enormous difficulties around control, needing to be in control, with having to share me with anyone else. Losing is also a real difficulty for the children here; they haven't been able to play with other children: because of their difficulties they've spent all their time with their mums, so they haven't had any experience of taking turns.

Lena: Yes, they don't know how to interact in the playground, because they've have had so little experience of it. In his old school Alek would last ten seconds in a game of football at break, because if someone got the ball off him, that was it, they were going down and he was off.

Fiona: I think individual therapy began to put Alek more in touch with what he was missing in terms of friendship and understanding people. He could be upset that people weren't friends with him, that he was on his own, and he began to be more interested in talking about these things. He began to learn that it wasn't acceptable, how he treated people, and to realize he could lose a lot—good things, like having friendships. He became a bit more remorseful, a bit more thoughtful, a bit less black-and-white. He got a more nuanced understanding of how the world works and that he wasn't the centre of it. Something became a bit lighter for him.

Lena: Yes, I think that's right. He was "heavy" before, because life *is* a heavy burden when you think everyone is so stupid.

Fiona: I think in the group work he needed to have the experience of taking turns and listening to others again and again and again. And he really wanted to be part of the group—as all excluded children do, they want to be in the group. Alek had felt alienated, so, when he started getting interested in other people—"what are all these others about"—that was an important part of the process, trying to allow other people in, and to feel empathy.

Lena: Yes, he lacked empathy. And now he has tons of it. Sometimes I have to reassure him: "It's OK. They're fine." He's quite extreme like that. But he also has friends now. He's in a WhatsApp group that's constantly pinging. I think he's realized how beneficial it can be to bite your tongue, that sometimes you've got to be kind if you're going to enjoy the social side of things. That is still a difficulty—thinking before he speaks. But he also has a girlfriend now, and I think girls quite like him because what you see is what you get. There are no mind games. He'll tell you exactly what he's thinking!

Fiona: It is amazing that he's in a class with 30 children now, given he couldn't really cope with four or five before. I don't think therapy is a quick fix. It doesn't always fix things "now". But I think the conversations you have in therapy can go on working. I think there is a sleeper effect. What happens in one setting can then help in the next.

Lena: Yes and back then it took a long time for things to change—till Year 6, really. In the first four years there were little, subtle differences. You'd miss them if you blinked, but they were still a relief. To see him laugh! To come here and hear him laughing about something, having fun, that was huge. He also began learning. His attitude had been: "I can't read, so I won't read."

He felt above it. If he couldn't do it the first time, then he gave up. I think it was to do with feeling vulnerable, about not being the cleverest in the room, so he'd try to disguise that.

But he developed a strong relationship with his teacher and went from not reading to reading literally anything. He allowed himself to trust her, and she really got to know him, inside out, which is very nice for a child that has been misunderstood a lot. I always say about here that nobody would do this job, and take the abuse, if they didn't love the kids and want to help. The staff form strong relationships with kids who've never had relationships before because they can't maintain them. Then the kids start feeling safe and wanted.

There was a discussion in Year 6 about whether he should continue his therapy, did he need the extra hour in class? But he said: "No, I really want to carry on." I felt we couldn't take that away. He really trusted Fiona. In his head, I think he thought he was the most special person to Fiona. He'd be like: "What's she going to do without me? It's not fair on her. I don't want to upset her."

Support for parents, and parents supporting each other

Lena: You could get support here every day, coming in. But I also got referred for some counselling and did that for about six months. They thought I might have a bit of Post-Traumatic Stress Disorder, from all our struggles, getting kicked. . . . You've gone through a lot by the time you get here. I was in such a weak and vulnerable state. My life revolved around him, and containing him, and it was exhausting.

The autism assessment service also had an EarlyBird course for parents, and that changed our lives. Parents don't like being told they might have to do it a different way, because parenting is personal, but I think I realized, this is not working for this child. I was low in confidence. It was like I was kicking my legs underwater and getting nowhere. For me the challenge was discipline. I felt so sorry for Alek, that he couldn't help it, that it was punishment enough how he was feeling. But I learnt about structure and routine, and that was key for Alek.

I learnt about picture charts, that he needed to know what he was doing every second of the day to feel safe, about giving him warnings, about seeing things through. I had to untrain your brain to stop you doing the things you've been doing. But the woman there said to me: "You'll do it this new way so many times, it will become normal." So if he broke something or lashed out, I'd tell him I was going to take it away, and why. I'd take it away and tell him when he could get it back and what I'd expect him to do to get it back, and not give in after an hour, which I used to do . . . stuck to my guns. Together with the counselling, I became more confident in my parenting. And the stronger I became, the safer he felt, because he could tell I was in control. He had been running our lives for a long time, running the house. I think they saw a big difference in me here, over the years.

There was also a group for parents here, and there'd be different topics and themes, but really it was about getting together and offloading. After a few months, I thought: "Thank you, Jesus, for this group." It feels like the first time you've got people not judging you, that you're not embarrassed in front of, because whatever your child has done, their child has done, too, and that's huge. You'd be like: "You'll never guess what he did the other day . . ." But you'd be laughing, not crying, because they knew where you were coming from. I was lucky, because I had a lot in common with the mums here at the time. They were "joining-in" mums, like me. I am still good friends with them. So it did something for me socially, too. We could go out together with the kids, because we weren't going to be embarrassed in front of each other.

Progress, setbacks, and getting ready for secondary school

Lena: So there were subtle changes, but things went on being hard for Alek. I still had to be spoken to four times a week at pick-up. He'd just laugh when he was in trouble and think everybody else was wrong. But something happened in Year 6, where he just decided he was going to stop a lot of things, that he was going to try to be good, that he wasn't going to act like that any more, and that he wanted to go to mainstream secondary school.

There was a serious incident at the beginning of Year 6, and I think that was the start of him changing. He'd lashed out and kicked a teacher in the head with football boots on, concussed him, and was excluded, which is serious here. But he was broken, devastated, to have hurt someone he knew well. It scared him, and I think it's the first time I knew him to feel real shame. A lot of teachers would have refused to teach him again, but this one didn't, didn't give up on him, and they stayed friends.

For the children here, getting back into mainstream is seen as *the* prize. They're very competitive and combative about everything, here, even about who's got the sharpest pencil, so going back to mainstream feel likes being the "winner". I think it was part of his stubbornness and being very strong in his convictions. He also convinced himself that the change was all down to him. "None of you did anything!"

But when he got accepted into secondary school, it was gobsmacking, everybody was gobsmacked, because even quite far into Year 6 no one had any expectations of that. I had been feeling really scared again at the thought of him going to a specialist secondary school, now knowing what it was going to be like, would it be violent with the older kids, not knowing what he'd come up against. I had started the appeals process. Looking back, I felt the local authority should have given more support with that transition process.

Fiona: It was amazing that he went back to mainstream, because a lot of our children don't, and, if they do, they don't stay. I think the staff are scared, too, during that process; they don't know what will happen and how the children will manage the transitions.

Lena: And he has stayed. He has a teaching assistant hovering around like a helicopter, because he can't be left to his own devices for too long. So he gets a lot of one-to-one in class, and that keeps him really focused. He needs that, because he's obsessed with what everyone else is doing and whether they're behaving. He has a pass for leaving class when it gets too much, but he's gone from using that about 18 times a day to about three.

He did nearly get kicked out once when a kid shoved him and he took it too far, kicked off in the classroom, went on a rampage. But he felt awful, real remorse, and then said: "I've decided I'm not doing that again. I'm going to get A*s." I've been getting texts this year saying how well he's doing. I said: "Why didn't you just do that before?!" I also say to him: "Just get to the end of Year 11, and then you can get to college and do something you're interested in." We have to focus on what's working, because he finds it very hard not to be good at things. But he has found something he's really good at, that he wants to do—design—and that makes him feel worthy.

He has therapy once a week in school and has done for a few years. He enjoys that, like he did seeing Fiona, because he wants to tell somebody all about it. He likes talking, likes to offload. I am not sure he'd be doing that if he hadn't had therapy before;

it's quite something for a teenage boy to admit he needs help. He has a sense of humour now, too, so says he's an expert at therapy now: "They can throw anything at me because at my old school you got counselling just to go to the toilet."

So he knows he needs it. I've told him: "You're in a strong position in life now, because you can accept help." He knows curve balls are always going to be thrown his way, because he doesn't think the same as everyone else, and he has accepted that, and I think quite likes the quirkiness of who he is now.

Fiona: Do you think he's less problematic at this age than you expected?

Lena: When he was 5, I used to occasionally think: "He's going to end up in prison because he's going to hurt someone. *That's his future.*" There is still a lot he will have to grapple with, and he still has his moments. He gets caught up in the moment, sometimes can't remember what's happened. But then you can reason with him. He's brilliant at home. Moody, but brilliant. He doesn't shout any more, which is lovely, and he hasn't broken anything for years. I used not to own anything that wasn't broken. We do a lot together. He's got a good relationship with his sisters, and he wants to be like the oldest, go to college, which helps. He sees his dad at weekends, and they get on well. He's still very clear that it's got to be just him and me. But I am encouraging him to go to university in Aberdeen!

I can never thank this place enough, because without it he wouldn't have been happy, he'd have got himself in trouble in a big way and ended up somewhere residential. And I would be in a looney bin. I mean that. I was on my way to a breakdown.

He has fond memories of here, and I'm happy about that, that he knows what they did for him here and that he talks about that. I hope when this appears, it doesn't seem like it's all about this *"troubled kid"*. Because you can see we're laughing, that there's humour here. When I first came here, there was no humour. I was not a happy person. So I'd say to other people going through the same thing, you've got to roll with it, you can't sweat the small stuff, and if you can do it with a bit of a smile on your face, relax a bit, it will rub off on the kids.

Acknowledgement

Alek and Lena have given permission for this interview to be published.

CHAPTER TWELVE

Working outside the therapy room in a therapeutic school

Ruth Glover

First thing on Monday morning, support workers, teachers, and nurses are standing ready at different points on the ground floor. Waiting for the day to start, there's a quiet buzz of anticipation, of not knowing how each child will come in, but a readiness to welcome them all as they come to begin their week.

Three boys arrive with heads down, shuffling one behind the other. They show little recognition of the hellos they receive. The boy in the middle smiles at the floor, not sure yet whether he is ready or pleased to be seen.

Bobby hurtles in through the corridor, screaming. He runs past his class-room and out the far door. He smiles. He looks both excited and scared.

Next is Abdi, animatedly showing a support worker his headphones from home. He gets close to her, his voice loud, keen to capture her full attention.

Then Amber strolls in. Smiling, she purposefully heads for the stairs. She sniggers. The adult says her bag needs to be checked before she goes up. Amber groans and rolls her eyes but seems pleased to hand it over.

Bobby rushes back through, still screaming. He slams into his classroom with a bang. Once inside, the screaming stops.

The day has started. The children are all coming in and coming back in their own way.

In these few minutes, the observing therapist sees the children's differing responses to beginnings and re-finding each other:

DOI: 10.4324/9781003185925-16

rigidity, hiding, testing, wanting to be found, and wanting not to be. Some are ready to connect, some are not. She sees how the chaotic muddle of transition from one space to another can feel like hurtling through space. All of the children are helped to find their way to their classrooms.

This chapter is about child psychotherapy within this specialist NHS therapeutic school. It is about what we do and what we bring to this setting. It is also about the lives of children, families, education and clinical staff within such a community, and how we work together to understand the confusing communications of troubled and troubling children. I will attempt to show from a child psychotherapy perspective what life looks like here.

Child psychotherapy within the school setting

I touch on the individual therapy that happens in this therapeutic school, but my focus is on how therapy and a child psychotherapy perspective is woven into the rest of school life. Those of us not seeing children for individual therapy work as child psychotherapists outside the therapy room, primarily through working with the team and the families. This includes joining the children for lunch, meeting them with their teachers, joining their community meetings, and facilitating groups. We may even go on residential school trips. We are there observing and being part of the constantly changing emotional fluctuations within the community. Yet, we are not there as teachers or support workers or nurses. What are we doing? I explore how we try to keep an eye on both inside and outside the therapy room and how we bring these different ways of understanding the children's lives together.

As child psychoanalytic psychotherapists, our first training is in observing and understanding early life and how aspects of our infantile selves stay with and in us all. We are trained to observe pre-verbal and non-verbal communication, what may be communicated without or before words, as well as alongside and behind what is said. We see how infants develop within the context of the ordinary loving, hating, distracted, and attentive minds and arms of their parents or carers. Infants take this experience in to form their sense of themselves and the world around them, each in their own way. In all therapeutic work we hold the baby in mind. We understand that irrational, emotional, and relational yearnings, as well as "crazy" or destructive states of mind, can link to very primitive feelings. In the therapeutic school setting, we bring this way of thinking about the complexity of development to the team. Most of the children in our specialist unit have not had an infancy that has helped them to develop emotionally into the age or bodies that they now inhabit.

A key aspect of what we see is shown in Bobby, in the observation above, who screams and looks terrified and excited at the same time. Many of the children in the school have learned to cope with terror and hurt by cutting off from fear, which then becomes muddled with excitement and even fun.

In team meetings and supervisions, in parent work and with children outside the therapy room, a space to observe and mentally digest can be helpful. Not every detail will be shared, but the psychoanalytic observational perspective offers a live sense of emotional temperature and contributes to working to understand the mass of feeling we all find ourselves in the middle of.

We know that children often do not communicate their anxiety or emotional conflicts in words. The children in the school usually communicate through behaviour that makes others feel what they cannot bear to feel themselves.

We know that children come to this school because trauma has flooded not only their own minds and bodies, but also the minds and bodies of those around them, their families and their schools. This is not about blame. It is not about pathologizing them, but it is about being able to talk about how sometimes it is children who have been most hurt, who hurt others the most. I write about this fundamental aspect of working with extremely disturbed children with some trepidation: it is also important to note that these are children who can be loving, fun, creative, ordinarily infuriating, and inspiring. However, in order to be helped, they make us see and feel the pain that they have felt.

Having child psychotherapy in the senior leadership team and supervising non-clinical members of the team, as well as providing psychotherapy to the children and working clinically with families allows this thinking to permeate the whole school structure.

This is not easy, and as in any other school where therapy is provided, there can be tensions about how to provide therapy and education—together and separately. The whole school team think about meaning and communication in the children's behaviour—this is not just the province of psychotherapy. Nurses and teachers are also working therapeutically. They are experienced and skilled. There can be difficulty with negotiating and allowing professional difference. We are all working within group processes and dynamics.

The children also need the teachers and other staff to teach and play with them, to tell them off, and to laugh with them. All of this is sensitive work and fundamental for the children's development. This is a therapeutic school, but the children do not need to be in constant therapy.

The aim is to work together, bringing our own skills and roles to the mix, and allowing ourselves to be different. But just as some children cannot allow their parents to come together because of anxiety about not being included, so we can also enact difficulties in being joined up as a team. In a service working with children who have had such fragmented experiences, this is not surprising.

For the child psychotherapists, part of the work involves not being drawn into fights. In this setting emotions run high, and it is easy for staff as well as children to become reactive. We have to work hard to balance enough closeness with enough distance to use our psychoanalytic observational capacity effectively.

Fragments: Bobby

I am going to present work outside the therapy room with two children in particular, whom the chapter follows at different points of their time in the therapeutic school. This section starts with Bobby. Bobby's story could represent many of our children, whose experiences in early development did not help them to grow.

Bobby came to the school at 5 years. He was the biological baby of an adolescent white working-class mother, who had herself grown up in care. It was not known who his father was. He was born addicted to heroin and was in an intensive care unit for the first three months of his life, experiencing painful withdrawal from heroin and lifesaving but traumatically invasive medical treatment. His mother took a lethal overdose shortly after his birth.

Bobby moved through a succession of foster homes before being adopted, just before he was 2 years old, by a white European middle-class mother and father. He had experienced significant physical and emotional pain from the very start. Much had happened before he had words. He had no way of making sense of it; few conscious memories. Yet fear, horror, and a powerful feeling of not belonging lived on inside him, and he took a version of this with him to every new relationship.

Bobby had been excluded from two nurseries and then finally from a mainstream reception class before coming to us. Running away, biting, throwing furniture at children and at adults, smashing windows, swearing: this little boy had never settled anywhere.

His parents were exhausted and on the edge of their marriage breaking down.

Like most of our children, he defended against feelings of terror by trying to be the one in charge.

First, a senior teacher and I met Bobby's adoptive parents. It was notable how far apart they seemed. His father said that school had just not understood Bobby. He hadn't really been as violent as they said. His mother remained quiet. I asked about her experience. She replied sadly that Bobby only came to her for food. She couldn't take him to the park because he ran away. If she tried to stop him, he shouted and spat at her. It was embarrassing. Everyone thought she was a useless mother.

The teacher asked about how he was doing educationally. His father said he was intelligent. His mother shrugged and said she didn't know. They talked to the teacher and me as though from a distance, without any expectation that, from our privileged professional perspectives, we would be able to understand how defeated they felt, or that we might see aspects of Bobby other than his violence.

In the next meeting we met Bobby. It was striking how young he looked. When hearing about him, it had been hard to remember that he was only 5. He was small and skinny, yet with an open, round face. When I greeted him, he murmured hello shyly, and I felt instantly drawn to him. Then, as if feeling my softening, he looked up at me with disdain and said, "This place is for babies. I am not a shitty baby."

All of the children come to the therapeutic school with a fear of learning. Bobby, for a long time, knew everything. It was not only bravado—he convinced himself. I heard in a team meeting how Bobby tried to join the older children in a complicated game that one of them had made up. He insisted he didn't need to be told the rules. He already knew.

Bobby was determined to know already the rules of a life he could not comprehend. He had been put into a family and had to just fit. Of course he could do it—what choice did he have? To learn, you have to be able to bear not knowing what comes next and to trust the world enough to let it in at least a little.

When I joined Bobby's class for lunch, I watched him and noticed that not only did he become aggressive when he felt he was not being fed, but, when actually given food, he would gobble it down as quickly as possible, almost without looking or seeming to get any pleasure from it. If he looked at the food first, it was with suspicion. He pushed it around his plate and stormed off —about something seemingly unrelated—without eating. He seemed to feel that taking anything in from the world and actually experiencing it—tasting or enjoying his food—might harm him. As he ran out of the room, his body seemed to move before his head.

Bobby began psychotherapy as part of his time in school.

In his therapist's supervision, I heard about how, to begin with, he was only able to come into the therapy room for brief periods. And in the room, he ran around desperately trying to break his way into cupboards and throw the things that were for him out of the window. Dropping, throwing, breaking, flooding seemed to be the main communications he passed on to his therapist, who had to work hard to hold the onslaught of terrified and disjointed experience. The locked cupboards were unbearable to him. But so were the things that were there for him. He seemed to have little idea that any of it might be to help him.

In gathering together fragments from the parents' description, the observations, the supervisions, the team, and the therapy, we could see there was a muddled mass of different feelings and experiences in and around this child. These included shame, rejection, confusion, violent aggression, denial, and failure.

Most immediately, for Bobby, safety was indistinguishable from danger. It may have been like this for the baby he had been, born withdrawing from heroin. Were those tubes pushed inside him helping him or hurting him? Was there a difference? For Bobby, the experience of softness from another threw him. It linked him immediately to terrifying vulnerability associated with babies or being babied. Being a baby was shit. He could not be one.

But among the disparate pieces, there were aspects of hope. This boy went to his mother for food. He made her feel useless in the process, but he went. His father had to limit what he noticed, but he knew that Bobby needed help. There were parents and a network who had got him here. Alongside the spitting, running, hitting, and pushing everyone away, there was a part of Bobby that was trying to reach out, break in, and hold on.

Lunchtime: Amber

Just as it can be difficult to navigate the professional boundaries within the team, so it can be difficult to navigate them within oneself as clinician, moving from one context to another within the school.

When the therapists join the children for lunch, we are not there to do therapy. Rather, we hold a midway point between observing and joining in. However, for some of the children, knowing I am a psychotherapist stirs something. All of the children are aware of psychotherapy happening in school: they may be in or have been in therapy themselves, or they see their peers going to and coming from sessions. For some children therapy is too intense, and they cannot manage (yet) to stay in the room. All of them have some degree of curiosity about it.

Amber, 10 years old, was living in her fourth foster placement. She was now with a black foster carer, who had originally come from the same Caribbean island as Amber's mother. Amber's birth family's history included experience of intergenerational profound mental illness, abuse, and neglect. Amber had been in and out of care until she was removed permanently at 7 years.

At the first lunch I joined with this class, Amber looked at me and told me fiercely not to use my therapist voice. I felt a bit taken aback and wondered aloud what a therapist voice sounded like? Nine-year-old Abdi said thoughtfully, "I don't know, I think she means calm."

This was not a therapy session, but I could still absorb what came from Amber and think about her need to aggressively push me away. This perhaps pointed to sharp worry and muddle, including about having a place at the table herself. I was not her therapist. Amber had rejected therapy.

Being part of school life in this way, having some experiences with the children in their daily groupings alongside the other staff, allows something different to happen. Amber was warning me: "Don't get too close!" or "Don't get inside!" or "Don't be fake with me—pretending you are calm or interested!" At the same time, she was letting me feel what it is like when you try to make contact and join in: you get shot down, it is public, it hurts, and it is humiliating.

Amber continued, annoyed by the connection that Abdi had made with me. She looked at me as if I was the most revolting thing she had ever seen, "You are a disgusting, paedophile!" Another boy joined in, laughing, "Paedo, paedo!" And the temperature rose in the group.

The support workers were firm and clear that Amber had to stop her attacks, and so did the others. If Amber really couldn't manage, she would need to move to a separate space, they said.

This boundary seemed to bring Amber some relief, and after protests of innocence and a brief, more curious glance at me, she managed finally to take a mouthful of lunch.

Another child shouted out, "Rapist!" to no one in particular. Amber turned on him with powerful righteousness. "You cannot call someone a rapist—that is disgusting. Paedophile is okay, but never rapist, that's just so bad."

I commented that the rules about what was okay or not to say here were confusing. Amber and the other child seemed able for just a second to hear this without feeling that contact from me as a therapist had become intolerably intrusive. The support workers built on this, and a conversation continued in a more ordinary way, which I also took some part in, about social rules and how confusing they could be. There was some sharing of ideas and debates about cultural experiences and expectations. The mood lightened. The support worker linked this to one of the topics in history that the children had been studying.

This was emotional, intellectual, and social learning happening simultaneously. Being able to feel Amber's attack and withstand it without throwing it back at her, alongside the firm and calm boundary given by the support worker, enabled a shift. Amber moved to a mental/emotional place in which she could begin to take something in: food, shared experience, and thinking.

Many children in our school have had their bodies invaded and hurt; for a significant proportion, this has included sexual abuse. Amber was the one who shouted out to the new person (me) about dangerous sexual contact, but she was (without realizing it) also communicating something for the whole group. Similarly, Abdi was the one who could thoughtfully consider that Amber might be troubled by the idea of a calm voice, representing another group point of view.

For Amber, an adult showing any interest in a child became paedophilia. The communication was intense, and the response she pushed for was collapse, hurting her back, or a wish in the other to run away. When the hostility was not turned on me, it was directed towards the other child, who became "so bad". The intensity with which Amber communicated to me what it is like not to have a secure place in the world (at the table) suggested that this was not something she thought I could understand. In what she saw, perhaps, as my comfortable, white middle-class therapist position, I was too far away from her. How could I possibly relate to feeling pushed out and voiceless, unless she made me feel it?

I did not say any of this. On top of the worry about what kind of a therapist–person I might be, there was another message: this isn't therapy, this is lunchtime in our classroom. I respected this.

Little by little, Amber began to relate to me in a different way. I observed over the weeks how much she looked at me, and to me. I noticed how acutely aware she was if my attention went towards another child.

In psychotherapy, a child is invited to the therapy room. Sometimes they might be encouraged firmly, but it is a separate space. In a wider school setting, such as lunchtime, the therapists can be part of the group with the children and colleagues. We can have contact with the children and take in their responses to us in a different way, using our observational training in an adapted form to enrich our understanding and work with the whole system.

What I processed for Amber in this brief example demonstrates a type of emotional communication that the rest of the team experience frequently throughout the day. The supervisory and team structures are there in part to help the frontline staff to recognize, manage, and understand the complex emotional states they carry for the children as a necessary part of the work.

Caring for ordinary toddlers can be exhausting work, emotionally and physically. Toddlers may snatch and push and bite, run away,

scream, and throw things. I have heard parents of ordinarily developing toddlers, who have had intact-enough starts in life, say they cannot
do it: they cannot physically manage them. When you see their actual
little child, you realize that this is not a physical reality, but the parent
can really feel it. Toddlers can be picked up, held, soothed, or firmly
contained with words. But for children of 7, 9, or 11 years who are still
as emotionally and physically reactive as toddlers, actual physical containment can be much harder. Many of the children in our school have
not had experiences that have held them physically or emotionally, so
they have not developed sufficient capacity to do this for themselves.

Learning

As case coordinators, the therapists meet the child with their teacher
and parents at the start of every term for a target setting and review
meeting. We hear how the holiday has been, and then together look at
the educational and behavioural targets set last term, at progress made
and consider what should be worked on next.

Bobby announced in an early meeting that his target was, "I'm not
doing learning!"

This was not only a response of defiance, but also an accurate self-
assessment of what could happen when he was the grip of anxious and
destructive states of mind. It was important not to avoid the aggression
while also seeing what else was there: Bobby is telling us he does *not* do
learning right now, and this is something he needs help with.

In the target review meeting two terms later, Bobby stood up on the
table and sang, with his back to us, "I don't want to leaaaarrrrn!" Then,
"I do want to leaaarrrn!" He sang one statement after another: "I don't,
don't, don't want to learn!", "I do, do, do want to learn"! His comment
about the battle inside him could be heard by everyone in the room.

Bobby's teacher then talked with him about his target from last term,
which was to attempt more maths work. They agreed together that he
had made real progress. "But", he said, now down from the table and
looking directly at her, "I want to keep this target—it's not done yet."
This seemed to show a fragile but developing wish to join (add) up the
emotional fragments inside him, and some recognition that he did not
know it all yet, he still needed time.

Movement

As education and clinical staff, we work as a team to notice the ways in
which the children may provoke us. This is integral to understanding

what they are communicating about aspects of emotional experience that are intolerable for them. Understanding why we feel the way we do can enable positions, roles, and identities to become a bit less stuck.

Bobby had now been with us for over a year. For the past month he had targeted one particular support worker, mocking her accent and making her feel worthless. Meanwhile, with another team member, he was learning to cook and showing infectious delight at discovering that he could make real food. Both support workers thought together about what Bobby was expressing. He was trying new things, but he still needed someone else to have the feelings that were unmanageable for him, such as fear of not belonging, located here in the support worker with an unfamiliar accent.

Bobby's mother's and father's parenting roles were also becoming less polarized. In parent work, his mother talked about feeling less judged, and his father seemed increasingly in touch with confusion and worry about his son. Bobby started to show some vulnerability at home. He could tolerate his parents being together as adults a little more, and his mother movingly described feeling that, for the first time, she had a bond with him. Both parents had become sensitive to when Bobby was particularly anxious about not fitting in or not being good enough. They could identify a little more with Bobby's furious distress.

Bobby started to bring more sexualized disturbance to his therapist, which he could now, just about, not let burst out everywhere else. There were poignant sequences of play with the toy animals. There were babies who didn't have mummies—sometimes they flew and sometimes they fell, they cried and died and fought and slept. Sometimes they even let the therapist hold and look after them.

He was developing a sense of things having a place and a time and of emotional experiences being possible to sort in a more ordered and manageable way. The cupboards no longer had to be broken into. He could trust (more of the time) that what his therapist brought for him was really for him and good for him; it didn't have to be thrown out—and nor would he be.

In his teacher's supervision with me, I heard how Bobby had drawn a picture of himself for the first time with other people in it, rather than just weapons. He was also beginning to dictate stories and could bear to face learning to read.

However, this progress was not linear. As Bobby began to manage better generally at home, when things were difficult, his behaviour was more extreme at school. Just before a school and therapy break—always a difficult time evoking separation and loss—his violence at school erupted.

There was movement, but for those working within the fragmentation, it felt near impossible to imagine that this might be part of development.

Working with abuse

Sometimes just walking through the school building can feel overwhelming. As if, rather than being there to help children recover from abuse, you are having to walk right inside it. Or that you are the neglectful bystander walking past while you hear it happening.

On a morning of Bobby's violence, I was bringing a new parent into the school.

As we walked up the stairs, we were hit by the noise. Two adults were standing outside the soft room, and Bobby was inside. "Fuck your mum!" The words echoed. He had managed to take a piece of wood in with him from the playground and started bashing at the glass. One of the support workers said, calmly but loudly, that she knew he had had a difficult morning, they wanted him to hold his body safely, but if he couldn't, they would have to come in and help him. The smashing continued. After a slight pause, louder, "Die, bitch!"

Prior to this, Bobby had head-butted his teacher hard in the face. Her nose had poured with blood. She had gone to hospital, concerned that it might be broken.

> I heard the two adults move in, talking to each other about how to hold him, and who would lead. They went in, and his shouts intensified. There was a scuffle, and his shouts tuned to screams. He tried to kick and bite. Eventually he was held, and his spitting subsided. Finally his fighting turned to deep and painful, guttural sobs.

> As I moved upstairs, two other children were running wildly round the building, with excitement on their faces.

Parents coming in to school experience the intensity in different ways. For some, there is horror: "Who are these children?" For others: "What are these adults doing to these children?" And for many there is relief: "This is somewhere my child will be looked after, helped and not rejected." For everyone—children, parents, and staff, versions of all of these responses are likely to emerge at different points.

An entrance like this—which is not how it always is—cannot hide the reality of working with a high level of disturbance. Imagining a therapeutic school that focuses on relationships, understanding, and helping troubled children can conjure an idealized image of calm care and reflection—of children learning in all senses of the word. Care and reflection are certainly part of the reality, calmness less so!

If troubled children communicate through action—making others feel what they cannot bear to feel themselves: terror, humiliation, demoralization, hopelessness—working with them is not easy. Sometimes supervisions are spent gathering people up. Like the mother that many of the children did not have, the front-line staff have to absorb the intensity of their distress.

In supervisions of different members of the team, I heard how shaken they were by Bobby's attack on his teacher. They did not want to work with him any more. They were worried about his impact on the other children. As Bobby was now better at home, his parents thought that this disturbance at school must mean that all the problems came from school, and he should be taken out. I felt myself filled with the despair and anger coming from all sides. The staff who were hurt, the parents—we were all filled with "no more" and "make this stop" feelings. It was tempting to act out and agree.

But what about Bobby? What was he communicating? I remembered his guttural sobs when he stopped fighting. I became aware of how separate and lonely I felt in trying to hold steady. There were questions that I experienced as self-accusations: What was I doing in the parent work? What was happening in his therapy? Or as accusations from school: What was happening at home? Or from Bobby's parents: What was happening at school? I felt aware of how hard I was finding it to listen to all of the perspectives and of how easy it was to retreat, or to be seen as retreating. I felt physically weak; I needed to close my eyes for a minute. I too imagined myself walking away.

We can see how a child like Bobby seriously risks education placement breakdown, even in a therapeutic school. Sometimes it does get to that point.

I had to notice in myself what unbearable communications I was now holding. Feelings of failure, anger, fragmentation, exhaustion. But by pausing and not retaliating or retreating, I could try to regain some perspective.

Of course, I was experiencing Bobby's catastrophe third-hand. He put his fury and distress directly into his teacher, the team, and his parents, and they each gave me their own account. I then had to feel and digest these different points of view in beginning to make sense of what had happened. The experience of having got through to another meant that the adults, in turn, were more able to provide a version of this for Bobby.

Team work

In the subsequent team meeting, my mind went back to the early observation of Bobby at lunch, his body moving before his head. I described this and linked it to how we knew that, when threatened, Bobby would move to action rather than thought. There was a mixed response:

> "He wasn't threatened?" "He chose to do this!" "He's not like he was then." A nurse reflected for the team that it felt so demoralizing not being able to understand what had led to the attack, or why this had happened. A therapist commented that it made us all want to get away. The mood changed, and a support worker said it felt so hard, everyone had tried to work with him, and it made her feel like a failure.

The teacher, thankfully, was okay and could be supported back to work. She seemed to be helped by the team's empathy and was ready to think in more detail about what had happened.

> She said that before Bobby had attacked her, he had built a tall tower out of Lego. Another child had crashed into the table, and the Lego tower fell to the ground. The teacher had gone to stop the other child from wreaking more destruction, leaving Bobby alone.

Bobby was starting to believe he had a structure around him and in him that was reliable. But, just before the holiday break, this Lego representation of trying to build—hope, life, relationships, himself—and then not being able to stop collapse was too much for him. And he felt alone with it. He fell back on having to generate his emotional crash on the outside—reaching others through brute force.

What did Bobby see when he hurt his teacher? When restrained afterwards, his words were, "fuck your mum" and, "die, bitch". Bobby had been a baby whose birth mother had died. He had then lost numerous other mother-figures as he moved foster placements. He now had a part of him that attacked hope and development inside him, pulling him away from trust and towards violence. The team was aware that in his therapy he acted towards his therapist in a way that would engender in her feelings that were unbearable to him. When he hurt others, he saw faces looking at him with horror and terror. He recreated a version of his own feelings in other people. Of course, this left him convinced that he was dangerous and bad, born a monster, who had caused death and destruction all around him from the start.

There was a moment of silence. Then a teacher said she thought we were all wanting to be like him at that early lunch—move our bodies first, we wanted to run without our minds.

With Bobby, things did not break down, though this was a painful and hopeless period of the work with him.

Like the children, the team needs space to express, stay with, and start to explore what can feel intolerable. There often needs to be room for this before we can move to thinking about the children, and part of the therapists' role in school is to facilitate reflective discussion. Later there can also be thought about practical learning from incidents like this.

Through staying with and investigating some of the unbearable feelings the children push into the school team and into their families, we facilitate change. The violent child can take in an experience of a world and relationships that sees and feels their horror, fear, and mess and knows their destructiveness. Thoughts and feelings can be experienced and thought about without having to be immediately expelled. Little by little, this helps the children to take in some reality-based emotional strength and stability.

Change

In a team meeting, I heard about Amber beginning to play basketball at play time. I also heard about her wanting to join the school anti-bullying committee. The team laughed when relaying this—but it was with warmth and good humour.

Working with education staff to slow down and look carefully at the detail of interaction with children can help all of us to see development and progress. The staff in Amber's classroom noticed the moment Amber looked to her support worker, as if drinking in her attention, before turning to the page in her book and reading: a fleeting moment captured of small but significant growth.

However, as Amber started to be less aggressive to others, the hatred turned in on herself. Often with the children in school, change can bring depression. Staff began to feel overwhelmed in a different way. Rather than worrying about their own safety, they started to worry about Amber's.

I was called to help a support worker, Jake, with Amber. She had been crying for hours and screaming that she wanted to kill herself. The classroom staff didn't know what to do. When I arrived, Jake looked exhausted.

Rather like the children, the team can become more used to coping with attack than with distress.

> Amber was sobbing and throwing herself against the padded walls of the soft-room. Earlier, she had tried to smash her head against the hard walls of the classroom. Jake told Amber that I had come, that she needed to be safe, she couldn't hurt herself or us. She cried okay. Once out of the door, she bolted to me and threw herself against me. I thought she was going to attack me. I buckled and we both staggered to the floor. But rather than attacking, she held onto me. She was clinging on and pushing her head into me. The three of us sat together as she cried. As I would in therapy, I let myself take in Amber's powerful distress. It hurt.

Unlike in therapy, I was sitting with Amber and Jake on the floor outside the soft room. This was a public space. Jake and I now had a child with us who, we could see, felt smashed up; we could see she needed looking after. I also noticed that Amber let herself recover when I joined Jake. I thought that she was not yet secure enough to feel that her furious distress would be manageable in a one-to-one situation. She needed two of us there to anchor her; and she had already communicated her idea that staying calm was my job. I encouraged her to go back with Jake to a quiet room near her classroom, where she fell asleep.

It was playtime near the end of term, and most of the children were in the playground:

> There was running, and there was a game of homie. The younger ones had been struggling with recent changes in staff. One of the support workers and a teacher realized that, in the context of this loss, the younger children needed a game that let them play at being aggressive and allowed them to feel connected. The staff introduced "sticky toffee", a game where the children chase and catch each other, all ending up in a circle holding hands, as if held together by sticky toffee.

After playtime, it was moving to see Bobby say to a new child, who kept swearing when waiting his turn, at the whole unit meeting, "I used to be like that—I'm not very patient." Several of the others spoke up that they were also not patient.

In the school, the children inevitably see each other's disturbance and are impacted by it. This is part of the reality of such children being together, and there are aspects of this experience the team wish we could protect them from. However, they also get to see parts of themselves in each other. They each get to be the helper of the child who is being aggressive; they each see how they and their friends can change and be helped by the adults around them.

Bobby joined the Nursing-led gardening group. His anxiety about development was still there, but not so all-encompassing:

> Initially Bobby shouted at his tomato plant that it was stupid and, if it didn't grow, he would shank it! Some of the children in the group laughed, others told him to shut up. His anxiety resonated with all of them. He stormed off but came back quickly and said, "I'm sorry for my overreaction." Amber nodded, "Just don't do it again, alright?" Then, with some thought, "Next time use your words."

Drawing on words used by adults in some of the school behavioural systems and structures, the children seemed to show that they had started to have confidence in the possibility of more benign development. Bobby shouted and stormed off, but he came back. Both Bobby and Amber valued this group. They could, now, stay in good-enough contact with others, enough to feel sometimes part of a world in which they could contribute and receive.

Bobby started to play at home. His father admitted he found it embarrassing when Bobby's cousin came over and Bobby wanted to be a cat (much like he had been doing in therapy). His mother said that it was not as embarrassing as when he was swearing or thrusting his genitals or being violent, as he had in the past, but it was disturbing to see this big now 8-year-old crawling around on all fours, miaowing. Both parents understood that Bobby had missed out on early play and could be helped to see that this was significant developmental progress, but it was still not without pain and shame.

Bobby now seemed more vulnerable, and his parents worried about him being bullied (which no doubt was what he had spent most of his life defending against).

In parent work and in meetings with the team, we thought about the shift from a Bobby who had to know everything—who knew the rules before being told—to a Bobby who sometimes crawled on all fours, like a baby, but made noises like a cat. He couldn't speak the language of those around him and had to try to make himself understood without words, sharp claws and spitting in reserve.

Inclusion

Watching the children, staff, and families together at the Winter celebration provides an example of what inclusion can look like. There is a sense of pride as parents are welcomed in for the show. Some of the children have written their own poems or stories, raps or songs. Some dance, some chaotically run around trying to keep both inside and outside the area they are performing in, forgetting what they are supposed to be doing, or adding impromptu extras. For some, it is too much to stay in for long, and they need to go out and get drinks.

They are all celebrated for what they bring and can do. One child sings about goodbyes. Amber listens and then hides her head in her hands. She has one more term with us. She can now let herself feel sadness, and separations are hard. This is a long way from the girl who appeared to feel nothing and who generated in others the wish to get away. The head teacher sits behind her and quietly puts her hand out. Amber takes it and curls up on the floor next to her; she smiles and says that she wants to stay in here with the others.

Families and children cheer each other on. Sometimes cruelty and humiliation leak out—there is laughter about the out-of-tune singer. A nurse puts a hand on the mocking child's back—giving just enough support to help them keep going and settle back down. The children are in school, with their families supporting them. They are doing something ordinary and extraordinary. Everyone here—support workers, teachers, clinicians, senior leadership team, children, and families—knows how much work has gone into this slice of taking part in life.

Bobby reads out, "Happy Winter Celebration to all!" His teacher catches my eye and smiles— and I know how much it means to her that he is reading in public, that she understands how big this is education-ally and emotionally for him. I know, too, that that she needs me to see her significant part in this. Bobby keeps his eyes on his mother. He is vigilant and watching her closely, but at least, now, he can let himself look for and find her gaze.

We know that tomorrow the children may come back in different states of mind, they may again leave their families and school with feelings of hopelessness. But that does not take away from the importance for them and those around them of having these experiences of things being better.

Child psychotherapy is not central to this event, but it is part of the fabric that helps it to happen in the way that it does.

This chapter has tried to portray something of how child psycho-therapists work, outside the therapy room, in a therapeutic school. By showing what it can look like here, I hope to have given a flavour of the thinking and observational approach that we use. Bobby's and Amber's stories illustrate how confusing and complex this work can be. They also show how, by helping to make sense of this confusion, we contribute to a multidisciplinary therapeutic educational approach, which enables hopeful and creative development for vulnerable children.

CHAPTER THIRTEEN

Personal perspectives across education and mental health in a therapeutic school

Interviews by Milly Jenkins

G loucester House, the Tavistock and Portman's specialist day school, sits at a crossroads of leafy Hampstead streets, an imposing red-brick Victorian villa with an ornate white porch. Passers-by might assume it was an expensive home if they did not notice the NHS sign. First opened in 1968, it educates and cares for around 20 pupils, aged 5 to 14 years, all of whom have had prolonged and painful struggles to manage in mainstream schools and are now funded by local authorities to attend a rare therapeutic school-community, often for as long as three years. A recent Channel 4 documentary called it *"The Last Chance School"*.

Its staff come from both education and mental health—specialist teachers, nurses, child psychoanalytic psychotherapists, support workers, and a psychiatrist—and work together to sustain, teach, and treat some of the most complex and challenging children from across London, working with their families and professional networks towards a hoped-for return to mainstream education.

In this chapter we hear from three members of the school's senior leadership team—head teacher, lead nurse/clinical lead, and child psychoanalytic psychotherapist—about how therapists work in the school and how education and mental health staff integrate their models of working to provide a holistic and bespoke service for children and families who have often experienced severe deprivation and trauma.

 DOI: 10.4324/9781003185925-17

Nell Nicholson, head teacher

I describe Gloucester House as a therapeutic school—a combined thera-peutic and education provision. We are defined as a school rather than a mental health service. Local authorities and families prefer that. We have an almost fifty-fifty balance of educational and clinical staff.

We provide therapy, but we also have a "therapeutic milieu". That means we are all thinking about what the communication is around behaviours, about what we are feeling and what that might be telling us. We have to balance that with the fact that education is also thera-peutic for these children, that they and their families need to feel they are learners, that they have something to contribute, and that they can become rounded and self-reflective individuals.

Therapeutic schools are often "therapeutic" in the sense that they provide speech and language therapy and occupational therapy, maybe get child psychotherapists in to do sessions with children and parents. But this is different, more like a therapeutic community, where all staff are working therapeutically, noticing their own feelings, noticing their interactions with one another, and trying to use that as "data".

That can be a difference that is hard to get across. But it is an impor-tant factor in our success, because the children we work with have had very fragmented experiences, and we see our job as knitting those frag-ments together to support them to become more integrated, internally and externally. It is a big ask of the children and families, but we are often successful in that. When children leave here, SENCos at their new schools say: "They have more insight than the staff!" That's because we have taught them language and skills to be always questioning, "What am I feeling" and "Why might I be feeling that?"

We have up to 21 children in three classes, so about six to seven in each. Every class has a teacher, therapeutic support worker, and progress support worker. Some children also have a one-to-one support worker. Therapeutic support workers are from the nursing team and do the nur-turing work, looking after the children in the classroom, helping with breakfast and lunch, maybe running social skills sessions. Progress sup-port workers are more focused on education, and they support learning in the classroom. Clinical staff are not based in the classroom but are providing individual therapy, groups, parent work, case co-ordination, supervision, and work discussion groups within the school.

All the children have had at least one or several Adverse Childhood Experiences (ACEs)—one or a series of traumatic experiences. We have lots of children with attachment difficulties, ADHD, autism diagnoses, or autistic traits, and some have learning difficulties, but they come here because their social, emotional, and mental health difficulties have become a barrier to learning. Local authorities are pretty good at know-ing whom to refer to us—children with very disrupted and complex backgrounds who, with our support, will be able to do the "unpicking" work, to understand themselves, and to build themselves back up. For some children and families, the therapeutic environment is too much; all the looking inward drives them mad.

It is hard to be a teacher here, because we expect progress. But the children can be at very different stages, and we first have to engage them as learners. Often the only way to manage them in previous schools had been through appeasement, so there may have been low or no expectations of them academically. I remember one boy, when he arrived, saying: "I don't do work, and I haven't for five years." We have to say: "Actually, you do work", and we have ordinary consequences when they don't. So we need to put boundaries in place *and* get them interested in learning.

We can't do that using mainstream methods. We use a carousel sys-tem, where lessons are broken up into four blocks of 15-minute tasks with different activities for different learners, as lots have attention difficulties. One might be doing some independent work—important because many are chronically dependent on adults. Another might be teacher-led, taking care about managing the children's strong rivalries about adult attention. Lots of the children can't tolerate whole-group teaching; they can't manage the interactions and feeling exposed and humiliated. And it doesn't work trying to teach social skills at the same time as educating them—they can't do both at once. Things like friendship groups and turn-taking games need to happen separately from learning. For me, that's therapeutic educa-tion, making sure we really do privilege that it's a school, that they are here to learn.

The child psychotherapists in the school provide therapy, but they also get psychoanalytic thinking into the school in a very practical and accessible way. We are all passionate here—the teachers, nurses, and child psychotherapists—about integrated practice, about getting differ-ent ways of thinking going across the team. This is the model we are continually developing. As well as being a teacher, I also have a masters in Systemic Family Therapy and bring that to the team, too—along with a family therapist, who also works here. At a recent conference we did a "live" whole team meeting and then asked the audience to reflect on what they'd heard. They commented on the psychiatrist talking about educational issues and the progress support worker talking about psy-choanalytic ideas. So we use each other's language. But there are also times when we need to just use our own—in professional development training for staff, for example, Ruth might present on psychotherapy and the psychiatrist on ADHD.

For me, child psychotherapy, together with psychosocial nursing, is what makes Gloucester House unique. It weaves psychoanalytic thinking into the whole of the school. But there can be tensions, sometimes: maybe a feeling that teachers are doers and therapists are thinkers—that's a bit insulting, because we all do a bit of both, but we try to bring those tensions into the open. Balancing therapy and education can also be a challenge, figuring out when a child will have sessions, what they are going to miss in class. The teacher might say, "How will they make progress if they always miss English?" The therapist might say, "How do you expect the child to come to therapy if they are always missing the fun part of the class day?" We have to work that out.

Sometimes there can be a honeymoon period when children begin here. Then they start therapy, and their behaviour goes crazy for a while. Teachers who have been here a while know that is normal and likely, and some will make sure a child has ten minutes before and after their session to do something quiet. For new staff, particularly if they've never had therapy, it can be harder to understand. I encourage them to imagine what it might feel like to have therapy and then straight afterward be asked to do a difficult sum. Sometimes teachers forget sessions, or haven't written it up on the board for the child, and that can be their ambivalence about therapy. It can be hard for support workers, too, if they have to sit outside therapy sessions to help the child and therapist if the child has a difficult session and kicks off.

In parent work, we are trying to develop the capacity to think about and understand what's going on. We can see real shifts—say, with a family with safeguarding concerns, where we have got a tight network around them, a child protection plan, support in the home and school, and when they have a capacity to retain the work. But others don't engage and can feel terribly challenged. We used to say parents had to be able to engage with us for their child to come here. But recently, with one family, we knowingly decided to make building the child's resilience our focus, and, ironically, as he became more robust, his parents became more able to engage with us. They were still not able to do parent work, but there was a real shift, especially in the father. The beauty of being small is that we can offer a bespoke service with individual packages. Those same parents found it hard to support their son having therapy, but he was able to make good use of the therapeutic milieu and flourished. Unlike a clinic, you don't have to rely on parents to bring children to the clinic, but we tend to find that for a child to really engage in therapy, it does need the family's support.

My hope is that children leave here with the resilience and self-awareness to be able to function in more ordinary settings. Some can go back to mainstream schools. Others still need a specialist school but might be able to join a football club, be in settings they couldn't manage before. One of the children in the Channel 4 documentary, when asked what he hoped for, said he wanted a house, a wife, a car, and a job. We want them to have those aspirations. But I am a realist, too, and I am wary when people think they're going to save the world. I don't think matching the children's omnipotence with our own is helpful.

So we get good outcomes, but we also have to be realistic about what is possible. We know early trauma has huge long-term effects. For some, a good outcome might mean we just make things a bit better for the time they are here. Others take away something longer lasting—a way of thinking and understanding that provides some sort of comfort. We hear good things about how some former pupils are getting on, and when we get visits and calls from families doing well, it's very moving.

We also run an outreach service, consulting to schools on individual children, as well as more broadly. In times of limited resources, I think the most important thing we can share with staff is about not squashing their feelings. When a teacher is feeling really challenged by a child, maybe feeling really humiliated by him, they think "I shouldn't be feeling this." But actually that feeling is important information about how small and humiliated that child feels. I tell them: "That fear of incompetence is his, not yours." Schools are under tremendous pressure, but it can help if staff get to reflect on their feelings so they don't act out on them.

Kirsty Brant, lead nurse/clinical lead

Nurses often have a seemingly ordinary approach that actually comes from a lot of experience. I might be sitting with a child and doing something that looks really routine, but actually my mind is tick tick ticking, trying to make sense of it. If you have worked on wards overnight, you get skilled at sitting with people in distress and in times of joy, and in being in that moment with them. Nurses get put in charge quickly on wards, and because we often work with very unwell people, we learn to manage difficult situations, to think on our feet. We don't just "do", we need a capacity to think alongside the "doing". So while I am sitting with that child, building a relationship, I am also gathering important information, piecing together a clinical picture, dynamically assessing risk, all leading towards making a formulation and care plan for treatment, together with my colleagues.

Our nursing team includes two other clinical nurse specialists and the therapeutic support workers based in the classrooms. Nurses here are a particular of kettle of fish. Most of us have worked in therapeutic communities and like working in the therapeutic milieu; we think of the whole school as a therapeutic space. In some ways we think differently from therapists, in some ways the same. Nurses here have opportunities to make therapeutic interventions that therapists don't—outside the sessions, in the classroom, and at playtime. But we then think about those experiences together, as a team, so we can all have more insight. We are an integrated team, and there are lots of forums for sharing our experiences and thoughts about the children.

So this is psychosocial work where you are always thinking about what is happening, what is being communicated, and giving the children a voice. That might mean, say, eating together at mealtimes, getting the children to serve the food to develop age-appropriate skills and a sense of shared responsibility. It might mean thinking about why Ben doesn't want to serve the food today, wondering about that to him and the group, trying to get them to work it out together. At other times in the day we might be wondering aloud or to each other: "Why is Rosa feeling so upset? Could it be she is a bit jealous that it is Christine's birthday?" . . . "Is he not doing his work because he is worried he can't?" . . . "Is he still thinking about what happened in the cab with Jake?" It is not that we sit there therapizing the children the whole time, but we notice and think what is happening; we might say something, we might not.

Although we do lots of one-to-one interventions in the school, whether it is in class or in therapy, we also feel strongly that life happens in groups, and if we can't support children to be in a group, then we are not doing our best to get them on an equal footing. But that is hard work, because they have historically had difficult family experiences, so sharing is a challenge, and there are strong feelings of deprivation and rivalry. The children have a limited capacity to sit with and tolerate uncomfortable feelings, which means a lot gets "thrown out" and pushed into other people. That makes being in a group difficult. You might think all these kids would understand each other and be kind to each other, and you do see bits of that, but they can be really horrible to each other and to staff because they want to get rid of feelings they can't bear to have.

The children who come here are on the extreme end of things. They haven't managed in mainstream settings. They have often had multiple agency involvement. Some families have fallen through gaps. Some have not been able to engage with services. We have children referred because of their violence, and, once things are settled, it becomes clear there is a significant social communications difficulty or a learning need alongside early trauma, which is almost always there. Because early trauma is pre-verbal, it is complex, and many children here have attachment difficulties. So this is a helpful, relationship-based model for them. But the attachments they make are complicated, and the way they make other people feel is powerful. So we have to pay lots of attention to how we function as a team. I think that is quite different from other settings, but there are more schools like this coming now—trauma-informed and ACE-aware.

There can be layers of trauma and loss. At the moment we have a high percentage of adopted children. These tend to be particularly complex adoptions. There may have been drug and alcohol abuse in pregnancy, or they may have been removed from birth families late. Lots have been exposed to domestic violence. But there can also be children where it is hard to make sense of what is wrong. I have learnt over the years that sometimes you can't make sense of it, and that it's important to recognize that uncertainty, the not knowing, that there are missing pieces, but not to get stuck on it, to find a way to move on together. Sometimes, in fact, with complex children, things often don't fit together in a nice neat box, and why should they? Not many of us humans do! Parents and carers and networks often want certainty, to know: "What's the reason?" Of course we need to remain curious but not get paralysed by looking for definitive answers.

Some children have been seen in CAMHS services before and it has not been possible to contain them in the building; everyone has been clear they need input, but it hasn't been possible in that setting. Parents arriving here are often at the end of their tether when there is extreme behaviour at home, school has broken down, and children have not been able to access CAMHS. In those circumstances there is a strong argument for a service like ours that combines education and mental health.

All children are thought about therapeutically here, but not all will have therapy. It is not the right intervention for everyone. For some, once-a-week therapy is the best option. In some cases, intensive three-times-a-week therapy is what they need and that can bring real change. For some of our children, I can't really think how else we could help them with their level of disturbance, to make sense of it and process it: they need someone separate from the rest of the team—the therapist—to do that. When therapy is going well, they—gradually, over time—start taking their disturbance to the therapy sessions and stop acting out in a big way in school and at home. They use the therapeutic relationship to make sense of their feelings.

But that takes time, and, in the meantime, the whole team needs to support the therapy, the child, and the therapist. That can be hard for support workers, having to sit outside sessions. Sometimes they're the ones getting it in the neck, and that's tough, feeling that the therapist only has to manage the child for 50 minutes, but they have to manage them all day. There can be envy or a feeling that psychotherapists are precious. They can feel, "why does that matter", when therapists say they need to do things in a particular way, see the child at the same time, in the same room. That is really about training and helping all staff understand why certain boundaries are crucial for creating a therapeutic space that really holds children.

So we have to work in a joined-up way to support the therapy, but at the same time be careful about confidentiality. It needs to be a sepa-rate space. Although we are aware of themes in the therapy, we don't hear about the content of sessions. So the therapy has to be held and known about by the staff and institution, but not in a way where eve-ryone knows everything. The boundaries are hard for therapists, too. Sometimes there are situations with a child and they want to help but can't because of needing to maintain a therapeutic stance. I might, say, be in a big situation with a child, in a hold with two other staff, with the therapist walking past, wanting to help out but not able to do more than alert others to what's going on.

We work closely with parents, and I think it can be so helpful for them at review meetings to hear a child psychotherapist speak about *their* difficult experiences with the child in sessions. It makes parents feel that someone else understands how hard it is at home, how awful the child makes them feel, that it is not just their "bad" parenting. We recently had a meeting with parents who were really struggling, and the therapist talked about how useless the boy could make her feel, how he cut down everything she said. Hearing that can be especially important for adoptive parents when things aren't as they expected them to be, and there is shame and judgement about that, a worry that they are not good enough. Some of that feeling may, of course, be coming from the child.

The child psychotherapists bring hugely valuable thinking to the team. Although psychoanalytic thinking is part of the culture here, whatever discipline you are from, their particular experience and train-ing in infant observation and work discussion helps other staff notice tiny details and use those to make sense of what is going on; especially about how children use us as "vessels" for their feelings. Some child psychotherapists can talk about those things in a really ordinary way. They also help keep us thinking about children's early experiences. Sometimes other staff can experience that as making excuses for bad behaviour, but on the whole the encouragement to notice small details, "little" communications, and their linking those to early experiences helps make sense of why a child is doing what he is doing. It is not so much a consultation model because it is more collaborative than that.

What can we share with other schools? Well, when we do outreach work in schools to help them with their most challenging children, we talk about needing to know a child's history. That can be tricky with confidentiality, but it is important for staff working closely with children, especially adopted children, to know they have experienced trauma, loss, and deprivation that has had a huge impact and that, no matter how affluent and lovely their new family is, that doesn't just go away. Whenever we are struggling to feel empathy for a child here, we go back to their history, because it helps us remember and make sense of their behaviour. It is also important to remember that as well as being disturbed, these are also ordinary children—to notice their strengths and abilities, the ordinary moments of joy.

Also key is reflective practice in school teams. That is the first thing we always offer in outreach work, to think with the team about what is happening. It can really shift things. It is not about us coming in as "experts", it is about joining people, trying to understand their experience and make sense of the child together. Schools, including ours, need to acknowledge that not all staff are specialists, and they need support. They are working with children who are incredibly difficult to be around, and if they don't have anyone helping them to make sense of it, the dynamics get complicated. You don't need to be a specialist to make a good connection with a child, but you do need specialist support.

Ruth Glover, child and adolescent psychoanalytic psychotherapist

Gloucester House is a really unique provision. It is both a school and a mental health service. I have worked in schools, special schools, inpatient units, and therapeutic communities, and it's none of these things alone. It is something of an interesting cross between them all, in its own distinct way. We often call it a "therapeutic school", bringing together education and therapy in an integrated way that aims to permeate throughout the whole community. It's significant that the senior leadership team includes a head teacher, deputy head, mental health nurse, child and adolescent psychotherapist, and a psychiatrist. Therapy and mental health provision are together here like nowhere else I know.

We take children who are at risk of the worst trajectories. They often have horrific, traumatic histories, sometimes born addicted, with early abuse and neglect. They are often in foster care or adopted and have had multiple breakdowns in placements. They are children who have suffered unimaginable hurt and exclusion and who sadly go on to repeat their own sense of rejection everywhere they go. This makes them very hard to care for. Not only have they endured abuse and loss, they have also lost the stabilizing factors other children have—like school. They are the children that, as a society, we all feel very sorry for when we hear about the harm done to them. But they lose public sympathy as they get older and continue to struggle in the way that some hurt children do. They are excluded again and again and later on risk further punishment rather than care—maybe through prison.

Before they come here, they have usually been from school to school, had educational psychology assessments, maybe small group or home education, perhaps tried family therapy at CAMHS, or medication, or had some form of post-adoption support. In my experience, if they are not accessing school, they will also have struggled to access other consistent help. They come from different boroughs across London, some willing to pay for one child, others with a contract. Local authorities that have had good experiences with us come back. But we are a small provision and have many more referrals than we can accept.

So it is an important provision, but it is hard to work in, because these children push so much of what they feel into people around them—they can make others feel the terror, abuse, and uselessness they have experienced. We talk a lot here about children putting feelings into someone else. It is hard to be on the frontline of that, on the receiving end. But it is a service that works, because we use a combination of approaches, psychoanalytic child psychotherapy being an important one of them.

We work to not only support the children but also to create an environment that supports staff by helping them to think about what the children are communicating, what they have to hold emotionally in this work, and why. We help the team to understand the children through also noticing how they themselves feel. By containing and training staff, the hope is that the children also get to have a new experience of their feelings being made sense of and contained. And from our therapeutic experience, this is a crucial part of facilitating meaningful change.

Education is a fundamental part of what Gloucester House does. We understand that these children are all struggling to learn, at least in part, because of their emotional difficulties. And we know that if they miss out on education, they also massively reduce their life chances and increase their risk of social exclusion. So this is not just about mental health provision—we are trying to make sure they can learn and achieve academically. But also, education and emotional support go hand in hand here.

The teachers' input is huge, not only keeping children on track with learning but in joining us to think about emotional meaning. Together, we can help the team to notice, for example, when a child can't take enough risks to be able to learn and when, for the first time, he starts to be able to. The class teams have to hold and manage all the anxieties in the classroom—the rivalry and sometimes terror that these children feel, that can lead to them being disruptive and aggressive—and at the same time maintain a belief that they can carry on, learn, and develop. They also help create a sense of family.

Our clinical lead is a nurse. Nursing here has a crucial function. Nurses work creatively, using their own therapeutic skills to enable psychosocial interventions and therapeutic community thinking. They run the community meetings with the children, which function somewhere between therapy and education. Children or staff of any level can call a whole team meeting, as a whole community, if they feel something is concerning, or something needs thinking about.

We are a small team of child psychoanalytic psychotherapists. Not all children have therapy. For those who do, it can be weekly, or twice or three times a week. This is often long-term work—one to three years. We see parents and carers in parallel to that work, often for weekly or fortnightly parent sessions. Therapy is not the right option for all children. However, I question the idea that there are children who can and can't "use" therapy. What does that mean? It can be looked at in different ways—for example, if a child runs out of the therapy room after five minutes, is that a wasted resource, or does it tell us something really important about that child that we can then work with? This is a live issue for me and one I battle with.

But we have to be realistic. Child psychotherapy is a limited resource here, and we have to think about who will benefit most at any point in time. There may be children who really can't settle in the room yet, who find a lack of structure totally overwhelming and might benefit, say, from art therapy or a psychosocial intervention, where there is more direction. These decisions are not always easy to make, and sometimes we have to think about what can be tolerated by the team as well as, or as much as, the child. Like in other services, or perhaps even more intensely than in other services, we are sometimes working with the ordinary human dynamics of rivalry, ego, and anxiety about professional value. But when it goes well, what these children can do in psychotherapy, when given enough time, can be exceptionally moving. We see them slowly start to lift off their armour.

It is different from providing therapy in a clinic. It's more like an in-patient setting or therapeutic community, more complex and intense. The whole team—the mini network within the school—needs to be on board in supporting the therapy, because the children tend to divide their world into "good" and "bad" and relate to people accordingly. That means the therapist can become the "good" person to the child for a while, and the support worker, teacher, or children the "bad" ones who get a hard time. So staff need to work closely to think about what is going on in and outside the therapy room, and that means that child psychotherapists need to work more flexibly than they might in other settings. Also, with exceptionally deprived children, the level of violence is often more extreme than in clinics, and we have to think about safety—of the therapist, as well as the child.

Providing therapy is only one part of what child psychotherapists do here. We work with the team using ideas from child psychotherapy. So the children access a lot of our help without actually being in a room with a therapist. We work in the senior leadership team to think about the way the whole school functions and about the individual needs of children and families within the school system. That can be complicated, because the difficulties children bring can get played out in the system, so work needs to go into noticing and managing that, from thinking about practical things, like routines and structures, to thinking about team dynamics. We do observations that we then bring to team meetings, to help think about an individual child and his or her impact on the team and in the school.

All school staff get individual supervision, and child psychotherapists help to provide that. On Tuesday mornings the children are not in, and we have staff meetings—these include clinical discussions about individual children, but it's also about getting a sense of what's going on in the whole environment. We also have clinician meetings and do class supervisions with teachers and support staff, thinking about what is happening in a particular class, and work discussion groups, where staff can bring a particular child or interaction to help us think about what has been going on.

We try to think about interactions in detail, especially as we are working somewhere where things happen fast and staff are often having to work on their toes, on instinct, so it's important to have spaces where we slow down and think about what's being communicated. Thinking about unspoken communications and dynamics can help staff feel less persecuted and more hopeful. There can be dynamics in these meetings that reflect what is happening with the children. For example, staff might feel we are focusing too much on the children and not enough on supporting them. This might really be a reflection of the children's feelings, of never being given enough, and so it's helpful for us to notice and think about it.

Child psychotherapists and nurses are also case coordinators, which means helping an individual family from the pre-admission stages through to the end, linking with networks before they arrive, while they are here, and when they move on. Life for families is often really difficult and confusing and has been for a long time. Parents can feel collapsed, useless, and hopeless. Sometimes they come with the hope that Gloucester House is going to solve everything and then have to face the reality that their child will bring the same difficulties here as they have elsewhere; also, they find that there are other children here with similar difficulties—for children who are easily scared and overwhelmed, it can be upsetting and frightening to be faced with the aggression of others.

We have structures here to keep children safe, but those boundaries can be difficult for parents at first—they can feel blamed if their children are violent and need to be held or need time at home for their safety. For families, it can feel as if cycles are being repeated. So we have to support parents through that, to help them stick with it. We try to support them, sometimes practically, but also in thinking about the meaning of their child's communication and behaviour and in helping them to see progress when it comes.

For parents whose children are having therapy, we provide regular parent work in parallel with the child's sessions, meeting them once a week or fortnightly. There can be an idea that therapy will quickly make things better—that if their child has therapy, everything will be OK—so, again, parents need support around this. Therapy can stir up all kinds of feelings for the child who may then become disruptive around the sessions, running in and out, around the building. It can be hard to make sense of, to think about what is coming out, what the child is bringing to the therapist. Feelings like "I don't feel safe", "I need to escape", "I don't know I can trust this person", "I want to see if they will find me". We need to help families and the team keep faith that these are important feelings being communicated, that we need to understand, and that it isn't just a breakdown.

Together with other staff, we also run groups. There is a time-limited Discovery Group for new children that is partly for assessment purposes but also to give them a first experience of people paying close attention to what they are doing, with us very gently reflecting on what they might be showing and how they feel about each other or about staff. They can begin to discover themselves with other people in

Gloucester House and begin to take in the possibility that others might be interested in them. We do longer term groups, too. Again, you need to work closely with the team when children are coming in and out of class for groups, full of feelings. But, as in individual therapy, when you see change in how they communicate, their attempts to reach out, it is so moving.

Sometimes it doesn't work out for children here, and that is painful. Families can lose faith when it goes on being difficult at home and in school. It is asking a lot of them as well—they need to give lots of support to the child to stay here. Also, sometimes we have to think about whether it's the right place for the child, if levels of aggression and violence don't reduce, and it feels unsafe. Some children might go to a more behavioural school or a residential one. But it doesn't happen often.

We do lots of outcome measuring, and it is impressive. As a therapist, it's interesting to see how the outcome measures can capture a child moving from acting out to feeling more depressed in a healthy way. That means they are feeling more, not just trying to get rid of feelings. That is really significant, because it means that they are beginning to be able to tolerate difficult and mixed feelings.

I think child psychotherapy is really important here for helping to understand what is being communicated by children. I think we bring skills in close observation of non-verbal communication, of unconscious communication, and help to give meaning and context. This isn't to say that other professionals here aren't also working to understand meaning. But we have had a particular training in psychoanalytic and developmental thinking, in thinking about early experiences, and I think our contribution is valued by the team. It is pretty unusual for children to have access to this level of child psychotherapy, and for our thinking to be so central in a school, but I am so glad it is.

What can mainstream schools struggling with children like this take from this way of working? It is hard because resources are limited, but I think supervision spaces for staff are so helpful, because so often troubled and hurt children will trouble and hurt those working close to them. If that can be made to feel less personal and better understood, then it can be profound—for support staff not to feel that they are doing something wrong, not to re-enact those cycles of rejection. Supervision can help to make staff feel valued. What they are doing is so important, but it can be easy for them to not feel valued in that work.

My hope is that the children here become less likely to recreate patterns of rejection and destruction. They are at risk of ending up feeling not wanted in the world if they repeat those cycles. We try to help to change that. They may well go on being vulnerable, but I hope that Gloucester House gives them a solid experience of people trying to understand them, of understanding that their aggression comes from a place of pain and vulnerability. This can help children to internalize an idea of not expelling their hurt feelings but, rather, to look after them in a way that leads to them developing empathy and managing better in their families, in their learning, and with their friends.

PART IV

EVIDENCE FROM EXPERIENCE AND AUDIT

Evidencing child psychoanalytic psychotherapy in primary schools: A case example

Marta Cioeta & Jocelyn Catty

Despite the increased provision of psychotherapeutic interventions in schools in the last two decades, there has been relatively little research evidence produced as to their spread, nature, or effectiveness. While other chapters in this book attest to the range and depth of child psychoanalytic psychotherapy in schools, there has been little formal empirical research in this area, with most research into psychoanalytic and psychodynamic psychotherapy conducted in clinical settings (for comprehensive reviews in this area, see Midgley & Kennedy, 2011; Midgley, O'Keeffe, French, & Kennedy, 2017).

Given the paucity of research data on child psychoanalytic psychotherapy in school settings, how is such work to be evidenced? The state of the evidence places more, rather than less, pressure on service leads, who are obliged to justify their funding requests without recourse to large-scale studies that might support them.

This chapter is an attempt to bring alive the dilemmas and constraints facing service leads in school settings when they attempt to provide evidence to funders—and to demonstrate what can be achieved, despite these constraints. To that end, we shall use one schools-based project, the Tavistock Outreach in Primary Schools (TOPS) project, as a case example. Rather than provide the "evidence" for this project here, we seek to illustrate both the nature and achievements of the clinical work as evidenced in the "data" of various kinds and to stand back from the data to reflect on the process of collecting and interpreting it and the benefits and disadvantages of so doing.

DOI: 10.4324/9781003185925-19

First, though, we turn to the research evidence in this area to illustrate the context for this work.

Background

What research there has been has tended to examine secondary schools and their provision of counselling, often humanistic. In 2009, a review of 30 studies of 19 separate school counselling projects synthesized data on approximately 10,830 clients (Cooper, 2009). Ten of the reviewed studies were of person-centred counselling, while the remainder were an integrative mixture of humanistic and, in some cases, psychodynamic practice. The counselling services were providing between three and eight sessions on average, with some young people attending more. Encouraging outcomes were noted, including reduced psychological distress by the end of treatment, but only one of the 30 studies examined longer follow-up. The author noted that the reviewed studies might not be representative of national norms.

A pilot randomized controlled trial (RCT) of school-based humanistic counselling for psychological distress involved 64 young people, aged from 11 to 18, from ethnically diverse backgrounds, randomly allocated to receive either 12 weeks of humanistic counselling or "usual care". The treated group showed improvements in psychological distress and emotional symptoms and increased self-esteem at 6 and at 12 weeks but were no different from the untreated group at longer follow-up (6 and 9 months post-treatment) (Pearce et al., 2017). Meanwhile, the largest RCT to date of school-based counselling, the Effectiveness and Cost-effectiveness Trial of Humanistic Counselling in Schools (ETHOS) project, is yet to report. This study recruited 330 13–16-year-olds to receive either ten weekly sessions of humanistic counselling or the school's pastoral care as usual, following them up until 24 weeks after baseline (Stafford et al., 2018).

By contrast, a review of play-based counselling in primary schools provided by Place2Be (Daniunaite, Cooper, & Forster, 2015) studied the outcomes of 3,222 children, aged between 4 and 12 years, in 178 schools in the UK. The intervention was associated with a significant reduction in psychological distress, with a clinical improvement in 50% of the children. Greater improvements were found for children with higher baseline levels of distress, for girls, and for bilingual children, while children with special educational needs did less well. The researchers called for more research, both quantitative and qualitative, to explore the effectiveness of this intervention and key change factors.

TOPS: an evidence snapshot

The TOPS project has been providing annual reports to its funders since 2006, drawing on both clinical vignettes and a range of audit data to bring the work—and effectiveness—of the service alive. One such report is used here as the basis for a description of the project's work and as a way of demonstrating the creative ways in which data—quantitative and qualitative, systematic and impressionistic—may be brought together. It should be borne in mind that audit and research are distinct practices, with distinct methodologies (Twycross & Shorten, 2014). A key difference relevant here is that an audit does not aim to be representative or generalizable, but simply to describe the service: sometimes, in its most formal sense, against agreed service standards or norms. When considering the findings described in this chapter, it will be helpful to keep in mind that the numbers are small compared to most typical research studies. In the report used here, outcome analysis was performed against objectives set by the funding body.

The report used as the basis of this chapter presented data on the annual year 2017–18 (Cioeta & Ahlers, 2018), which was the third of a three-year programme funded by the John Lyon's Charity and the Big Lottery Fund. At that point, the service was operating in seven primary schools in one London Borough (Camden), employing 5 part-time child psychotherapists (equivalent to 1.4 of a full-time post), 14 honorary assistant therapists, an assistant psychologist, and an administrator. This is a service that typically provides such evidence by illustrating the clinical work with disguised vignettes, which provide a flavour of the range of interventions offered, as well as using a range of "outcome monitoring" data and other teacher and parent reports. We are not replicating the clinical vignettes here, as other chapters in this book bring the clinical endeavour to life, but it is noteworthy that this use of multiple methods is utilized to convey to funders and other interested parties what the nature of the therapeutic work is, as well as its outcomes against particular benchmarks.

Who was seen?

The first task facing any service lead is to demonstrate to the funder the scale of the work that it has been possible to achieve: the number of cases seen and their characteristics (demographic or clinical, such as how "complex" they are in various ways). This information tends to be easier to collect than other types, although it still requires a high level of administrative endeavour and accuracy, not least to check that the

time-span in question is being considered accurately and how any re-
referrals should be dealt with, to avoid counting the same child twice.

The TOPS project, in the year in question, was able to report that it
had seen 92 children in total, exactly half (46) being new referrals. Details
of their gender, age, and ethnic background are shown in Table 14.1.

To make this information meaningful, it is useful to know whether
the demographic breakdown is typical of previous years, and in this case
the report authors note an increase in referrals of boys, despite efforts
made by the clinicians to help school staff recognize girls' greater likelihood of expressing their psychological distress through internalizing
disorders. They note, however, that the preponderance of boys, at 65%
of referrals, is in line with national data on child referrals (NHS Digital,
2017). The larger numbers of referrals from the 5–9-year-old group is not
surprising, given that this would be a larger pool of potential referrals
than the 10–11-year-olds; but clinicians had put particular emphasis on
the need of Year 6s (the final year of primary school in the UK) for emotional support, given their forthcoming transition to secondary school.

It is also helpful to contextualize such data in relation to the wider
local or national picture. In this case, external data sources were used

Table 14.1 New referrals 2017–18: Demographics

Demographics	N = 46	
	N	%
Gender		
Male	30	65
Female	16	35
Age		
0-4	3	6
5-9	36	78
10-11	7	16
Ethnicity		
White British	16	35
Any other white background	2	4
Black African/Caribbean	13	28
Bangladeshi	3	7
Arab	4	9
Mixed ethnic background	5	11
Other	3	7

as comparators for the TOPS group: first, the 2011 National Census for Camden, and, second, data on the ethnic make-up of the seven TOPS schools. This indicated that TOPS referrals closely reflect the composition of the schools' communities but, like the schools, contrast with the ethnic profile of the borough, with what appears to be a higher representation of Black and mixed-heritage backgrounds. This information allowed the report writers to make the reasonable inference that TOPS was engaging well with families from minority ethnic backgrounds in the school setting.

Turning to clinical complexity, this was assessed using three different mechanisms: data on complexity collected by the school (referred to here as "need and complexity indicators"); qualitative, impressionistic data collected from referrers on the service's referral forms; and a comparison between school demographic data and the Borough average.

Of all the families worked with during the academic year in question, nearly half (38, 41%) were involved with social services. As Table 14.2 shows, slightly more than half the children were on the Special Educational Needs (SEN) register or had "action plus status" (indicating that

Table 14.2 Complexity indicators

	N = 92	
Participants	*N*	*%*
Children on the SEN register/had action plus status	48	52
Children in receipt of free school meals	48	52
Financial difficulties, e.g. family depend on benefits	43	47
Children had experience of abuse/neglect	42	46
History of parental mental health difficulties	40	43
History of social services involvement (now or in the past)	38	41
Families where English is an additional language	35	38
History of acrimonious separation affecting the children (now or in the past)	34	37
Families experiencing housing problems (e.g. risk of eviction)	21	23
Parent/carers with a substance misuse issue	15	16
Parents/carers with a disability	11	12
Families with refugee/asylum status	10	11
Children identified as a younger carer	10	11
Children in care/kinship care	8	9
Families with experience of war/torture/trafficking	7	8

they had additional support from the school), more than half were enti-
tled to free school meals (52%), and nearly half had families in financial
difficulties such as relying on benefits (47%), had experienced abuse or
neglect (46%), or had parents with mental health problems (43%)—all factors known to increase the likelihood of mental health difficulties developing in the children (Cregeen, Hughes, Midgley, Rhode, & Rustin, 2016).

These complexity data were triangulated with impressionistic data
collected on TOPS referral forms: an important opportunity both to
bring in additional perspectives and to bring the children more alive
for the report reader (the funder). The referrers—predominantly special
educational needs and disabilities coordinators (SENDCOs) and deputy
or assistant heads—highlighted a variety of factors that they considered
when referring a child to the service. They described "concerns regard-
ing the family, i.e. history of mental health issues, substance abuse,
domestic violence, immigration issues, trauma, family breakdown and
bereavement", as well as "moderate to severe emotional and behavioural difficulties in children", alongside "family history of involvement
with social services". This suggests that schools saw TOPS as a support
to the wider network around the child, and not just the child alone, and
demonstrates the wide reach of the TOPS service. (Referral form data
also attests to the staff's perception that there is a greater level of need
than TOPS can cater for, even though, during this academic year, the
service worked with eight more children than commissioned for. This
is a hugely significant statement, of course, for any project pressured by
more referrals than it is resourced for.)

This information on the complexity of the children and families seen
by TOPS could also be compared to local norms: in this case, to need
and complexity indicators in the population of the seven TOPS schools
and for the whole borough (see Cioeta & Ahlers, 2018).

Table 14.3 shows that TOPS children have greater financial needs, as
represented by free school meals, than either the whole population of
the TOPS schools or the borough as a whole; likewise, far more children
are on the SEN register or with "action plus" status (although the data
here are not exactly comparable).

By drawing on this range of data, a picture thus emerges of TOPS
providing a service to children with high levels of complexity who are
broadly representative of the rest of the children in the schools covered.

What did TOPS do?

The next task for the service lead is, naturally, to give an impression of
the work achieved by the project: not just in theory (such as in a position

Table 14.3 Need and complexity indicators: TOPS cases vs TOPS schools vs Borough

	TOPS cases (N = 92)		TOPS school populations (N = 3,028)		Borough total (N = 12,219)	
	N	%	N	%	N	%
Free school meals	48	52	11,414	46.7	4,924	40.3
SEN	48	52[1]	660	2.0	623[2]	5.1
EAL	35	38	1,759	58.1	7,294	59.7

[1] For TOPS cases, this is percentage on SEN register or with "action plus status".
[2] This figure includes mainstream schools and the schools working with only SEN pupils.

statement or service description) but in practice. To do so, it is helpful to be able to report the amount of each type of therapeutic work that was taken up: again, an apparently simple task but, in fact, one that requires a high level of commitment. These kinds of data can also incorporate issues such as how long the child or family had had to wait to be seen, how long they attended for, and whether they dropped out or missed many sessions.

TOPS offers a variety of different types of direct therapeutic work—weekly individual, group, parent, or family sessions—and assessment sessions, which may involve children, their parents or carers, and other professionals. In the academic year studied, 1,636 appointments were offered, of which 65% were child therapy sessions, 16% were work with parents, 15% were assessments, and the remaining 4% were family therapy sessions. Waiting times for appointments were relatively short, as Table 14.4 shows; attendance rates were high, as seen in Table 14.5.

Table 14.4 Waiting times

Referral to first appointment (N = 46)	Weeks
0	14
1	13
2	8
3	6
5+	5

Table 14.5 Attendance

Attendance (appointments) (N = 1,636)		Cancelled		
	Attended	Total	By Trust[1]	DNA[2]
Assessment	285	34		15
Child therapy	732	67	13	0
Work with parents	382	64	9	2
Family therapy	52	2		1

[1] Sessions cancelled by the Trust sessions, which are included in the total number of cancelled sessions.
[2] DNA = Did not attend.

The data thus show a service that is very responsive to referrals, with extremely short waits compared to other settings, while also achieving a high attendance rate.

What do we know about outcomes?

Outcome monitoring, or outcome measurement, is the aspect of service delivery that is most likely to excite, but also perhaps alarm, service leads. It requires more sophisticated tools to be used, with attention to how, when, and why they are being used. It also requires staff to commit themselves to using measures that may or may not sit comfortably alongside their clinical thinking, such as goal-based outcome measures (Emanuel, Catty, Anscombe, Cantle, & Muller, 2014). Even among highly committed staff, measures may get forgotten amid the turbulence of school life or the particular clinical ups and downs of an individual case. The service lead, turning at the end of the academic year to the tasks of audit, may find a far from complete set of outcome measures and then needs not to despair but, rather, to work out what can helpfully be used: what can be reasonably claimed from the amassed evidence, and how any gaps can be filled by other means. Data analysis may need to be outsourced.

TOPS was able to make use of data from different sources: routine outcome measures (ROMs) collected from clinicians, parents, teachers, and SENDCOs; specially designed questionnaires for parents and teachers; and more impressionistic data taken from review meetings conducted by therapists with parents, carers, and staff. To evaluate the impact of TOPS intervention, questionnaires were used from initial assessment (pre-therapy) and compared with either: (a) end of treatment (post-therapy) or (b) the six-month point in the case of children who were still in treatment.

Data were utilized from a broad range of measures: "off-the-peg" measures such as the widely used *Strengths and Difficulties Questionnaire* (SDQ; Goodman, 1997), which asks the recipient to rate a range of statements and answer other set questions; the *Children's Global Assessment Scale* (CGAS; Shaffer et al., 1983), which asks the clinician to give a global rating from 0 to 100; the *Goal Based Outcome Measure* (GBOM; Law, 2009), where the user—child, parent, or clinician—sets and rates the goals for themselves; and measures designed by the service itself. This led to a data-set comprised of:

» 221 parent-completed SDQs;
» 211 teacher-completed SDQs;
» 89 parent–clinician-completed GBOMs;
» 150 children's CGAS questionnaires;
» 39 TOPS Teacher Questionnaires (TOPS bespoke measure);
» 41 TOPS Parent Questionnaires (TOPS bespoke measure).

As this list demonstrates, a vast amount of data was collected by the service across the year. Yet even so, some outcome monitoring data were not available, for a range of reasons: the forms were not returned, cases closed prematurely so as to preclude using the measures, or (in a small number of cases) the families did not consent or it was not clinically appropriate to ask them. Where ROM data were missing, some further data could be gathered from therapists and teachers relating to the child's progress. An additional limitation on the findings was that the data-analysing service used by TOPS could compare only complete data-sets for each measure (such as all CGAS scores obtained at baseline compared to all CGAS scores obtained at treatment end) rather than the data for the smaller group of children for whom data at both timepoints were available (that is, with CGAS scores at both baseline and treatment end). This means that the results risk inflating the degree of any improvement, as the follow-up data-set excludes children for whom no forms had been completed.

The three main findings from TOPS were:

1. Children improved their social relationships, reducing negative incidents and increasing positive friendships.
2. Children improved their capacity for school learning and relationships with teachers, enabling increased achievement of school targets.

3. Parents/carers improved family relationships through better under-
    standing their children's needs and engaging better with school-
    based services.

These three areas had been identified in discussion with the funding
body—perhaps unusually, as many services would simply present data
on the range of measures they had used. Each area was not straightforward to measure, and how this was done in each case is described in
what follows.

Outcome 1: social relationships

*Children with severe emotional/behavioural difficulties will manage their feel-
ings better and will improve their social relationships. This will increase their
positive friendships and reduce negative incidents in school.* There might be
various different ways of measuring such an outcome, but here the
service agreed to look at two key indicators:

*   making and keeping helpful friendships (reported by children/
    parents/teachers)—i.e., positive change in peer relationships;
*   for children seen due to conduct difficulties: behaving appro-
    priately (reported by school data and teachers)—i.e., improved
    management of social relationships.

Of the 92 children seen, all were reported by their school and/or family
to have some degree of difficulty with social relationships, although to
differing extents. To assess the children's progress in this respect, the
SDQ peer relationship problem subscale and the SDQ prosocial subscale
(measuring the child's ability to make and maintain positive peer relationships and capacity for empathy) were used.

There were 301 questionnaires available to assess the children's progress from beginning of treatment to either the six-month point or the
end of treatment, depending on which stage of therapy the children had
reached for this reporting period. (Some 131 forms had to be excluded
as they were used at different points outside the reviewed periods.)

Combined figures from the Parent and Teacher SDQ prosocial subscales indicate that the children's ability to operate in a prosocial manner (their capacity for empathy and their ability to make and maintain
friendships) improved following TOPS intervention. Before therapy,
the combined average for the parents' and teachers' assessments of the
children's capacity for prosocial behaviour was 7.0: less than both the
parent-assessed "normal" child sample average of 8.6 and the teacher-
assessed "normal" sample average of 7.3 (https://www.sdqinfo.org/
norms/UKNorm3.pdf). This means that these children were assessed by

their parents and teachers as exhibiting less empathy and less positive friendship-making skills than the average child in the UK. Following intervention, however, the children's capacity for prosocial behaviour was assessed to have improved, meaning that they were able to behave in a more socially positive fashion. The children's mean score rose to 7.6: a small change, but one that might be meaningful in practice.

Looking at the SDQ Teacher subscale for peer relationship problems, the average rating given by teachers at the start of therapy on the peer relationship problems subscale was 2.5, which is above the national average of 1.4 for peer problems (Meltzer, Gatward, Goodman, & Ford, 2000). At the end of treatment, this had decreased slightly to 2.1.

Of the 144 SDQ data sets completed by parents and teachers at the beginning of treatment, 48 (33%) (24 for SDQ-P and 24 for SDQ-T) scored in the clinical or borderline range for prosocial behaviour, meaning that those children had a low or very low capacity to feel and show empathy towards others and to make and maintain positive friendships. At end of treatment, a combined 19 forms completed by teachers and parents still scored in the clinical/borderline range. This figure represents 22.6% of all the forms (84) collected at treatment end. This suggests that some children were supported by TOPS therapists to develop their empathy and improve relationships with peers.

Analysis of the CGAS data was conducted on 63 cases that either closed during the reporting period or were six months into treatment. At assessment, the children's mean score was 52, in the "moderate clinical" range, indicating that some form of mental health intervention is required. At six months or the end of treatment the children's overall mean score was 60, which is at the top end of the clinical range. This shows an average shift towards the borderline range, where children have "some difficulty in a single area but generally function pretty well". A positive trend for improvement over the course of the treatment can thus be seen.

Using the TOPS Teachers' Questionnaire, teachers were asked to assess children's capacity to make positive friendships. Responses indicated that the majority demonstrated positive change in relation to making friendships: 71% showed either a "significant" or a "small" positive change. In 24% of cases, the children showed "no change". Although this might seem disappointing, it might, equally, represent meaningful work preventing their peer relationships from deteriorating: a delicate balance of interpretation is needed here, as this might be more difficult to "evidence" but might make good clinical sense to staff in the service. Overall, the questionnaire findings closely matched the finding from the

SDQ that teachers found the great majority of children seen by TOPS to be able to demonstrate a positive change in peer relationships.

Parents were asked to complete the GBOM in discussion with the lead therapist once the assessment was completed and treatment had been agreed. The agreed goals then informed the nature of the therapeutic work. (A goal scored as 0 indicates that the goal has not been met at all, while a score of 10 means that it has been fully reached.) Using this measure, a number of parents identified peer and social relationships as areas of particular difficulty for their children, such as: "be happier in social situations in school"; "become more assertive in a helpful way when she likes to speak up to peers/adults"; "improve his relationships with other children"; "help her with managing peer relationships and social interactions at school"; or "build stronger peer relationships". Examining those goals that were focused on social relationships, the mean rating at assessment stage was 4.2, whereas at the end of treatment (or at six months for ongoing cases) it was 7.4—an average improvement of 3.2 points out of the full 10-point range.

Termly review meetings also generated outcomes that could be collated for 84 cases. These meetings between parents, teachers, and therapists confirmed that the children had improved their social relationships following TOPS intervention: 59 children were reported to have improved their social relationships, 14 stayed the same, while 21 did not improve in their social relationships. (The remaining 4 cases had not yet been fully assessed at the time of the review meetings.)

Turning to social relationships in the school environment, the conduct and hyperactivity subscales of the SDQ were utilized, as these provide an understanding of the children's needs in relation to their concentration and behaviour. Research suggests that hyperactive behaviour is associated with conduct difficulties in children (Iizuka et al., 2010).

Of the 144 SDQ questionnaires completed by teachers and parents at the beginning of the work, 61 (42%) scored in the clinical or borderline range for conduct problems, compared to 18 questionnaires (21%) out of 84 completed at the end of treatment. For hyperactivity, 66 (46%) out of 144 combined questionnaires produced scores in the clinical or borderline range at assessment stage, compared with 23 (27%) out of 84 at the end of treatment (Table 14.6).

Additionally, the questionnaires completed by teachers rated the average child as having a hyperactivity score of 5.6 at the beginning of treatment—more than the teachers' assessed "normal" child sample average of 3.0 and into the borderline range. At end of treatment, the teachers' average score was 4.1, which is well within the normal range, showing a trend towards a reduction of hyperactivity.

Table 14.6 SDQ: Borderline/clinical range for conduct and hyperactivity problems

| | Treatment | | | | |
| | Beginning (N = 144) | | End/six months (N = 84) | | Improvement (%) |
Parent–Teacher-rated	N	%	N	%	
Conduct	61	42	18	21	21
Hyperactivity	66	46	23	27	19

Outcome 2: school learning and relationships with teachers

Children with severe emotional/behavioural difficulties will improve their capacity for school learning and relationships with teachers. This will enable increased achievement of school targets.

To measure this, change in relationships between children and teachers and changes in the child's capacity for school learning were examined by analysing data from the TOPS Teachers Questionnaire and the Teacher-rated SDQ, as shown in Table 14.7.

On the 39 TOPS Teachers' Questionnaires completed at the end of each academic year and/or at end of treatment, in 66% of cases teachers reported a "significant" or "small" positive change in their relationship with the children following involvement from TOPS, while in 28% of

Table 14.7 TOPS Teachers' Questionnaire (n=39)

| | Change | | | | | | | | | |
| | Significant positive | | Small positive | | None | | Little negative | | Significant negative | |
	N	%	N	%	N	%	N	%	N	%
Teacher-child relationship	13	33	13	33	11	28	2	5	0	0
Avoiding conflict[1]	9	24	13	34	16	42	0	0	0	0
Meeting learning targets	12	31	15	38	11	28	1	3	0	0

[1] One case is missing here, n = 38.

cases they reported that it remained the same. They also reported a "significant" or "small" positive change in avoiding conflict with adults following TOPS intervention for 58% of cases, with no change reported for 42%.

Following TOPS intervention, they reported that 69% of children improved their learning; of these, 30% showed a significant improvement, and 39% showed some improvement. For 28% of children, no change was reported in their learning targets achievement, and for 2% (one case) some slight regression was reported.

Data from the Teachers' SDQs shows that in relation to achieving learning targets, teachers reported that when referred for therapy, 34% of the children's learning was being affected "a great deal" by their difficulties and 34% "quite a lot", with 22% of the children being "only a little" affected in their learning and 10% not at all. The teachers then reported that following therapy, 43% of children's learning was affected "only a little" by their difficulties and 25% "not at all", with 18% of children still affected a great deal and 14% quite a lot. This correlates with the 69% rating for the children's learning having improved.

The SDQ-P and SDQ-T questionnaires ask parents/carers and teachers to rate how much the children's difficulties interfere in several areas of their lives: home life, friendships, classroom learning, and leisure activities for SDQ-P; peer relationship and classroom learning for SDQ-T. For this outcome, the classroom learning answers given by parents/carers and teachers were used. Using SDQ data rated by parents/carers, it was found that before treatment, 11% of them reported that their child's difficulties interfered "a great deal" with their learning and 37% "quite a lot"; 37% indicated that these difficulties only interfered with school learning "a little", and 15% rated it as "not at all". At end of therapy, no parent assessed that their children's difficulties affected their learning a great deal, while 23% rated that learning was affected quite a lot. Positively, 53% of parents viewed learning affected only a little, and 24% not at all. (See Table 14.8)

Differences in ratings between teachers and parents might be accounted for by teachers having a more direct view of the children's struggles with learning at school; parents, on the other hand, infer it from what the children and teachers tell them or from how children manage homework at home. By contrast, the finding that the children's behavioural difficulties decreased, which was rated consistently by both parents and teachers, shows the parents having a more positive view of what might be happening in class.

A number of parents set goals using the GBOM that reflected their concern about learning targets, such as: "to be more settled in class, less

Table 14.8 Impact of difficulties on classroom learning (SDQ)

| Classroom learning affected | Treatment | | | |
| | Beginning of | | End of | |
	N	%	N	%
Teacher rated	(N = 59)		(N = 28)	
A great deal	20	34	5	18
Quite a lot	20	34	4	14
Only a little	13	22	12	43
Not at all	6	10	7	25
Parent-reported	(N = 54)		(N = 17)	
A great deal	6	11	0	0
Quite a lot	20	37	4	23
Only a little	20	37	9	53
Not at all	8	15	4	24

walking around"; "less distracted with school work"; "have better concentration"; "feel more able to do school work independently"; "more consistent with reading"; "to get less frustrated from homework;" "to be able to stay in the classroom for longer periods of time". Analysing these goals as a group (10 GBOMs at each time), the average learning goal was rated at the start of treatment as 4.8, rising to 8 at end of treatment (an average improvement of 3.2 points).

Termly review meetings between parents, teachers, and therapists relating to 84 children also confirmed that the majority of children improved their learning following TOPS intervention: 60 children were reported to have improved their capacity for learning, 13 stayed the same, 6 had not been fully assessed yet for this aspect, and 5 had not improved.

Outcome 3: improving family relationships

> Parents/carers will improve family relationships through a better understanding of children's needs and engaging more with school-based services.

This outcome was assessed in a variety of ways. Engagement with school-based activities was demonstrated by the high attendance rates for parents: 85% of parent sessions and 95% of family therapy sessions being attended. The number of appointments cancelled (rather than the parent failing to turn up) (11%) also shows some commitment to working with TOPS, and these rates are also particularly positive given the complex family backgrounds involved.

To measure parents' capacity to understand their child's needs, to listen more to their child, and to respond more appropriately—a subtle concept—data were utilized from the GBOM, the TOPS parents' and teachers' questionnaires, the SDQ-P, and review meetings.

A number of the goals chosen by parents with support from the lead therapists demonstrated that they were able to think about and identify their children's emotional needs, as well as their own role in supporting their child. These included: "help parents to help [child] to feel more contained"; "for mother to be more confident to support [child] with the issues related to his parents' separation"; "for [child] and Mum to be able to understand better the meaning of her behaviour towards mum"; "for [child] and Mum to improve their relationship when they feel angry"; "for Mum to feel more comfortable to support [child] at home when he tells her about school problems"; and "for parents to be able to support [child] more in moments of upset and frustration". At the beginning of treatment, these goals, as a group, received an average rating of 4.1, whereas at the end of treatment or at six months this had increased to 7.3.

As part of the TOPS questionnaire, parents/carers were asked how effective their method of supporting their child was when their child was distressed. Before TOPS intervention, 6% of parents and carers completing the measure assessed their approach as "not at all" effective in managing their child's distress, while 34% said it was "slightly effective"; by contrast, 47% said it was "effective", and 13% "very effective". Thus 60% rated their own support positively, and 40% were less confident. At six months/end of treatment, 37% of parents/carers assessed their approach as "effective" and 29% judged their approach as "very effective"—a total of 66% feeling that they were effectively helping their child—whereas 32% assessed that their approach was "slightly effective", and the remaining 3% reported "not at all". This represents a slight shift in a positive direction and suggests that the parents became more confident in their way of helping their child. Moreover, before intervention, 21% of the parents completing this questionnaire stated that they did not have alternative ways of engaging their child if their first approach did not work, whereas at six months/end of treatment, this was reduced to only 5% of parents.

Parents completing the parent-rated SDQ were asked whether their child's difficulties interfered with everyday life at home. At the beginning of treatment, 34% felt that these difficulties did have an impact, either "a great deal" or "quite a lot", whereas at the end of treatment, this had decreased to 12%, with 35% of parents stating that these difficulties did not interfere at all, and 53% only a little.

Teachers in the TOPS questionnaire were asked to assess whether there was a change in the quality of the parent–child relationship during and following TOPS intervention. In 30% of cases teachers assessed that they had observed a positive change in the relationship between children and their parents at six-months/following TOPS intervention (27% small positive change; 3% significant positive change). For 64% of children accessing the TOPS service there had been no change. For 3% (two cases) there was a "little negative" change and for another 3% the teacher said that this was not applicable. For those teachers answering "no change", there may not have been an obvious observable issue in the first place.

In review meetings conducted with the parents and teachers of 84 children, 56 of the parents reported that they had reached a better understanding of their children, 17 said that they had an understanding that was similar to when treatment had started; 7 parents felt that they did not improve their understanding; and for 4 of them this aspect could not be fully assessed yet. This use of the review reports illustrates another pragmatic limitation: depending on the progress of the case, the clinician might not be in a position to assess and discuss all the outcomes.

Feedback from children and parents/carers

The views of children and parents/carers were ascertained at the end of treatment with use of the Experience of Service Questionnaire (ESQ; Brown, Ford, Deighton, & Wolpert, 2014), to which some additional questions were added specifically to explore views about having the therapeutic service delivered in school settings. Feedback was obtained from 23 children aged 9–11 and from 25 parents or carers.

Overall, the parents/carers and children felt that TOPS responded appropriately to their needs—for example, that their views and worries were taken seriously, that they felt listened to, and that the therapist discussed the treatment options with them. All said that the TOPS service was more convenient and accessible in school settings, with the therapist and school staff working together to help with the children's difficulties. The children reported that they would prefer greater flexibility around appointment times, and parents reported that they would like more written information about TOPS before their first appointment.

Asked specifically about the therapeutic service, all the parents/carers and 82% of the children reported that they were treated "very well" by the therapist. Virtually all of the parents "felt listened to" and found it "easy to talk" to the therapist and said that their "views and worries were taken seriously": only 3% said that these statements were only "partly true". Similarly, 97% of parents/carers and 84% of the children felt that, overall, the help that they received from TOPS was good. Of the child respondents, 76% reported that they were "listened to" and that their "views and worries were taken seriously", while 24% said that they were "partly" listened to. In relation to whether the "therapist discussed the treatment options", 69% of the parents/carers felt that this was true, 9% thought it was partly true, and the remaining 22% did not answer.

Qualitative feedback was also sought. Feedback from the children who accessed the TOPS service was positive ("I felt really treated well when I got help"). They felt listened to and comfortable to talk to the therapist during their sessions ("She listened to my worries"). They also felt that they received helpful support from their TOPS therapists: for example, they spoke about the positive impact on their emotional wellbeing and their ability to manage their feelings.

Feedback from the parents/carers who completed the ESQ was also positive and supportive of the service. They felt that the therapist helped them in supporting their child with his/her presenting difficulties ("helped us to think about how my child was feeling and how we could act to help her") and saw a positive improvement in their child and family life following the sessions ("it was extremely helpful for my son and myself to be able to talk about any situation of concern").

Discussion

As this chapter has illustrated, a service like TOPS is able to evidence its work with children with high levels of complexity through the use of multiple data sources: routine quantitative outcome measures, specially designed questionnaires, impressionist data from clinical review meetings, and school- and borough-level demographic data. This is a very significant undertaking, and we have tried to demonstrate what can be achieved, while also acknowledging the very real limitations encountered by anyone in a "real life" setting as opposed to a research study.

Despite these limitations, a clear picture emerges in the TOPS project evidence of a population of children with high levels of need, whose emotional and behavioural difficulties lead to difficulties at home and in the classroom if untreated. Yet they are making progress through TOPS intervention that is meaningful both on outcome indicators and in the views of their teachers, parents, and carers. Often the latter are more clinically meaningful: outcome measures over relatively short periods of time may pick up changes that seem relatively modest if not interpreted and triangulated with impressions "on the ground".

The need to focus on the outcomes discussed here is self-evident. Increased prosocial capacities and better peer relationships will be essential to support good functioning for these children throughout their childhood and into adulthood, while reduced hyperactivity leads to better concentration: in turn having a positive effect on a child's ability to engage in classroom activities. Reducing hyperactivity is positive in supporting children to make and maintain relationships with other children and with adults. Improvements in hyperactivity are also likely to be associated with a lower likelihood of children going on to develop attention deficit-related disorders and experiencing internal school exclusions which are often correlated with these diagnoses. Improving relationships with teachers and reducing conflict is clearly crucial in facilitating children's willingness and interest to learn. Indeed, at six months into treatment (or at its endpoint) 68% of the children were assessed as having their learning "only a little" or "not at all" affected by emotional or behavioural difficulties and having made either some or a great deal of progress in learning. This is likely to be due to the fact that the psychotherapeutic work these children received gave them the chance to process and work through difficult experiences and emotions which can act as a block to learning. It is also meaningful that parents seemed to have an improved understanding of their children's needs which would be expected to facilitate improved communication and relationships between them at home.

Evidencing a school-based psychotherapy project, then, ideally requires a range of different kinds of data to be used. We have tried to demonstrate how this may be done but also to give a flavour of the kinds of decisions the service lead must take: how to provide quantitative data without over-burdening staff, or how to weigh up the competing evidence of, say, teacher reports and parent-rated measures. Sometimes something as simple as "feedback" from parents or teachers seems the most telling. Certainly, in TOPS's case, the fact that the families surveyed unanimously wrote about the convenience of having the service located in the school and described the project as working very collaboratively with the school, is no small matter. Having child psychotherapy in school would have fostered the families' perception of school as a place which cares for the holistic development of the children, increasing trust and collaboration between families and school, so furthering the chances of fruitful development for the children. The project's high attendance rates for both children and parents or carers across the various types of appointments (with peaks of 95% for family work and 93% for children therapy) is also testament to this.

While robust prospective empirical research into child psychoanalytic psychotherapy in school settings is urgently needed, the combination of routinely collected quantitative, qualitative, and impressionistic data described here—a key element of practice in this leading psychoanalytic schools project—goes some way to demonstrating the vital role of such work in supporting vulnerable and complex children and families.

REFERENCES

ACP (2018). *Silent Catastrophe*. Available at: https://childpsychotherapy.org.uk/acp-report-silent-catastrophe

ACP (2019). *Children and Young People's Mental Health: Specialist Provision for Complex Needs.* Available at: https://childpsychotherapy.org.uk/news/children-and-young-peoples-mental-health-specialist-provision-complex-needs

Aldgate, J., & McIntosh, M. (2006). *Looking After the Family: A Study of Children Looked After in Kinship Care in Scotland.* Edinburgh: Social Work Inspection Agency.

Alvarez, A. (1992). *Live Company: Psychoanalytic Psychotherapy with Autistic, Borderline, Deprived and Abused Children.* London: Routledge.

Alvarez, A. (2012). *The Thinking Heart: Three Levels of Psychoanalytic Therapy with Disturbed Children.* London: Routledge.

Armstrong, D. (2010). Bion's work group revisited. In: C. Garland (Ed.), *The Groups Book. Psychoanalytic Group Therapy: Principles and Practice* (pp. 139–151). London: Karnac.

Ashley, C., Johnston, J., & Hall, J. (2020). *Kinship Carers' Experiences During the Coronavirus Crisis: Report Produced on Behalf of the Parliamentary Taskforce on Kinship Care.* Available at: https://frg.org.uk/publications/kinship-carers-experiences-during-the-coronavirus-crisis

Barnard, M. (2003). Between a rock and a hard place: The role of relatives in protecting children from the effects of parental drug problems. *Child & Family Social Work, 8* (4): 291–299.

Bion, W. R. (1961). *Experiences in Groups and Other Papers*. London: Tavistock Publications.

Bion, W. R. (1962). *Learning from Experience* (chap. 27). London: Karnac, 1984.

Briggs, S. (Ed.) (2002). *Surviving Space: Papers on Infant Observation*. London: Karnac.

Brown, A., Ford, T., Deighton, J., & Wolpert, M. (2014). Satisfaction in child and adolescent mental health services: Translating users' feedback into measurement. *Administration and Policy in Mental Health and Mental Health Sciences Research, 41*: 434–446.

Burgess, C., Rossvoll, F., Wallace, B., & Daniel, B. (2010). "It's just like another home, just another family, so it's nae different." Children's voices in kinship care: A research study about the experience of children in kinship care in Scotland. *Child & Family Social Work, 15* (3): 297–306.

Canham, H. (2002). Group and gang states of mind. *Journal of Child Psychotherapy, 28* (2): 113–127.

Children's Commissioner (2019). *Childhood Vulnerability in England 2019*, Available at: https://www.childrenscommissioner.gov.uk/publication/childhood-vulnerability-in-england-2019

Cioeta, M., & Ahlers, I. (2018). *Tavistock Outreach in Primary Schools (TOPS): Summary Report. September 2017—August 2018*. London: Tavistock & Portman NHS Foundation Trust.

Cooper, M. (2009). Counselling in UK secondary schools: A comprehensive review of audit and evaluation data. *Counselling and Psychotherapy Research, 9* (3): 137–150.

Cregeen, S., Hughes, C., Midgley, N., Rhode, M., & Rustin, M. (2016). *Short-Term Psychoanalytic Psychotherapy for Adolescents with Depression: A Treatment Manual*, ed. J. Catty. London: Karnac.

Daniunaite, A., Cooper, M., & Forster, T. (2015). Counselling in UK primary schools: Outcomes and predictors of change. *Counselling and Psychotherapy Research, 15* (4): 251–261.

Daws, D. (1985). Two papers on work in a baby clinic: (i) Standing next to the weighing scales. *Journal of Child Psychotherapy, 11* (2): 77–85.

Daws, D., & Boston, M. (Eds.) (1977). *The Child Psychotherapist and Problems of Young People*. London: Wildwood.

DeJong, M. (2010). Some reflections on the use of psychiatric diagnosis in the looked after or "in care" child population, *Clinical Child Psychology and Psychiatry, 15* (4: 589–599.

Department of Education and Skills (2003). *Every Child Matters*. London: Stationery Office. Available at: https://assets.publishing.service.gov.uk/government/uploads/system/uploads/attachment_data/file/272064/5860.pdf

Department of Health/Department for Education (2017). *Transforming Children and Young People's Mental Health Provision: A Green Paper*. Available at: https://www.gov.uk/government/consultations/

transforming-children-and-young-peoples-mental-health-provision-a-green-paper

Department of Health (2004). *National Service Framework for Children, Young People and Maternity Services*. London: The Stationery Office. Available at: https://www.gov.uk/government/publications/national-service-framework-children-young-people-and-maternity-services

DfE (2014). *Court Orders and Pre-Proceedings*. London: Department for Education.

DfE (2019). *Schools, Pupils and Their Characteristics: January 2019*. Available at: https://www.gov.uk/government/statistics/schools-pupils-and-their-characteristics-january-2019

Downie, J., Hay, D., Horner, B., Wichmann, H., & Hislop, A. (2010). Children living with their grandparents: Resilience and wellbeing. *International Journal of Social Welfare, 19*: 8–22.

Durban, J. (2014). Despair and hope: On some varieties of countertransference and enactment in the psychoanalysis of ASD (autistic spectrum disorder) children. *Journal of Child Psychotherapy, 40* (2): 187–200.

Early Intervention Foundation (2020). *What Is Early Intervention/Why It Matters*. Available at: https://www.eif.org.uk/why-it-matters/what-is-early-intervention

Edwards, J., & Maltby, J. (1998). Holding the child in mind: Work with parents and families in a consultation service. *Journal of Child Psychotherapy, 24* (1): 109–133.

Emanuel, R., Catty, J., Anscombe, E., Cantle, A., & Muller, H. (2014). Implementing an aim-based outcome measure in a psychoanalytic child psychotherapy service: Insights, experiences and evidence. *Clinical Child Psychology & Psychiatry, 19* (2): 169–183.

Farmer, E., Selwyn, J., & Meakings, S. (2013). "The children say you're not normal because you don't live with your parents": Children's views of living with informal kinship carers. *Child & Family Social Work, 18* (1): 25–34.

Freud, S. (1917e). Mourning and melancholia. *Standard Edition, 14*: 237–258.

Freud, S. (1920g). *Beyond the Pleasure Principle. Standard Edition, 18*, 1–64.

Freud, S. (1937c). Analysis terminable and interminable. *Standard Edition, 23*: 216–253.

Goodman, R. (1997). The Strengths and Difficulties Questionnaire: A research note. *Journal of Child Psychology and Psychiatry, 38*: 581–586.

Grandparents Plus (2017). *State of the Nation 2017 Survey Report*. Available at: https://www.grandparentsplus.org.uk/state-of-the-nation-2017-survey-report

Harris, M. (1968). Consultation project in a comprehensive school. In: M. Harris & E. Bick, *The Tavistock Model: Papers on Child Development and Psychoanalytic Training* (pp. 317–343). Harris Meltzer Trust Series. London: Karnac, 2011.

Holtan, A., Ronning, J., Handegard, B., & Sourander, A. (2005). A comparison of mental health problems in kinship and nonkinship foster care. *European Child and Adolescent Psychiatry, 14* (4): 200–207.

Iizuka, C., Yamashita, Y., Nagamitsu, S., Yamashita, T., Araki, Y., Ohya, T., et al. (2010). Comparison of the Strengths and Difficulties Questionnaire (SDQ) scores between children with high-functioning autism spectrum disorder (HFASD) and attention-deficit/hyperactivity disorder (AD/HD). *Brain and Development, 2* (8): 609–612.

Jackson, E. (2002). Mental health in schools: What about the staff?, *Journal of Child Psychotherapy, 28* (2): 129–146.

Jackson, E. (2008). The development of work discussion groups in educational settings, *Journal of Child Psychotherapy, 34* (1): 62–82.

Kinship Care Alliance (2019). *Kinship Care Alliance Agenda for Action 2019.* Available at: https://www.frg.org.uk/involving-families/family-and-friends-carers/kinship-care-alliance#agenda-for-action-2019

Klein, M. (1946). Notes on some schizoid mechanisms. *International Journal of Psychoanalysis, 27*: 99–110.

Lanyado, M. (2009). The impact of listening on the listener. In: *Transforming Despair to Hope Reflections on the Psychotherapeutic Process with Severely Neglected and Traumatised Children* (pp. 117–132). London: Routledge, 2018.

Law, D. (2009). *Goal Based Outcomes (GBOs): Some Useful Information.* London, UK: CAMHS Outcome Research Consortium.

Leadsom, A., Field, F., Burstow, P., & Lucas, C. (2014). *The 1001 Critical Days: The Importance of the Conception to Age Two Period. A Cross-Party Manifesto.* Available at: https://www.wavetrust.org/Handlers/Download.ashx?IDMF=e1b25e67-b13b-4e19-a3f6-9093e56d6a31

Maiello, S. (2012). *Point–Line–Surface–Space: On Meltzer's Concept of One- and Two-Dimensional Functioning in Autistic States.* Unpublished paper presented at the 2012 Meltzer conference, London.

Malberg, N. T., Stafler, N., & Geater, E. (2012). Putting the pieces of the puzzle together: A mentalization-based approach to early intervention in primary schools. *Journal of Infant, Child, and Adolescent Psychotherapy, 11* (3): 190–204.

Maltby, J. (2008). Consultation in schools: Helping staff and pupils with unresolved loss and mourning. *Journal of Child Psychotherapy, 34* (1): 83–100.

McLoughlin, C. (2010). Concentric circles of containment: A psychodynamic contribution to working in pupil referral units. *International Journal of Child Psychotherapy, 36* (3): 225–239.

Meltzer, D., Bremner, J., Hoxter, S., Weddell, D., & Wittenberg, L. (1975). *Explorations in Autism: A Psycho-Analytical Study.* Strath Tay: Clunie Press.

Meltzer, H., Gatward, R., Goodman, R., & Ford, F. (2000). *Mental Health of Children and Adolescents in Great Britain.* London: The Stationery Office.

Midgley, N. (2008). The "Matchbox School" (1927–1932): Anna Freud and the idea of a "psychoanalytically informed education", *Journal of Child Psychotherapy, 34* (1): 23–42.

Midgley, N., & Kennedy, E. (2011). Psychodynamic therapy for children and adolescents: A critical review of the evidence base. *Journal of Child Psychotherapy, 37* (3): 232–260.

Midgley, N., O'Keeffe, S., French, L., & Kennedy, E. (2017). Psychodynamic psychotherapy for children and adolescents: An updated narrative review of the evidence base. *Journal of Child Psychotherapy, 43* (3): 307–329.

Miller, L., Rustin, M., Rustin, M., & Shuttleworth, J. (Eds.) (1989). *Closely Observed Infants*. London: Duckworth.

Music, G. (2007). Learning our lessons: Some issues arising from delivering mental health services in school settings. *Psychoanalytic Psychotherapy, 21* (1): 1–19.

Music, G. (2016). Biology and the brain. In: *Nurturing Natures: Attachment and Children's Emotional, Sociocultural and Brain Development* (pp. 89–106). London: Routledge.

Music, G., & Hall, B. (2008). From scapegoating to thinking and finding a home: Delivering therapeutic work in schools. *Journal of Child Psychotherapy, 34* (1): 43–61.

Nandy, S., & Selwyn, J. (2013). Kinship care and poverty: Using census data to examine the extent and nature of kinship care in the UK. *British Journal of Social Work, 43*: 1649–1666.

NHS (2019a). *Communicating with People with Profound and Multiple Learning Disabilities (PMLD)*. Available at: https://www.jpaget.nhs.uk/media/186401/Communicating_with_people_with_PMLD__a_guide__1_.pdf

NHS (2019b). *The NHS Long Term Plan*. Available at: https://www.longtermplan.nhs.uk/publication/nhs-long-term-plan

NHS (2019c). *Overview: Learning Disabilities*. Available at: https://www.nhs.uk/conditions/learning-disabilities

NHS Digital (2017). *Mental Health Bulletin: 2016–2017 Annual Report*. Available at: https://digital.nhs.uk/data-and-information/publications/statistical/mental-health-bulletin/mental-health-bulletin-2016-17-annual-report#key-facts

Pearce, P., Sewell, R., Cooper, M., Osman, S., Fugard, A. J. B., & Pybis, J. (2017). Effectiveness of school-based humanistic counselling for psychological distress in young people: Pilot randomized controlled trial with follow-up in an ethnically diverse sample. *Psychology and Psychotherapy: Theory, Research and Practice, 90*: 138–155.

Pines, M. (2004). Isaacs, Susan Sutherland (1885–1948). In: *Dictionary of National Biography*. Oxford: Oxford University Press.

Pitcher, D. (2002). Placement with grandparents: The issues for grandparents who care for their grandchildren. *Adoption and Fostering, 26* (1): 6–14.

Reid, S. (1987). The use of groups for therapeutic interventions. *Educational and Child Psychology, 3–4*: 171–179. [Special Issue: J. Thacker & R. Williams (Eds.), *Working with Groups*]

Reid, S. (1990). The importance of beauty in the psychoanalytic experience. *Journal of Child Psychotherapy, 16* (1): 29–52.

Reid, S. (1999). The group as a healing whole: Group psychotherapy with children and adolescents. In: M. Lanyado & A. Horne (Eds.), *The Handbook of Child and Adolescent Psychotherapy: Psychoanalytic Approaches*. London: Routledge.

Reid, S., Fry, E., & Rhode, M. (1977). Working with small groups of children in primary schools. In: D. Daws & M. Boston (Eds.), *The Child Psychotherapist and Problems of Young People*. London: Wildwood.

Rhode, M. (1999). Echo or answer? The move towards ordinary speech in three children with autistic spectrum disorder. In: A. Alvarez & S. Reid (Eds.), *Autism and Personality: Findings from the Tavistock Autism Workshop*. London: Routledge.

Rustin, M. (2007). John Bowlby at the Tavistock. *Attachment & Human Development, 9* (4): 355–359.

Rustin, M. (2008). Work discussion: Some historical and theoretical observations. In: *Work Discussion: Learning from Reflective Practice in Work with Children and Families*. London: Routledge.

Salzberger-Wittenberg, I., Williams, G., & Osborne, E. (1983). *The Emotional Experience of Learning and Teaching*. London: Karnac.

Schore, A. (2010). Relational trauma and the developing right brain: The neurobiology of broken attachment bonds. In: T. Baradon (Ed.), *Relational Trauma in Infancy: Psychoanalytic, Attachment, and Neuropsychological Contributions to Parent–Infant Psychotherapy* (pp. 19–47). London: Routledge.

Shaffer, D., Gould, M. S., Brasic, J., Ambrosini, P., Fisher, P., Bird, H., & Aluwahlia, S. (1983). A Children's Global Assessment Scale (CGAS). *Archives of General Psychiatry, 40*: 1228–1231.

Stafford, M. R., Cooper, M., Barkham, M., Beecham, J., Bower, P., Cromarty, K., et al. (2018). Effectiveness and cost-effectiveness of humanistic counselling in schools for young people with emotional distress (ETHOS): Study protocol for a randomised controlled trial. *Trials, 19* (1): 175. Available at: https://trialsjournal.biomedcentral.com/articles/10.1186/s13063-018-2538-2

Turner, A. (2020). *Pandemic 'Amplifying' Unrecognised Needs of Kinship Carers, Putting Placements at Risk, Charity Warns*. Available at: https://www.communitycare.co.uk/2020/05/06/pandemic-amplifying-unrecognised-needs-kinship-carers-putting-placements-risk-charity-warns

Twycross, A., & Shorten, A. (2014). Service evaluation, audit and research: What is the difference? *Evidence-Based Nursing, 17* (3): 65–66.

Wade, J., Sinclair, I., Stuttard, L., & Simmonds, J. (2014). *Investigating Special Guardianship: Experiences, Challenges and Outcomes*. London: Department for Education.

Whitehead, J. (n.d.). *The History of Woodberry Down Comprehensive School.* Available at: https://www.locallocalhistory.co.uk/schools/woodberry/index.htm

Wijedasa, D. (2017). *Children Growing Up in the Care of Relatives in the UK.* Available at: http://www.bristol.ac.uk/media-library/sites/sps/documents/kinship/policy-bristol-report.pdf

Wilkinson, J., & Bowyer, S. (2017). *Research in Practice. The Impacts of Abuse and Neglect on Children; And Comparison of Different Placement Options. Evidence Review.* London: Department for Education.

Williams, D. (1992). *Nobody Nowhere.* London: Transworld.

Winnicott, D. W. (1953). Transitional objects and transitional phenomena—a study of the first not-me possession. *International Journal of Psychoanalysis, 34* (2): 89–97.

Winnicott, D. W. (1963). Morals and education. In: *The Maturational Processes and the Facilitating Environment* (pp. 103–105). London: Hogarth Press.

Wood, J. (1993). Limits and structure in child group psychotherapy, *Journal of Child Psychotherapy, 19* (1): 63–78.

Wood, J., & Argent, K. (2009). Group psychotherapy: The role of the therapist. In: M. Lanyado & A. Horne (Eds.), *The Handbook of Child and Adolescent Psychotherapy: Psychoanalytic Approaches* (2nd edition). London: Routledge.

Youell, B. (2006). *The Learning Relationship: Psychoanalytic Thinking in Education.* London: Karnac.

INDEX